Zero Tolerance

Zero Tolerance

■

Resisting the Drive for Punishment in Our Schools

A HANDBOOK FOR PARENTS, STUDENTS,
EDUCATORS, AND CITIZENS

Edited by
William Ayers, Bernardine Dohrn,
and Rick Ayers

THE NEW PRESS   NEW YORK

Published in the United States by The New Press, New York, 2001
Distributed by W. W. Norton & Company, Inc., New York

LIBRARY OF CONGRESS CATALOGING-IN-PUBLICATION DATA

Zero tolerance : resisting the drive for punishment : a handbook for parents, students, educators, and citizens / edited by William Ayers, Bernardine Dohrn, and Rick Ayers.
    p. cm.
    Includes bibliographical references.
    ISBN 1-56584-666-4 (pbk.)
    1. School discipline—Social aspects—United States—Handbooks, manuals, etc. 2. School discipline—Political aspects—United States—Handbooks, manuals, etc. 3. Classroom management—Social aspects—United States—Handbooks, manuals, etc. 4. Classroom management—Political aspects—United States—Handbooks, manuals, etc. I. Ayers, William. II. Ayers, Rick. III. Dohrn, Bernardine.

LB3012.2 .Z47 2002
371.5'0973—dc21   2001030814

The New Press was established in 1990 as a not-for-profit alternative to the large, commercial publishing houses currently dominating the book publishing industry. The New Press operates in the public interest rather than for private gain, and is committed to publishing, in innovative ways, works of educational, cultural, and community value that are often deemed insufficiently profitable.

The New Press, 450 West 41st Street, 6th floor, New York, NY 10036
www.thenewpress.com

Printed in Canada

2 4 6 8 10 9 7 5 3 1

Contents

Foreword

REVEREND JESSE L. JACKSON, SR.

"An error means that a child needs some help, not a reprimand or
ridicule for doing something wrong."

—MARVA COLLINS IN "MARVA COLLINS: TEACHING SUCCESS
IN THE CITY," *MESSAGE*, FEBRUARY 1987

Fear of our children is at the heart of zero tolerance policies in our schools. Guided largely by fear, the education system has sought to exert power and control over our children, and has abdicated its responsibility to guide, nurture, and protect. Our greatest challenge, then, is to transcend a preoccupation with "power over" and to refocus energies toward developing the "power to do." Exerting "power over" children fuels the jail industrial complex but does nothing to advance our collective aspirations. The "power to do" all that we can to insure that all youth have the opportunity to become self-sufficient and productive adults fuels the education industrial complex and utilizes scarce resources toward the task of empowering rather than punishing.

"Power over" focuses attention on personal, rather than societal, misdeeds. In this context, it becomes rational to focus on youthful indiscretions and turn a blind eye to societal indiscretions like inadequate funding for public schools or inadequate health care for all youth. Our charge is a simple one. We must arrest and abate irrationality.

Each and every day across America, we are leaving children behind. In our state legislatures, on our school boards, in our schools, and in our homes, we have given up on America's greatest promise—our children. This amounts to a tremendous loss of human capital and to underdeveloped talent, which in turn has a devastating impact on our communities and our nation as a whole. We must insure that all children, despite race or socioeconomic status, receive the support and resources that they need to traverse an increasingly complex world.

A commitment to insuring that no child is left behind must decidedly begin on the individual level. As adults, we must first be persuaded that all life is precious and that all children have the potential to make a contribution to our society. Without this heartfelt recognition, all other efforts fail. The sanctity of all life must decidedly be at the foundation of all of our efforts on behalf of our youth. When we do not commit to the sanctity of all life, contempt rather than love becomes the guiding force behind our actions.

When we commit to loving all children as we love our own children, we create a world rich with promise and hope. When we commit to leaving no child behind, we are motivated to nurture rather than punish, to intervene rather than incarcerate, and to love rather than to loathe. When we commit to leaving no child behind, the adage that says "it takes a village to raise a child" acquires new meaning, beyond that of a hackneyed phrase that is only applicable to our own children or those whom we regard as redeemable. Instead, it becomes a rallying point to insure that no child—that no life—is lost to hopelessness and despair.

When teachers recognize that all children have promise, they teach differently and seek creative solutions to persistent problems. When legislators and school administrators recognize that all children have potential, they legislate differently and channel resources toward educating and away from incarcerating.

The greatest threat to harmony is segregation. Segregation has created divergent and conflicting realities that lead to misunderstanding and mischaracterization. We separate the poor from the rich and white from black and are befuddled by the fact that we act and respond differently to similar stimuli. If we desire a world with common frames of reference, we must begin at the same reference point. Children conform to the dictates and expectations of their environment. If we desire loving children, we must create loving environments.

The enemies in the war on our children are least defined by the color of their skin or by their ideology as much as they are by their capricious rule-making, rigidity, irrationality, and arbitrary cruelty. The proliferation of zero tolerance policies is merely an expression of these characteristics and of the escalating anger toward our children. Zero tolerance policies represent macho posturing taken to the extreme. We must make those who lodge daily assaults on our youth understand that macho posturing is no substitute for sound and rational policy or fair and measured discipline. As former U.S. Secretary of Education Richard Riley has said, no punishment should result in the loss of educational opportunity. It is not beneficial to the child nor is it beneficial to society as a whole.

This book, written by child advocates ranging from teachers to attorneys, details the proliferation and subsequent impact of zero tolerance policies on our youth, families, and communities, and provides commonsense alternatives that promote learning in a safe environment. The authors unequivocally demonstrate that "get tough" policies do not work. Rather than promoting safety, zero tolerance policies provide the illusion that something is being done. In the process, these policies promote an irrational climate of fear that excludes countless youth from a quality education and the support that they need to become independent and self-sufficient adults.

All of us are directly or indirectly impacted by the unintended consequences of current school discipline practices. As citizens, we owe it to ourselves to turn the tide on policies that simply do not work toward promoting a quality education in a safe environment for all youth. We owe it to ourselves to insure that those who impact the lives of our children share our collective vision. We must make sure that they are forever mindful of the results that we desire and that we expect them to develop policies directed toward these results.

Those of us who have made a commitment to the sanctity of all life must stand in the forefront of a new movement—a movement toward our children rather than away from them. Be it in Decatur, Appalachia, or Chicago, we must venture to leave no child behind. This book represents a good first step in the process. Our collective involvement in reclaiming our youth is, however, the most crucial step. Where there is hope there is life, where there is life there is possibility, and where there is possibility change can occur. Keep hope alive!

Rev. Jesse L. Jackson, Sr.
President and Founder
The Rainbow/PUSH Coalition

Introduction

Resisting Zero Tolerance

WILLIAM AYERS, RICK AYERS, AND BERNARDINE DOHRN

Not long ago, the principal in a Chicago high school announced a new policy—*zero tolerance*. From now on, she said, there would be no excuse for violating certain school rules, notably the ban on student use of drugs and alcohol. At first, the announcement seemed harmless, if a little odd—after all, there had never been any murkiness or ambiguity about alcohol or drug abuse in the school. Everyone already held the same standard of behavior: kids shouldn't drink or do drugs. What could a zero tolerance policy possibly add? Further, drug and alcohol abuse suddenly now had a new and privileged position in the hierarchy of misbehavior—fighting wasn't on the list yet, nor were racial bigotry, disrespect, sexual assault, and a whole lot more.

Shortly after the new policy was implemented, we asked the principal about it. She explained that zero tolerance was simply an attempt to refocus on existing rules, something to get the kids' attention. "We want to clarify what we already do," she explained, and she assured us that zero tolerance was a contemporary way of expressing what we already believed and practiced.

The new policy, however, was not simply her invention. It was instead, like many developments in education, the application of a new and ubiquitous buzzword, an idea that has caught on in school policy throughout the country and the world.

Zero tolerance policies have by now become commonplace practically everywhere—certainly in our schools and increasingly in our workplaces—and the phrase has been reduced to a platitude through overuse and misuse.

Clichés are never clarifying, but a closer look at zero tolerance in practice reveals a disturbing pattern:

- A high-school boy pulls out a steak knife in the cafeteria to peel an apple, and is expelled for weapon possession.
- A fifteen-year-old Chicago youth is assigned to bring an object from home in order to write a report for his English class; when he enters the school with a large, elaborately carved cane, he is expelled for bringing a weapon to school.
- A fourth grader forgets his belt at home and is suspended for violating a school dress code.
- Another Chicago boy, in a disagreement with a teacher over writing "I will not misbehave" on the board several hundred times, says, "I'm going to take this to the limit," and is expelled for threatening a teacher's life.

In criminal law there are standards of intent and there are assumptions of innocence as well as procedures of due process. Zero tolerance incorporates no such standards. What began, perhaps, as clarification has morphed rapidly into Frankenstein's monster, destroying children in its path.

Some 90 children, overwhelmingly African American and Latino, are now suspended or expelled from Chicago public schools each week. The vast majority are excluded from their schools for nonviolent misdeeds. Schools everywhere—public, private, urban, suburban, rural, and parochial—are turning into fortresses where electronic searches, locked doors, armed police, surveillance cameras, patrolled cafeterias, and weighty rule books define the landscape. Ironically, elaborate security hardware fails to create school safety. Recent research indicates that as schools become more militarized they become less safe, in large part because the first casualty is the central, critical relationship between teacher and student, a relationship that is now being damaged or broken in favor of tough-sounding, impersonal, uniform procedures.

A safe environment for kids can be achieved only as part of something comprehensive. "Safe haven" is another high-sounding idea that educators promote, but there can be no safe havens in a treacherous world. In Chicago, for example, one high school last year had five shootings right outside its doors. Prohibiting weapons in school while failing to engage a larger community is a fool's errand. While youth crime was down by 50 percent over the past four years, most youth crime occurs *after* school and *outside* of school, in the hours from 3 to 6 P.M. If adults want to protect our youth, we will keep schools open late, fill them with exciting programs and activities, add healthy food and academic support, and help their working parents. If we want to protect youth, we will remove handguns from children's environments, address the issues of family violence (both child abuse and domestic violence), and assure evenhanded methods of justice, not racially disproportionate punishment for some and opportunities for others.

Zero tolerance began as a prohibition against guns. This worthy intent of getting guns out of kids' hands is sensible overall public policy. But gun removal is an adult responsibility, not an excuse for sending more youth into prison. If we must have zero tolerance, let it be for gun makers, gun dealers, and gun owners who encourage or allow youth access.

We need teachers, educators, parents, and school boards to reclaim schools as sites of learning and growth—places where incidents of misbehavior, poor choices, wrongdoing, and, yes, even crimes are generally handled *within* the school setting based on principles of repairing the harm, recognizing the consequences, and developing talents and assets. There are numerous models of school sanctioning which work for all but a few behaviors: old-fashioned remedies like detention halls, time-out, letters of apology, contacting parents, and losing school privileges, as well as more modern restorative-justice approaches such as peer juries, community service, community panels, teen courts, and intensive supervision.

Obviously, any such system can become either mechanical or abusive, but these remedies could be part of a context of learning which engages youth themselves in a question of vital interest to them: What's fair?

School-based discipline might become, then, a pedagogy borrowing from the common practices of many parents and most early childhood educators, a concept that is a sharp rebuke to zero tolerance: "the teachable moment." When a group of four-year-old boys excludes the girls from the block corner, when two children tell another "You can't play," when a kindergartner hits another child on the playground, this is recognized as a teachable moment, an occasion for conversation, for reflection, for empathy, for reconsideration. There are consequences and sanctions, yes, but always in the service of learning something important about the complexity of learning to live together.

This is more possible in an intimate community, a place where every child is known well by a caring adult, where parents can come together in common cause, and where teachers are fully responsible and accountable for the learning and growth of a manageable group of kids. And this helps explain a growing phenomenon that began in cities but is sweeping now through rural and suburban schools as well: the small-schools movement is transforming big schools into smaller sites of learning. Small schools are safer, on every measure: suicide is down, violence dramatically reduced, attendance and grades up, graffiti and vandalism down. In small schools, every student is known, no one gets "lost," and there is a stronger parent presence. These are sites where teachers and students and parents create culturally relevant learning contexts, where teachers and learners can experience true collaboration.

While teachers or parents may be fearful of, or angry at, "other" youth we perceive as troublemakers, we want second chances, recognition of unique circumstances, and opportunities to recover when they are our children, or when we get to know them individually. This is what all children deserve. And so schools cannot abdicate teaching in favor of criminal punishment if we are in pursuit of a common, productive future. Teachers, parents, and educators cannot cede their authority to police and prosecutors. We must stand with our children, saying, "We know you and we care for you; turn to us."

Now is the time for parents, teachers, citizens, and youth themselves to come together sensibly to resist zero tolerance. We must begin by remembering that a child is a child, and that teenagers are negotiating a particular stage of human development. Adolescence, of course, is a border—on the other side, adulthood. It is impossible to think of adolescent development entirely outside the conflicts of our own adolescence, but neither do we think of teenagers outside the context of being here, where we are now, having made the passage with relative safety, residing now on the far shore of adulthood. Perhaps, most fatefully, we forget that adolescence is by definition a time of immaturity, of experimentation, of predictable mistakes. No human being, after all, is experienced before being inexperienced, wise before naive, polished before clumsy.

Adolescents need steady grown-ups to talk to, to think with, to bounce off of. Closing the door is a form of abandonment, of neglect. Closing the schoolhouse door as well can become an economic death sentence or a straight line to prison, for school attendance is a critical protective factor in keeping kids out of juvenile and criminal justice systems and away from a life on the streets. In a recent national survey, adolescents responded that the single thing they most wanted was an adult who listened. When adults become anonymous or unavailable to teens, when adult protection ceases, adolescents are left with only their peers and, then, a pseudomaturity that heightens their vulnerability.

Children are different from adults and are likely to recover from misbehavior and mistakes when given proper guidance, challenge, and support. And each child is, of course, an individual, with particular strengths and needs. No one is entirely understandable through their worst actions, and so adults cannot give up on kids, even those who get into trouble again and again, even those who have been involved in a serious offense. The seven young men in Decatur, for example, who in 1999 came together in an unsavory and typical teenage brawl that frightened more than it harmed, are clearly distinct people with dramatically different records, needs, hopes, and challenges. A fair approach, a commonsense approach, to their misbehavior would be to fashion a punishment that would teach but not cripple, educate and develop but not destroy. But in Decatur we also see another all-too-common underbelly of zero tolerance—the racialized use of the concept in practice. After all, when everyone keeps insisting, "This isn't about race," race is the thing it is most assuredly about.

Teenagers are intensely curious, often idealistic, willing to work hard on projects that interest and engage them, willing to commit to a cause. They are easily engaged in the arts, for example, in conversations concerning the ethical; in fact, the creative power of youth acting together transformed the world in Little Rock, Birmingham, Soweto, and Tiananmen Square. Yet, it is abundantly clear that purposelessness and despair can result in an obsessive interest in shallow sensationalism, substitution of consumerism for identity, and scapegoating others when part of a crowd—group behaviors which we adults display in treacherous variety.

In the pages that follow, we explore the dangers of zero tolerance policies and examine the real alternatives. Educators and students tell real stories from the schools and classrooms. Legal experts examine the dangerous precedents that zero tolerance ushers in, creating a downward spiral of further punishment and greater social alienation. We look at how the media have promoted zero tolerance and attacks on youth, and at how zero tolerance resonates against children with disabilities. We deal with the big questions that zero tolerance policies seek to obscure: three hundred years of refusal to educate African-American youth in America, the criminalization and fear of youth today, the effort to destroy public education, the current testing mania, and the strange alliance of gun activism with antiyouth agitation. Finally, education researchers allow us to visit the larger statistical and theoretical perspective on discipline policies.

Let this volume serve as a handbook for citizens. Let students and teachers, school-board members and community activists, juvenile courts attorneys and legislators examine these stories from the front lines. Yes, it is a battle, but the enemy is not the youth of today. The enemy is those who advocate unthinking, knee-jerk repression, disguised as accountability, and then congratulate themselves in the ensuing chaos of the self-fulfilling prophecy of a society split against itself and at war with itself.

For almost every kind of adolescent behavior, our response must be, "It depends." It depends on the context and the consequences, the intention and the competence. Like most ethical questions, it may not be immediately obvious. Is it right to rat on your friends? It depends. Is it right to fight back for your friends or family honor? It depends. Dimensions of complexity, of conflicting interests, of cultivating judgment among youth are part of the glory and challenge of working with adolescents.

Those fortunate youth with caring, if flawed, families—those who are not dedicated to sheer survival—are immersed in the developmental work of separation. Theirs is tough, heavy work, an effort undertaken to rid oneself of dependence and to gain fulfillment in freedom. Their boundary crossing is a time of push and pull, letting go and hanging on, falling and catching hold. It demands an engagement with caring and competent adults. We can neither accede nor withdraw.

Zero means none or nothing. Tolerance gestures toward understanding, generosity, kindness, benevolence, justice, forgiveness. Our children need maximum understanding, sensible standards, benevolence, justice, and then a chance to grow beyond their transgressions. We need to teach tolerance . . . and we need to practice it, too.

To read more, including important contributions that would not fit in this volume as well as updates on the zero tolerance debate, and to give feedback or seek support, visit the webpage for this book at www.zero tolerancehandbook.org.

Zero Tolerance

PART ONE

Narratives

"From a distance," sings Bette Midler, in protest of the racism and wars of this earth; from up in space, the earth looks beautiful, peaceful: "From a distance / you look like my friend, / even though we are at war. / From a distance, / I just cannot comprehend / what all this fighting is for."

If it's all about perspective, sometimes we have to step further back to see how ridiculous our actions are. But at other times, we have to move up a whole lot closer. From the comfort of the congressional floor, the newspaper office, the ivory tower, it seems so easy to prescribe the medicines to "fix" our schools and "straighten out" our youth. For so many in America, our own kids are wonderful but kids in general are crazy; our own kids' teachers are heroes but most teachers are incompetent; even our own school is a mainstay of the community but in general we think schools are sinking ships.

Indeed, it seems that in our collective unconscious, in our broad social discourse, young people have become frightening aliens and schools have become places of horror and dread. And as in so much of the social discourse in the United States, we find archetypal stories and code words to discuss those terrifying schisms whose names we dare not say. We never talk about racism, but we are gripped by the trial of O. J. Simpson; we can't address race, but everyone clings to the Decatur football fight drama. Through these public rituals, we are all given permission to make the most racist observations, to give voice to hateful thoughts. Those students acted "like animals," these youth can "never be reformed." Public lynchings are mostly a thing of the past; tabloid pack mentality is alive and well.

We conveniently live in a different world with our own children and remember a different world from that of our youth. Our memories are at once hyperintense and hazy, and growing up is in some part an act of forgetting, a kind of ordinary amnesia. We wrap ourselves, then, in an illusion: we remember some of the facts and events of our youth, but not the all-encompassing atmosphere; we forget the despair and the soaring ecstasies, the profound loneliness, the vivid perception of adult hypocrisies, the anxiety, self-criticalness, and powerlessness, as well as the joy and energy and heightened expectations, the moments of discovery.

For white adults in America, the discrepancy is much greater . . . from sympathizing with their own childhood, all the way to the matter of understanding the realities of a youth of color in America. Where is the allowance for mistakes? Where is the opportunity to teach and learn? Where is the understanding of often harsh and difficult circumstances that our society has placed this young person in? Dangerous youths fill the headlines since poverty and lack of power do not make good copy. Worse than that, even when white youths commit atrocities, as in the explosion of violence at Columbine High School in the spring of 1999, somehow it is black and brown youths who bear the brunt of the supposed correctives. What's wrong with this picture?

It is common for us to make convenient dismissals of young people "from a distance." It is only when we are on the ground, in the lived lives of youth, that the picture comes into focus in a whole different way. Now take a look at that young Chicana detained for fighting; now find out the story behind the gun; now get real. Narratives from those who are the true experts, the practitioners in the classroom and in the community, give a face and hand and heart to these "perpetrators." And they remind us of our own children, our own youth, and what it takes to go forward from here.

Ground Zero

GREGORY MICHIE

My friend Mara was sitting in the reception area of a small Catholic school on Chicago's North Side, where she'd gone to inquire about registering her daughter for the 1999–2000 term. She wasn't sure she'd be able to afford the school's monthly tuition bills, but she'd decided to check things out anyway—ask a few questions, pick up some forms, maybe even begin the application process.

The principal, a pleasant, conservatively dressed woman of about fifty, welcomed Mara and then quickly ran through her sales pitch, emphasizing the school's small classes and exemplary level of parent involvement. She explained that Mara would be expected to put in her share of volunteer hours, then buzzed through basic information about student uniforms, tuition payment plans, and disciplinary procedures. "Oh, yes," she added, pulling a piece of paper from a file folder and handing it to Mara. "You'll also need to sign this."

Mara took the form and glanced at it. At the top of the page, in capital letters, it read "Zero Tolerance Agreement."

"All of our parents have to sign it," the principal said. "When you read it over, you'll see that it's a first-strike-you're-out situation. That means first offense—no discussion, no excuses."

Mara was taken aback by the conversation's sudden change in tone.

"We haven't had any complaints about the policy," continued the principal, perhaps noting the confusion on Mara's face. "The parents all think it's a good thing. With all the school shootings lately, we just . . ." Her voice trailed off. "Well, we just don't want to take any chances."

Mara scanned the list of offenses that could result in a student's swift and automatic expulsion—weapon possession, drug use, gang activity, fighting. But all she could think about was that her daughter was only five years old.

I don't think I'd ever heard the phrase "zero tolerance" when I began teaching in the Chicago public schools in the fall of 1990. That was before Paducah, before Jonesboro, before Littleton. But even before school shootings became a regular item on front pages and nightly newscasts, the idea that schools were dealing with a frightening new breed of violent, amoral youth was beginning to take hold. Newspaper and television reports of rising crime rates played alongside stories of drive-by shootings, gang-related murders, and children killing children. During my first year in the classroom I remember listening to an older colleague's running commentary as she read a magazine article about youth violence: "These kids get worse every year," she said, shaking her head. "They'd just as soon shoot you as look at you."

It was in this climate of fear—some of it justifiable, some not—that zero tolerance policies began to be seen as a reasonable response to school safety concerns. Proponents argued that the measures would make educators' jobs easier by providing a clear framework for handling serious disciplinary cases. They said schools would be safer because students who caused problems would be removed and other students would be deterred from engaging in violent or criminal activity. Critics countered that zero tolerance policies would unfairly target students of color, who already often faced stiffer punishments than their white counterparts for similar offenses. But proponents insisted the policies would be fair—there would be no ambiguity. If kids messed up, they were out. Period.

It didn't take long for the idea to gain momentum, and soon it was appearing frequently in the speeches and policy statements of school board members, politicians, and teachers' union representatives across the country. Parent groups also jumped on the bandwagon, circulating petitions and doing grassroots organizing. To many, zero tolerance made perfect sense. After all, what teacher doesn't want his job to be a little less stressful? What parent doesn't want her child's school to be as safe as possible? What student doesn't want to receive the same treatment as her peers?

As a new teacher struggling to keep my head above water, I didn't pay much attention to these early rumblings. Not that I didn't think it was an important issue. I'd been as bombarded by media stories as the next person, and there were times—inside and outside the classroom—when I felt the paranoia creeping in. But I was more worried about getting LeShawn to come to school and getting Jason to pick up a book than about hypothetical situations involving weapons or drugs. I knew there was a real possibility that I might someday have to confront such a circumstance, but I guess I figured I'd cross that bridge if I came to it. I came to it about two months into my third year as a teacher.

The tardy bell had just rung at Seward Elementary, a mammoth 100-year-old building in a mostly Mexican-American neighborhood known as Back of the Yards. I was at my third-floor hall-duty post, a blur of young people blowing past me in both directions. I said hello to passing kids, a little preoccupied because I had nothing planned for my first-period class, which began in ten minutes, but otherwise feeling pretty good given that it was Monday morning. Then up walked Julio.

Lumbering, baby-faced, and—to use his understated self-description—"kinda chunky," Julio was an eighth grader who liked school a lot more than it liked him. He'd had little official academic success during his elementary career, but he showed up every day seemingly undeterred—cheerful, eager to learn what he could, ready to give it his best shot one more time. I didn't know him that well, but I sensed that he was a kid with a huge and generous heart.

"Hey, Michie," he said, reaching out one hand to shake mine, as he often did. He was carrying a dirt-smudged gym bag in the other.

" 'Morning," I answered, grasping his pudgy palm.

He glanced over his shoulder, then looked down the hall in the other direction. It was almost empty. "I need a favor," he said.

"OK," I replied.

"It's a big one," he said, a hint of worry showing on his face. "A real big one."

"OK. What is it?"

"But you can't tell nobody," he said, grabbing his gym bag with both hands. "I mean, I don't wanna get in trouble. I don't wanna get kicked out."

As far as I knew, Julio had never been in trouble for anything, not even minor rule bending, so I couldn't imagine why he thought he was at risk of getting booted out of school. More puzzled than concerned, I motioned him into my classroom.

"I need you to hold my bag for me," he said in hushed tones. "Just till the end of the day."

"OK. You wanna tell me why?"

"Um, well, it's . . . uh," he stammered. "I brought something to school I wasn't supposed to bring."

I relaxed. I'd dealt with this one before: a kid brings some sort of technically-against-the-rules-but-really-not-such-a-big-deal piece of contraband to school, suddenly is fearful of being discovered, and wants me to stash it for the day. I wondered what Julio wanted me to hold for him. A tape with explicit lyrics? A pack of cigarettes? A hand-me-down copy of *Playboy*? A pager?

I asked to see what he had, and he partially unzipped the gym bag, pulling it open at one end. I peered inside and saw the unmistakable butt of a rifle.

I could hardly believe it. A gun? Contrary to popular belief, there wasn't a .22 in every desk and a knife in every backpack in Chicago public school classrooms. This was the first time I'd seen an actual weapon in school, and I had no idea how to handle the situation. I had no precedent to fall back on, no well of experience to draw from, nothing from my teacher education courses that seemed relevant. I knew that the Board of Education had a detailed "uniform discipline code" that spelled out five categories of student misconduct and a range of disciplinary options for each. I'd never used the code, but I'd looked at it enough times to know that weapon possession was a Group 5 offense, the most severe—a minimum of six to ten days' suspension and a maximum of arrest and expulsion. I remembered a clause buried somewhere in the document that mentioned mitigating circumstances, but I also remembered stories of kids getting suspended for possessing objects that fit the definition of a weapon far less neatly than a gun—nail files, box cutters, X-Acto knives.

All of this spun through my head in a matter of seconds, but it didn't help me figure out what to do. Relying on instinct—or maybe just stalling for time—I started asking questions.

Julio told me that it was a BB gun and that it wasn't loaded, though he had a box of BBs in the bag as well. He said he'd been visiting his uncle in the suburbs over the weekend and that he'd used his gym bag as a makeshift suitcase. His uncle liked to hunt, so Julio had taken along the BB gun, hoping the two might get in some target practice, though that didn't happen. He'd come home from his uncle's late Sunday night, woken up late for school, thrown on some clothes as fast as he could, and rushed out the door to beat the tardy bell. He pointed to his crazily cowlicked hair as evidence. It wasn't until he was inside the building that he'd remembered the gun.

I had no doubt that he was telling the truth. And it was obvious that he had no intention of using the gun, that he wasn't plotting any sort of attack, that bringing it to school was a complete accident. He wouldn't have told me about it otherwise.

So what did I do? I took the bag, locked it up in my closet, talked with Julio about the seriousness of the situation, and made him promise never to make such a mistake again. I returned the bag to him at the end of the day, watched him leave with it, and—until years later—never breathed a word of it to anyone. I had some further conversations with him about the dangers of guns and the risks involved with gun ownership, but other than that, nothing more ever came of the incident.

Julio graduated from eighth grade that June, scraping by with Ds in almost every subject, and went on to high school. I didn't think much more about the incident until several years later, when I read a story in *Teacher* magazine about an eleven-year-old student in Redwood City, California, who'd accidentally brought an unloaded BB gun to class. By this time Congress had passed the Gun-Free Schools Act—which mandated that any student caught with a firearm on campus be expelled—and school boards across the country had embraced zero tolerance as an all-purpose, get-tough, commonsense solution to school safety problems (the Chicago Public Schools adopted the policy in 1995). The boy in California was an honor student and had never been in trouble of any kind, but he was expelled from his elementary school under its zero tolerance policy for his entire sixth-grade year.

I flashed back to that morning with Julio and began wildly second-guessing myself. What if another kid had somehow gotten the gun out of my closet? What if on the way home Julio had decided to show off the gun and had accidentally shot someone? What if he'd been emboldened by my inaction and had shown up with a real gun later in the year? I knew I hadn't handled the situation perfectly. It was poor judgment not to tell any other adult at school what happened, and I could have been more thorough in my follow-up. But the more I thought about the situation and my response to it, the more I was sure I'd done the right thing. Maybe I should have worked out some sort of creative punishment—have Julio do a project on gun violence or arrange for a guest speaker on the topic—but what good would it have done to suspend him or arrest him or expel him for a year? It wouldn't have made our school a safer place, it wouldn't have sent any message to the other students that they didn't already know, and it sure wouldn't have helped Julio.

But in many other zero tolerance cases around the country, those factors didn't seem to enter the equation. Blind adherence to rules was winning out over doing what was in the best interest of children. Kids were being suspended or expelled for things like sharing a cough drop or a Midol capsule, bringing a steak knife to cut a piece of lunch-box chicken, or displaying a one-inch-long pocketknife during show-and-tell.

Even more troubling than the absurdity of the punishments in these instances was the willingness of adults in positions of authority to abdicate responsibility. Don't blame us, the administrators and school board members seemed to say. Our hands are tied; there's nothing we can do. It was an easy out. And that, I realized, had been part of the appeal of zero tolerance from the beginning: the promise of a simple solution to a tough and complex problem.

Maybe that was why I hadn't been completely turned off by zero tolerance proposals at first. Like most new teachers, I was still halfheartedly searching for magic pills—instructional methods that would work with every student, classroom-management techniques that would never fail. Deep down, I sensed that one-size-fits-all approaches were unrealistic, yet on the days—which were many—when I felt my classroom was like a torpedoed ship, I found myself looking for quick fixes. But the longer I taught, the clearer it became that one size didn't fit all. There was no one way to teach reading effectively, no single method of motivating students, no perfect way to bring history lessons to life. And as much as some educators might have wished it were otherwise, the same went for questions of discipline and school safety.

The week before Thanksgiving in 1996, Armando, a seventeen-year-old former student, came by my house to visit. He told me he'd been suspended from his South Side high school yet again, this time for cutting class. "Man, I'm sick and tired of that," he said. "I mean, they're just dropping kids like it's nothing. Sometimes my teacher takes a kid to get written up, and she'll come back and say to us, 'OK, who's next? I'll suspend you for five days right now!' If teachers want kids to do better, why do they suspend them? They should be keeping them in school, not kicking them out. The guy in the detention room, he tells us, 'If you're doing so bad in school, why do you even bother to come?' Sometimes you feel like they don't even want you there."

The zero tolerance policy the Chicago Public Schools adopted—which covers kindergarten through the 12th grade—had a dramatic impact in its first three years. According to Board of Education figures, student suspensions systemwide increased more than 51 percent (from 34,307 to 51,873) during this period and expulsions jumped from 21 in 1994–95 to 668 in 1997–98—an increase of over 3,000 percent. But as usual, the numbers tell only part of the story. While CPS's written zero tolerance policy targets violent and drug-related offenses, more and more students like Armando, who had no such marks on his record, found themselves kicked out for far less serious transgressions—excessive tardiness, skipping class, and failing to wear a student ID were a few of the most common. The uniform discipline code also allowed schools to suspend students for up to five days for repeated violations of catchall infractions such as "failing to abide by school rules" and "defying the authority of school personnel."

Critics of the Board of Education charged that schools were intentionally pushing students out in an effort to improve test scores. The central office denied the allegations, insisting that keeping students in school was a top priority. But while the board had initiated some legitimate efforts to curb the perennially high dropout rate, it had also turned up the heat on administrators to raise standardized test scores by any means necessary. Principals, fearing the threat of probation or school reconstitution, seemed to feel less of an incentive to hold on to kids who might be considered "problems." If those kids weren't in class, their low scores couldn't drag down the school's averages.

Once they were on the streets, it usually wasn't long before they got arrested for one petty offense or another, usually loitering. If schools had zero tolerance, some of the cops who worked in the community seemed to have even less. "All this neighborhood is," a white officer visiting my school once told me, "is one big gang." That sentiment isn't lost on the young people who live in the area. "The cops around here, they take advantage of their badge," says twenty-year-old Paco, who read books about Houdini and dreamed of becoming a magician back when he was in my sixth-grade classroom. "They push people around. They look at us and they think, 'You're a gangbanger, you ain't got no goals. You ain't gonna be nobody in life. You belong in jail.' So they try to lock us up for any kinda reason."

It was disheartening, to say the least, to watch so many of my students graduate from eighth grade and then get pushed out of school only to wind up on the streets or locked up. I knew most of these guys well enough to see that, although they'd made some poor choices, they still had plenty of potential. What they needed was another chance.

I was getting ready to leave for school one morning in February 1998 when I flipped on the radio to check the weather. I was only half listening to the news reports when the phrase "4900 block of South Paulina"—which isn't too far from Seward—caught my attention. "Double murder last night . . . fourteen- and fifteen-year-old are dead. . . . Teenager in custody. . . . Police say it could be gang-related." Feeling my stomach tighten, I turned off the radio, grabbed my book bag, and headed out the door.

Soon after arriving at school, I found out that the twelve-year-old arrested for the murders was a seventh grader who was in my reading class. He'd been serving a week-long suspension from Seward for drawing gang signs in his notebook—the final straw in a series of run-ins he'd had with teachers and administrators at school over the previous several months. I'd visited the boy's house the previous afternoon, just hours before the shootings, to take him some assignments and a book to read. I found it hard to believe he'd committed the crime, but according to the police, witnesses said he got out of a car just after 6:30 P.M., walked up to the two other boys, and fired several shots at them point-blank. He tried to run, but a squad car caught up to him a block or so away. Once handcuffed and in the car, police said, he confessed to the killings.

For the next few days my classroom was crawling with reporters, and the story was front-page news in the *Chicago Tribune* and at the top of nightly newscasts. The coverage was often sensationalized—a headline in the *Salt*

Lake City Tribune read "Double Murder Halts Career of Chicago Gangster, 12." I could see zero tolerance supporters using the case as evidence of why such harsh measures were necessary. They could argue, "It's a good thing the accused student was suspended at the time of the shooting—just imagine what might have happened had he been in school that day."

But some people saw the shootings as evidence that inflexible disciplinary policies weren't working. One of them was Father Bruce Wellems, a priest at Holy Cross Church, which sits directly across the street from Seward. He saw the killings as a wake-up call, a clear sign that something needed to be done, but he was looking for a better solution. "With something like zero tolerance, you're not dealing with the problem," he says. "You're not facing what the issues really are. It's like the Ten Commandments—'Thou shalt not, thou shalt not, thou shalt not.' OK, but what *will* you do? What's the other side of that?"

Born and raised in Albuquerque, Wellems had come to Chicago in the early 1980s to study for the priesthood. He'd landed at Holy Cross in 1991 with only a vague idea of what an inner-city ministry should be about and little commitment to the neighborhood's struggling youth. "I remember Tim McGovern, who was the park supervisor at the time, working with some of the gang kids, taking them on trips," Wellems says. "He'd always try to get me to come along, but I really didn't want to get into it. I was afraid. I kept trying to turn away from them, and Tim would keep turning me back again. One day we were at the park and I said, 'Tim, you know, these gang kids are really bad kids, they're really dangerous.' And I'll never forget what Tim told me. 'Bruce,' he said, 'these gang kids are your kids.' And he was right. They are our kids."

Wellems started working extensively with dropouts and gang members in the community, and he quickly discovered that most of them wanted one of two things—a decent job or the chance to continue their education. But finding schools that would accept the kids was hard, and keeping them enrolled was even harder—especially after zero tolerance became the rule.

When Eddie, a fourteen-year-old who'd recently dropped out, was shot in a drive-by, he asked Wellems to help him get back into school. Wellems got him enrolled in a Catholic high school, and Eddie sailed through ninth grade until the final month, when a teacher caught him scribbling gang graffiti on a desk. In short order, he was expelled and given no credit for the course work he'd completed. Wellems tried to intervene, but the principal wouldn't budge. "We don't tolerate gang activity," the principal said. "That's our rule, and we follow our rules."

Fine, Wellems thought. If other schools don't want to help these kids, I'll start my own. He'd tossed around the idea of a community high school before but hadn't known how to get the right people behind it. When the city's attention turned to Back of the Yards in the wake of the two murders, he decided to try to use it to make something good come out of the tragedy. In late February, Chicago Public Schools' CEO Paul Vallas visited Seward, and Wellems tagged along on the tour, championing the idea of an alternative school at every opportunity. By the end of the morning, Vallas had made a verbal commitment.

Launching the high school became Wellems's mission. He decided to call it the Sister Irene Dugan Institute after a Religious of the Cenacle nun who'd worked with some of the neighborhood's gang members during the last year of her life. "Irene always used to tell me, 'Bruce, teach them to read,'" he says. "And that really made sense to me—the importance of learning to read. It does so many things. It raises their self-awareness, their awareness of what's going on around them, what they know, what they're able to know. And as they come to an appreciation of that, they calm down, they grow."

In the months that followed, Wellems formed a coalition of neighborhood educators, business leaders, community activists, and volunteers who worked together to map out details and build support. He visited alternative schools in Los Angeles to gather ideas about scheduling, curriculum, and encouraging parental involvement. Every Tuesday night he and a counselor, Sergio Grajeda, met with a group of 15 to 20 guys who were interested in signing up for the school—getting their input, keeping the momentum going.

As the weeks passed, Wellems cleared or kicked aside hurdle after hurdle, and by August 1998, Dugan Institute was up and running. Housed in a small brick building on the back lot of Holy Cross that had once been used as overflow classroom space for Seward, the school opened with 19 students, many of whom had police records or were gang members. Several had been pushed out of other schools, often for minor offenses. "Society can say they won't tolerate this type of individual, and so can schools," Wellems says. "But what does that do? It makes the kid feel rejected. They're in a corner, and they give up. They're back out on the street affecting ten other kids in a negative way. How does a kid have room to screw up and grow when you have something like zero tolerance? How about having a kid atone for something? How is there any atonement if you just flat out reject a kid?"

The following June I watched as Dugan's first graduating class of six students walked across the front of Holy Cross's sanctuary to receive their diplomas. Four of them were the first in their families to graduate. The valedictorian, Federico Vega, was twenty-one years old, married with a baby boy, and working a full-time job in addition to his five hours of classes at Dugan. He'd been suspended from high school for fighting at the beginning of his senior year and had given up on returning until Dugan opened. "My life has changed a lot in this past year," he said in his commencement speech. "If I could turn back time I would change all of the negative choices I made in my life, and I would trade them with positive ones. But as you all know, that is impossible to do. I can't change the past, but I can change my future. I can learn from my mistakes and change my ways. I think all of us can."

So we find ourselves at a point where, in order to enroll her five-year-old for kindergarten, a mother must acknowledge the possibility—and the consequences—of her child bringing a pistol to school or attacking a classmate. I guess it shouldn't be surprising. During the ten years since I began teaching in Chicago, young people have become the enemy in America. In the media and in our imaginations, kids have become the scapegoats for our own worst misdeeds. But, examined more closely, this is clearly a distorted view—one that confuses cause for effect. If anything, the reverse is true. Urban children, particularly youth of color, are under attack. Whether through zero tolerance measures, or cuts in funding for arts programs, or antibilingual education crusades, or the exclusive use of biased standardized tests to evaluate student progress, city kids—particularly African Americans and Latinos—are suffering. The question we must ask ourselves is: How will we respond?

In his recent book about the mid-1990s Rwandan genocide and its aftermath, *We Wish to Inform You That Tomorrow We Will Be Killed with Our Families*, Philip Gourevitch tells of being stranded on a remote, muddy road in the mountains of central Rwanda one night when all of a sudden he hears a terrible scream—a woman's voice—off in the distance. The woman continues, in a kind of whooping sound, and soon other voices join in, seemingly mimicking her cry. The hollering rises to a peak and then subsides. About an hour later, Gourevitch sees a group of soldiers emerge from the hills with a prisoner in tow.

When Gourevitch asks one of the Rwandans he is traveling with what happened, the guide explains that the man in custody had been trying to rape the woman Gourevitch first heard scream. And the other voices? asks Gourevitch. The guide says the woman's call was a traditional signal of distress, and that it carried an obligation for anyone within earshot. "You hear it, you do it, too. And you come running," the man says. "This is how Rwandans live in the hills. . . . I cry, you cry. You cry, I cry. We all come running. . . . This is simple. This is normal. This is community."

Our challenges as educators are obviously far different from those of the people living in the Rwandan hillsides. But, as youth workers like Father Bruce Wellems have shown, our responses can mirror theirs in terms of their compassion, their bravery, and their activism. "The ills of this society affect all of us, and it takes all of us to work together to do something about them," Wellems says. "We can try to blindfold ourselves to it or try to turn away from the kids who need our help, but they're not going away. We turn away because we're afraid to know them. But once you make the effort to get to know them, what you find is a lot of life in these guys. I really believe some of our best leaders are going to come from these kids."

Two Punches, Expelled for Life

It all started on a Saturday night. Just after my wife and I got home from a friend's birthday celebration, the phone rang. It was Esperanza Herrera, a fellow teacher at Berkeley High School who is responsible for its Chicano/Latino program.

She opened with, "Hi, Rick. You haven't heard anything about Lisandra?"

"No. . . . What?"

"I'm going to have to be the one to give you the bad news then. . . ."

I waited. "She was arrested on Friday with two other girls for beating up on another girl, an ESL student."

We made some plans to find out what we could about the incident, to try to get them out of custody, and to keep in touch. Esperanza was going to a meeting at the church with Father Crespin and all the parents, both those of the alleged attackers and those of the victim. One of the arrested students was in my world literature class: Lisandra Gonzalez. The Latino students have dubbed her La Silent. During the first week of school, I had barely noticed her. Small in stature, with a white, moon-round face, she gazed at the world with large, unblinking, Keane-painting eyes. At first I thought she was afraid; she had that deer-caught-in-the-headlights look. Later, I learned that that stare was just her way of taking things in; she had plenty to say when she was ready. It took a while before she smiled. Then she revealed a mouth full of braces, furthering the look of innocence.

I had known Lisan's aunt, Alma, since before our daughter Sonia was born. We both worked at Centro Vida Preschool in West Berkeley; I was the cook for five years and Alma eventually became the director. Lisan had grown up in the Mission District of San Francisco and had attended ninth grade at Roosevelt High School there. She had lived in a neighborhood where you don't join a gang, you are in it by virtue of where you live. She had gotten into trouble as a youngster and her family was moving her to Berkeley to get her away from the life.

Of course, Berkeley had the same cycles, the same claiming of colors and names—the Sureños with the blue and the number 13 and the Norteños with the red and the number 14. Lisandra was on the fringe of the girl group called Berkeley Norteños (their graffiti said simply "BN"), although Alma was keeping close tabs on her, dropping her at school, keeping her home on weekends, trying to break the cycle.

November 10, 1997

To: Juvenile Hall Referee
Via Alameda County Probation Department
2200 Fairmont Drive
San Leandro, CA

From: Rick Ayers, Director
Communication Arts and Sciences Program
Berkeley High

I am writing in regard to the case of Lisandra Gonzalez, who was arrested at Berkeley High on November 7, 1997. I have no knowledge of the event that led to the charges against her. I write as the teacher who best knows her disposition in school and progress this year.

We started the Communication Arts and Sciences program at Berkeley High in order to find ways for school to be more successful for all students. Students have a chance to do video production and to work in closer collaboration with staff and peers.

Lisandra is one of the stars of the program, a young woman who has been turning her life around academically and socially this year. She has taken a leading role in getting fellow students to complete a major video project (filming a scene from *Macbeth* in Spanish). She has completed and rewritten all her assignments. She has been a leading staff member on a new publication at Berkeley High put out by and for Chicano/Latino students (see enclosed articles, including one by Lisandra, and photo).

And she has been selected to read her poetry onstage with renowned author Luis Rodriguez at New College of California on November 16.

I know the court is interested in steering students like Lisandra into programs that will engage them and get them on the right path. I believe she is already in such a program and has been making great progress. I ask the court to allow us to continue our work with her and to prove the successes she can achieve.

I would be glad to speak over the telephone or in person to anyone who is interested in investigating these matters further.

Thank you.

Sincerely,

Rick Ayers

I am wondering about all these things as I get up early on that following Monday at 7:15. Here I was seeing great motion in Lisandra, great ideas and enthusiasm. She was participating in the Teaching Project, working with fourth graders at Washington School across the street. Yet sometimes she just wanted to stay in her world. She hated being put in groups without her friends—in fact, that made her clam up almost entirely. But she was willing to lead ten kids on a video trip, to argue some major literary connections, to write poetry. When we found out Chicano writer Luis Rodriguez would be doing a poetry reading on the night before he was to speak at Berkeley High, and that some students would be asked to read with him, she immediately volunteered and began working on a piece for the special event.

All this bundle of contradictions, all these pedagogical dilemmas I was working on to make Lisandra succeed, all this was interrupted by this stupid action the girls took—the fight, the getting busted. And that was compounded by the stupid actions taken by the authorities: the school administration calling the police instead of their parents; the police shipping them to Juvenile Hall after holding them at Berkeley Police Station for three hours. It was a small fight, some blows thrown, a kid with a puffy lip. Nasty stuff, not good, but qualifying for time in Juvie? I could not believe it.

Fifteen (by Lisandra Gonzalez)
Everyone who is fifteen years old hates it.
You have to.
It's part of being fifteen.

But you have to think, if you're forty you
Would give a lot just to look fifteen
And to go back to your days when you were
Fifteen.
You might think older and look older
But you're only fifteen.
I'm too young.
I think.
Too young to have some real fun.
I think.
Just old enough to get on the best ride
At Great America.
Old enough to have a couple of babies on the side.
But not old enough to see a scary movie just yet.
I hate being fifteen.
How old am I again?

[From Lisandra's journal] It was a pretty Saturday morning from what I saw from a shadow in my window. I waited every minute until it was visiting time. I didn't get to talk to my mother yet so I was scared and worried. The police had told me they didn't get a hold of my mother and that there were better things my mother had to do than see me. So I thought about that all day. I thought about a way to get out. I thought about if I opened the window and escaped and wondered where I would go. I thought about everything you can think of.

All I could think of was what I would tell my family and my only trusted friend [Jorge]. I looked really bad at that point. I prayed as much as I could. And for a moment I was giving up on praying. I felt that it wouldn't do no good and there was no use.

But I remembered that my Abuelita always told me to pray to God. I didn't want to let down my grandma so I had to promise myself to keep praying. I went to church at Juvie and listened to a lady preach to me. I felt so much better. During the time I waited, I would lay down on my bed and think, what could have happened? Why was I here? I questioned everything. I was so bored. I had nothing to do but cry. And wait for the worst food I ever tasted. I never really ate anything. I didn't have an appetite.

On Saturday nights, everyone went to a Rec Center where you play games.

But I was so confused and lost that I decided not to go. I was mad at B-Eyes the most. But more mad at myself for letting this happen. I felt sorry for me and Anna the most. It was time to sleep and the music went on. There was a radio on the ceiling that you can't turn off. I felt like I was being tortured.

On the door there was a small glass window that you can see out. I wished so much that there would be someone to take me. Every time someone would pass by, you could see everyone running to the window to come and get them. And not one time was it for me. I closed my eyes and fell asleep on the cold cement floor.

After a whole day of trying to speak to parole officers, district attorneys, or turnkeys who control visiting, I'm finally told that Lisandra is to be released.

It is so pedestrian, this routine of captivity and release. I check in at the desk; the woman in charge of buzzing open the door locks at two different ends of her cubicle directs me to take a seat in the waiting area, awaiting the arrival of Lisan's mother. Like everyone else in this sprawling institution, I soon get bored and stare dully at the painted cement-block walls.

Finally, after another hour passes, Lisandra Sr. and Alma arrive. The rain is coming down again. We hug and exchange news. They check in at the desk. OK, the attendant will call for Lisandra to come up.

Suddenly there is Lisandra at the other side of the cubicle. She looks smaller than usual, paler. She has her lips pursed tight, looks intently at the form she is directed to sign. She looks up and spies her mother and the rest of us, and a smile blooms on her face. Then she is back to work with the attendant, completing paperwork, emptying a plastic bag with her personal belongings, getting her backpack.

[From Lisandra's journal] And then it was Sunday. I got up and was getting excited about me maybe leaving on Monday. It was visiting hours and I had gone to see my mother. She fell to the floor crying, she was so sad and mad. I hugged her and cried with her. I had four hours with her to talk and the time flew by. It was time to go back.

I never felt out of place when I would cry in front of the kids. I had gone back to my room and it was time to shower. I had took a shower with another girl, she talked to me about her case and how she killed a girl. All I kept thinking was, oh shit, what if she tries to drown me? I left so quick and that was the first time I was anxious to get to my room.

I had one more day. That Sunday night was very long. I prayed that the hours would skip by and I closed my eyes and thought of all the good things in my life and things I'm going to change when I get out. And before I knew it, it was morning.

I got up and made my bed and laid on top. I started practicing Baile Folklorico. I felt stupid but I was bored out of my mind. I sat on the floor and that stopped me. I remembered how ignorant I thought my older brother was, when he talked about the governor and the system and how he always wants to burn the USA flag and always "Fuck Pete Wilson." I never looked at it his way. I thought he was wrong.

But when I sat down, I thought to myself that the people who treat me like shit in here can do that. That's their job. I permanently changed my ways of thinking, ever since that day, how people who are innocent have no choice.

I heard the door open and it was a black woman and she said, "Get your ass up, you're going home." I was so happy. I went to a room to put my clothes on and went to the front where they come to get you. I saw Mr. Ayers, my Mommy, and my Tia.

I was very thankful for these three people. If it wasn't for them, I would have given up. I had left that day without seeing or hearing from the girls and N——. I didn't care.

I did lose something. I lost my way of thinking in life. I now understand my brother and I have no respect for the people up there in the White House. And I have a permanent mark on me that I can never forget and [I can] never forgive the way of how Berkeley High and the system takes care of things.

The doors buzz and she is released to us, swinging her backpack like a kid on a field trip. She hugs her mom, leaning into her and shaking slightly, as if cold. We all hug, then head out the door, bunched together to talk and share in the comfort of community.

At home later in the day, I can't shake the images of the morning, the buzzing doors, the shoes outside the surreal blue doors of the lock-up, the boredom of the clock.

What can we really do to save Lisandra? Move her to another city? The great maw of the cities in the '90s will eat you up. What happened to our dreams, our sincere belief that we were going to change the world, that the dispossessed would actually achieve political power and overcome poverty, alienation, defeat?

Back at school on Wednesday, I write a sharply worded memo to the principal, Edgar Flynt, Bob Tierny, the district guy who will deal with any expulsion hearing, and vice principal Carl Winters. I also attach one copy of the letter I gave to the PO at Juvie. I give a copy also to Betty Crowden, another vice principal.

I get no response from Mr. Flynt. In fact, I never receive evidence that he has read any of my memos. Lisandra is suspended until a meeting with Mr. Flynt the following week in which she will learn if there is to be an expulsion hearing.

Betty stops in my room, however, to raise just one thing. "I understand you are deciding to go to bat for this girl Lisandra," she says. "But I question the wisdom of you using the stationery of Communication Arts for your letter to the Parole Officer. I mean, then it is not just a letter from you; it carries the weight of or suggests that it is from the whole program."

I find myself speechless at first. What's this about? It seems that she wants to avoid a straight-ahead debate on all the issues and is choosing this technical issue, the stationery, as a place to pick away at it. But she's wrong. I respond, "Well, actually, no, I don't think this implies a vote of the students or parents or kids. If Mr. Flynt writes a letter on BHS stationery, does this mean he has the vote of the school behind anything he says? Of course not. I am the director of the CAS program and am trying to show the PO something about the program."

She backs off this point and starts bringing up the issue that is behind all the administration moves. "Maybe you don't know about the gang involvement here. It is not just about this fight. There are girls going around hurting other girls. There are girls who have even left the school in fear, not of Lisandra but of one of the other accused. This has to be nipped in the bud."

"Okay," I respond. "Look at it this way. I have been trained in educational theory; when I teach a lesson, I have some pedagogical reasoning behind it. Usually there is research behind any teaching approach, usually there is countervailing evidence on both sides of a decision of how to teach something. I teach the lesson. Sometimes it works, sometimes it doesn't. But it is all embedded in some theory, some rationale and professionalism about teaching.

"When this administration picks up students, though, when it sends them to Juvenile Hall for four days without charges, when it moves to expel someone for a brief fight in which minor injuries were reported, what is your penological theory? Did someone tell you that a trip to Juvie would do them good? What if I brought you evidence that a trip to Juvie would make them criminals? But we aren't even at that level of discussion. This administration has no training in criminology. It has no theory. The theory is at the level of a couple of guys talking in a bar: 'Yeah, if we weren't coddling these criminals, we would not have so much youth crime.'

"You can't even argue with this. If you put forward an alternate point of view, they just look at you like you are crazy."

Betty agrees with the complaint I am raising. She is not sure how to push the discussion ahead. I tell her I'm going to keep sending memos, that I want to go to any hearing that is coming up on expulsion, and that all her other teachers want to write letters and do what they can to keep working with her.

November 18, 1997

To: Edgar Flynt, Carl Winters, Bob Tierny

From: Rick Ayers

This is a follow-up memo to my one from last week. I know you are having a discussion with the mother of Lisandra Gonzalez today. I have spoken with Carl and Betty about the situation and have made clear my concerns and my evaluation of this student. I want to reiterate a few points:

1) Lisandra is a student who has made great advances this year. . . . She has taken on numerous responsibilities in class projects (including leading a group of students to do an ambitious video project—taping a scene from *Macbeth* in Spanish). She has written her assignments as well as extra credit. She has taken leadership in Ms. Herrera's Academic Prep class, becoming coeditor of the newspaper they are working to put out.

2) Lisandra has been in trouble before and has not extricated herself fully from the influences that have led to this trouble. But she has been clearly moving in this direction, shown by her statements and actions, as well as by her serious approach to school.

3) I think the best approach to dealing with troubled teens is to get them engaged with genuine and authentic tasks in school, get them active in work that has meaning to them. In the absence of this, punishment is meaningless, and for some only becomes a badge of courage. These two philosophies—engaging school work and punishment—clash all the time, and they are tested precisely in a case like Lisandra's.

4) It is simply hypocrisy to try to sweep the "gang problem" under the rug by failing to address it directly, failing to have any programs or interventions on it, on the one hand, and to try to expel students for a minor fight because it is allegedly "gang related." Refusing to admit the presence of gangs as a PR measure (to not scare off the "hills parents") is like burying our heads in the sand. And trying to expel away the problem will only make it worse.

5) I've been told that the school must first concern itself with the victim. This is a subjectively compelling argument. Who can argue with it? But it does not constitute a coherent theory of criminology. The approach of punishing the defendant in the name of the victim is exactly what has driven our society to build the greatest number of prison cells per capita in the world (South Africa used to lead the U.S. but that has fallen since the apartheid regime fell). Subjectively it feels good to get the offender, to have sympathy for the victim. But with no programs that bring the offender back into a productive role in society, guess what? Crime gets worse.

For these reasons, I think Lisandra is exactly the type of student we should be working with. If Communication Arts and Sciences and Academic Prep are going to turn students around, then we have to have the chance to work with them. Give us a chance to show that this way works.

The next days are Kafkaesque. I keep talking to Carl, Mr. Flynt, then later to Bob Tierny. They nod their heads, then go ahead with the expulsion hearing. They say they have no choice. Of course, the real issue suggested underneath the whole thing is the suggestion that the BN, the Norteños, are involved.

Another irony, of course, is that after Alberto Perez was killed, Esperanza was struggling with the school to take on the gang problem. But the administration had no commitment to gang intervention, to creating alternatives. They only have a repression policy.

Again, the philosophy of the guys in the bar.

[E-mail from Alma, Lisandra's aunt]
Dear Rick,

Thanks again for all your help. I really hope this does not get you into any trouble with coworkers or supervisors. Oh yes, Lisan asked if you could ask Mrs. Helms—the other teacher in the CAS program—[for a letter of support]? There is one security guard Lisan describes as a very nice lady. The lady took it upon herself to take Lisan's homework to her teachers when she was arrested. Do you think we could get her name and ask her for a letter? Lisan seems to think that Mr. Wayne [school security chief] would not like this idea. Lisan describes her as someone really nice and who knows she isn't like the others. Who could it be?

De nuevo, muchas gracias, Ricardo, por toda tu ayuda!

Abrazos,

Alma

Finally, I get a response, a letter from Mr. Tierny. He is defensive about the legal responsibilities of the district. He points out that "the police act independently of the school district, and the Welfare and Institutions Code (Section 625) allows police officers the power to take a minor into custody even at school. In fact, past opinions of the California State Attorney General's office, Ops 54–96, Ops 34–93, and Ops 32–46, state that school officials have no right to prohibit the police from interrogating children while in school." As far as the expulsion issue, he also quotes the Education Code (Section 48915a) on the question of expulsion. According to him, any fight with injuries must result in an expulsion hearing at which the final decision is made.

While he expresses concern about the need for social intervention in such cases, and frustration that we do this too little, Mr. Tierny is also convinced that the district must provide a consistent response, especially to gang violence.

He adds, "I'm saddened by the denial of our society to recognize the inequities, by the low esteem in which it holds our schools, by the hypocrisy of saying one thing and doing another. The priority of our budgets is wrong. All of this is true and it is through education and the reprioritizing of our resources that the cycle will be broken. However, in the meantime we must also be realists in dealing with those elements of the school population that are, for whatever reason, intimidating the majority of students who are attending to business. All students have a right to a safe environment in which to pursue their studies and socialization. I propose that we do this by applying the law and policies dealing with discipline in a just fashion, balancing the rights of the accused and the victim to the best of our ability."

Now this raises important issues. It is quite clear that we have to give teenagers limits. It would do them no good to simply declare them free and stand back and hope that everything goes well. Am I guilty of naïve denial of the problem?

I don't think so. The problem is that limits and consequences can be built very strongly if there is a community that the student belongs to. With community, the expectations are strong. Community does not mean everyone is alike; indeed, the history of communities is the history of dealing with the ones who don't do well, who cause problems. But there is fundamental commitment to the needs of the group.

The security imposed on the modern high school, however, is the opposite of community. It is the height of alienation. The school becomes a large institution which can barely tolerate your presence. It is teachers who have contempt for your culture and your yearnings. It is law-and-order efforts based on repression and control, not group standards. So we talk about setting limits, but we cannot divorce this from the reality of the classroom culture, even from curriculum. The law-and-order educators say we shall create order first, then the students will have their butts in the chair and be quiet, then teaching can happen. The chaos of the modern schools is a tribute to their folly.

November 25, 1997

Dear Alma,

Thanks for your note. Yes, I did get homework from [the science teacher] Ms. O'Leary. She stopped by and was very interesting. She had given Lisan an F for the quarter. But she felt she was actually a good student, understood the material, was conscientious about her work, usually. The F came from the fact that she missed the work around a major project and it did not come in. But she really wants to keep her in the school. She said she'd write a letter (I showed her Ms. Helms's as an example). AND she would like to be at the hearing on Wednesday. I also saw the letters from Roosevelt—recommendations for Lisandra. What does this girl do that wins such enthusiastic support from so many adults? I think it is her honesty and thoughtfulness—vague words but ones that apply so strongly to Lisan.

I spoke to a security guard who is a friend of mine. He said there were fights with injuries (minor) about every 2 or 2½ weeks. Obviously there is not a suspension for fighting every time, though the administration says a fight with injuries demands expulsion, by law.

Also, I spoke to Charles at the health center at BHS. I wanted to know how often a kid comes to the health center with an injury from a fight, even minor like a cut requiring a Band-Aid. On Wednesday, I got a note from him in my box: "11/25/97. Rick—Approximately *once a week*, according to our front-desk person."

Did you see Lisandra's poetry? She brought it in in the notebook she submitted. Again, I have to say it is stunning. There are spelling errors and some clichés, etc., but each one also has a core that is very deep, well thought out, and expressed in language that is powerful and rich. Again, the honesty is the core. I'll send you a copy over e-mail after I scan it into my computer.

Talk to you soon. . . . Hey, everyone should be thanking YOU for all your work on this and for taking in your niece, acting as her guardian, advocating up at the school. I hope you get some major appreciation from your family and friends cuz this is quite a load you carry.

Best wishes,

Rick

The hearing was held on December 3. Rita Martin, the assistant superintendent, headed the board and there were two other principals on it. She pointed out that they usually take only a half hour. This one took three and a half. Partly it was because we had a lawyer and all the issues were challenged. In addition, there were three teachers there to testify (me, Esperanza, and Kate O'Leary) and a mom and two aunts. Suffice it to say that the district people were nauseating. They were in no way pursuing an expulsion because they "had to." They were going well beyond obligation. They were doing everything they could to get her kicked out.

The district lawyer led off with an overview concerning the incident and concluded, "We need to expel this student to send a clear message that this kind of violence will not be tolerated." He questioned security chief Wayne and Carl Winters to develop his case. Their evidence was shoddy; the allegations of gang affiliation were wrong (Mr. Wayne: "I can tell who is in a gang by who hangs on a certain corner, and who hangs with them, plus they display the red."). They used the fact that the victim did not want to testify against Lisan (she was in communication through the church and wanting to resolve it in the community meetings) and that other students at the park would not testify as evidence that Lisandra was guilty, since she must be intimidating them.

We came back again and again to the theme Lisan's lawyer had defined: "I would remind the board that we are not here to 'send a message.' We are here to decide the future of this young woman's life. We can't forget that."

I said that if there was any message to send, it was that a kid from difficult circumstances can make it. We can send a message to all the other young women like Lisandra, that you can turn your life around; we can send this message when she graduates very successfully in two years. Esperanza, the aunts, everyone spoke.

Then we were dismissed so the hearing board could decide. The next step would be a vote by the whole board if they recommended expulsion. We had to wait for the following Wednesday.

On December 5, I attended a youth speak-out in West Berkeley, at James Kenney Park. There, Lisan and her sister Xochitl arrived. Lisandra was bursting with something to say. She came over to me.

"Mr. Ayers. I got a call from Mr. Tierny. He says I can come back to school. Something about I have to wait until next Thursday. I'm not sure what it all means, but you can call my mom."

She beamed. We had won! It turned out to be an "expulsion, suspended" which means any more trouble, even cutting class, can result in expulsion.

Then Alma, her aunt, came over. She hadn't heard. Lisandra went up to her.

"Tia, guess what?"

"What?"

"I get to go back to school. . . . Yeah, they said we won!"

Alma stared at her, started smiling, then pinched her nose. "Ooooh, you, Lisan!" They had a long hug while Xochitl and I looked on.

We had a cake and party for Lisandra when she returned on December 11, Thursday. She jumped right into the class, helping lead her group's Latin-American book circle.

Afterword

Following is Lisandra's college application essay, written two years later. A year after the incident, she came clean and said she had been messing around, posing, she said, on the fringes of the gang. She also finally described the role she had played in the assault. But she was also getting her life together, getting on track, as they say. This was the girl the authorities would have put on the street in her sophomore year. Which path would be better for her?

College Essay

When the door shut, it slammed so hard I heard the room echo. The room looked so pale and cold, like something you would only see in the movies. Everything was cement and tightly compacted. I sat on the thin layer of cushion that was laid out on the bed for hours, asking myself a hundred questions, repeating myself over and over.

My first idea was to escape. It hadn't kicked in that I had no options. I tried to pick the automatic lock to my door. I even tried to think of a way to melt the nine-inch-thick plastic window to get out. I wondered if anyone even remembered that I was in this room or if I even existed. No sounds. No visitors. Nothing but the deep thump of my heartbeats and the sound of my deep breaths.

The next morning I woke up to the horrible sound of the Juvenile Hall guard's voice telling us to get up and make our beds. I had barely opened my eyes, thinking my bad dream was over. But it wasn't—it had just started.

I was so terrified about what was going to happen. I was in trouble with the law and my family. I was more afraid of coming out than staying in. I was going to be dealing with the toughest family and teachers. I had a lot to think about in 48 hours. I had a weird feeling about worrying my teachers, as they had become a big part in my life. I never thought I would even become close to one. I thought they gave me Fs because they just didn't like me. The truth was that I was at the best high school, where teachers love their students and will take that extra step to make sure that we succeed.

When I was 15, I could have sworn my birth certificate said 21. I even got to live like an adult. But when I was 16, that's where it got bad and my adulthood paid me back. "Lisandra Gonzalez, please strip and bend over. Then cough." Those were the words of the woman who left me bare and cold and ashamed. Assault and robbery was what it was called, for my case. The finger-prints, the mug shot, everything I've watched on "Cops" is what I experienced.

At the age of 15, I was known as a juvenile delinquent. Who would have ever thought I would follow in my brother's footsteps. Life was surrounded by gangs, in my eyes. I grew up in a neighborhood where the majority were Lati-nos who immigrated from all over Latin America. Gangs came in the late '60s, which carried on from generation to generation. The people I looked up to and the people who I thought I could be with, the ones with the so-called power, were failures, gang members.

The four days I was in Juvie felt like four months. Every time they closed the doors behind me, I felt this bitterness that the system had the key to my life and in reality they did. Who was I to blame at the age of fifteen? "The white man put me here," I thought, but the fact was I couldn't blame anyone but myself. It was the Chicana girl that put herself here.

The two people that I was mostly worried about were my aunt, Alma, and my teacher, Mr. Ayers. They both had done a lot for me to achieve. I was embarrassed and ashamed. They both had tried to keep me out of trouble, but there was nothing they could say or do to change my mind. I had to find it in my eyes. Two thoughts, giving in to my gang or proving myself for the rest of my life. It had to be one or the other that was more important to me.

When I was a little girl. I always wanted to be like my Tia Alma, who I thought was mean and smart, a very strong Chicana with a perfect family that included a dog. I could only think she was very lucky, but now I was starting to realize that it had nothing to do with luck. At this point, I had to think about what was best for me—having everything she had or not knowing if I'm going to live the next day or not. I had to think if my gang was going to make me happy or if I should go to college, get a good job, education, and have a family of my own.

All these points laid out for me made me change so quickly. My outlook, my views, my friends, my attitude changed. Here I am today, May 1999, at UC Santa Cruz, getting some help from college students. They are helping me to write this college admission essay. Sitting with one of my classmates who I hated during my sophomore year because I thought she was too smart, telling her my story and asking for her opinions.

I never once thought that I would make it this far or even visit a college to write an essay for my future. I'm thinking right now—and looking back, even *if it was a few months ago—how stupid and selfish I was. I was making my-self think I was going to become someone bigger with power. The real power is what good things you do with your life. I know that college is just the beginning of those good things for me.*

Lisandra is now attending a California state university.

Arturo's Case

STEVEN DRIZIN

Introduction

Tears moistened the principal's eyes as she watched the axe fall on twelve-year-old Arturo, a student she had known since she first became the principal of the elementary school on Chicago's South Side. A twenty-three-year veteran of the Chicago public school system with seven years under her belt as a principal, she was visibly torn by her concern for the safety of her staff and students and for the future of Arturo, a good kid from a good family who had never before run afoul of the school's disciplinary code. But there was no wiggle room under the school's zero tolerance policy against bringing guns to school. All the mitigating circumstances in the world couldn't save Arturo from his preordained fate. He was going to be expelled. The only question was for how long.

Arturo's case was my first encounter with the Chicago public school system's zero tolerance policy and my first case representing a child who had brought a weapon to school since a number of school-related shootings had compelled President Clinton to push for the Safe School Act, a federal law requiring that schools expel students who bring guns to school for up to two years. The Chicago Public Schools' zero tolerance policy was one of the harshest in the land. Much broader than the federal law, it required mandatory expulsion for a wide range of student misconduct, growing to include even activity which took place off of school grounds. Arturo's father, Hector, had contacted my office, a teaching legal clinic at Northwestern University School of Law, only a few days before his son's hearing. Anxious for new legal experiences for our students and eager to see zero tolerance in action, a colleague and I agreed to represent Arturo and each of us assigned one of our law students to the case.

I came to Arturo's case with mixed feelings about the new and growing trend to crack down on kids for school disciplinary violations known as "zero tolerance." As a parent of four children, two of whom were in elementary school at the time, I have no tolerance for guns in school. But who does? No one in their right mind would support the idea of allowing guns in schools. The very school district in which my children were enrolled was still haunted by the tragic day over a decade earlier when Laurie Dann, a mentally ill young woman, opened fire on elementary school classmates, killing one child and wounding eight others, before turning the gun on herself. That day will live in infamy in our school district and it forever disabused me and other parents of the fantasy that such tragedies couldn't strike in "our" schools.

At first blush, the idea of expelling kids who bring guns to school also did not give me much pause. But I knew that the devil is always in the details of zero tolerance policies, and I had many concerns and questions. Would schools who expel kids be required to provide them with quality alternative educational programs while they were expelled or would the kids end up back on the street, unsupervised, easy prey to the temptations of the criminal life? How fast would expelled kids be mainstreamed back into regular schools and would the regular public schools accept them? Would these policies be disproportionately applied to minority youth? Would school districts use these policies to get rid of difficult, emotionally disturbed kids—kids who are eligible for special education services?

My biggest concern, however, was that such zero tolerance policies would rob school principals and educators of the discretion to take into account the individual circumstances of each case in deciding how to appropriately sanction school misconduct. My mother was an elementary school principal and a teacher with over twenty-five years under her belt, and my father had devoted almost forty years to teaching and coaching children in Philadelphia's public school system. Both of my parents were the kinds of teachers for whom teaching was much more than a profession—it was a calling. It would be a serious mistake not to allow such educators on the front line—those who know their students better than anyone else—tremendous say-so in a decision with such serious consequences as expulsion. My fear was that the zero tolerance policies would be used by administrators as an excuse not to make the hard decisions with which we trust them and for which we pay them.

As an attorney whose primary expertise is in representing children charged with crimes, I came to Arturo's case having seen the damage done to kids from similar policies which have robbed judges of the discretion to decide what to do with kids who commit crimes. The so-called "automatic transfer" laws, which require that children charged with certain crimes proceed directly to adult court, have led to an exponential increase in the number of kids sent to adult court. Once there, they are subject to "mandatory minimum" sentences which prevent judges from taking their youth into account in sentencing them. It no longer matters whether the kid is a first-time offender, whether he was a bit player in the crime, or whether he gave in to peer pressure or other influences which often drive teenagers to break the law. Children today are defined by one factor and one factor only—the seriousness of the charged offense. They are defined by the worst thing they have ever done in their lives—a narrow and myopic way of defining any person and which negates all of their strengths, their special qualities, their idiosyncrasies.

So I came to represent Arturo with mixed feelings. As a parent, I was horrified by his decision to bring a gun to school; as a son of teachers, I was sensitive to the difficult balancing act that teachers and administrators (like my parents) face in weighing the safety concerns of staff and students with the concern for the future of individual students. But as an attorney, I was concerned with justice for children; I was skeptical of any "one size fits all" solutions for dealing with kids who get into trouble. Arturo's case only reinforced my skepticism.

Representing Arturo

Arturo was a big, pudgy, Pillsbury Doughboy kind of a kid, if my memory serves me right. He was much bigger than most twelve-year-olds, but his face and body still carried the baby fat and sheen of childhood. From all appearances, he had not yet reached puberty. He had none of the telltale signs of that awkward transition between childhood and adulthood we call adolescence. He had no facial hair, no acne, no muscular tone, none of the signs of emerging manhood. He was clean-cut, respectful, and polite. He was genuinely remorseful for what he had done, recognized the potential consequences of his actions, and was anxious to get on with his life. My students and I liked him immediately.

Arturo's father, Hector, also impressed us at the first meeting. By the time we had met with him, he had already done a lot of legwork to see if there was any chance that Arturo could remain in the school. He was despondent when he learned that this was not a possibility but desperate that Arturo be expelled for the shortest amount of time possible. He also wanted to make sure that the hearing officer knew that Arturo was a "good kid." He felt some responsibility for having the gun in his own home, but he cut Arturo no slack, holding him responsible for violating his trust and for taking the gun to school. In the days after Arturo was suspended, he and other family members had all expressed their disappointment to Arturo, so much so that Hector feared that they had cracked down too hard on him. Hector feared that Arturo was getting depressed and sent him to live with his aunt to get away from the "negativity" at home.

Hector had gone to great lengths to get Arturo admitted to his elementary school. Dissatisfied with the neighborhood school and fearful that Arturo would be pressured to join the local street gang if he went there, Hector researched the best alternatives for him, working his way through mounds of bureaucratic red tape to enroll Arturo in the South Side Academy. Just getting to school was an adventure for Arturo, requiring that each day he travel over an hour by bus. But the long commute appeared to be well worth it. He was thriving at school, doing well academically and socially, staying clear of the negative influences in his community which so often tempt our children. Though his grades slipped as he entered the upper grades, he was still enjoying school and was performing at a level far above the neighborhood kids who had attended the local school.

After interviewing Hector and Arturo separately, my students and I pieced together the following story of what had landed Arturo in trouble. One day, near the end of the seventh grade, Arturo asked his father if he could borrow the key to his father's desk to get some markers for drawing. While looking for the markers, Arturo stumbled across a case. He opened the case and, to his amazement, inside was a handgun. The gun was not his father's but his uncle's. A truck driver from Arkansas, where it is legal to carry concealed weapons, the uncle had brought the gun with him on a trip to visit his family in Chicago. Arturo's father had taken the gun from his brother when he arrived and locked it away so that the kids would not be tempted to play with it. Before storing the gun, he required that his brother remove all the ammunition. The uncle had forgotten to take the gun with him when he left and planned on picking it up the next time he came for a family visit.

The gun mesmerized Arturo. He picked it up, pulled out the clip, put the clip back in, aimed it, and squeezed the trigger. After playing with the gun, he put the gun back in its case. The gun was a powerful magnet to Arturo. He was drawn to it, and over the next few days, he handled it several more times while ostensibly looking for markers. Each time, he carefully put the gun back in his case to conceal the fact that he had handled it.

One day at school, Arturo saw a group of classmates gathered around Sean, a boy who was not a close friend of Arturo's. The boys were looking at Sean's magazine, which was filled with pictures of guns and knives. Arturo mentioned casually that he had access to a gun. From that moment on, Sean relentlessly pursued Arturo about the gun. He talked to him several times a day at school about it. He even started calling Arturo at home, asking him each time to bring the gun to school. He even offered money to Arturo to borrow the gun. Finally, Arturo succumbed to peer pressure, agreeing to let Sean have the gun for a few days. The exchange took place in a school bathroom. Sean gave him nine dollars for the gun. Arturo agreed to give him the gun on one condition—that he give it back to Arturo a few days later.

After a few days had passed, Sean still had not returned the gun. Arturo started to panic. What if his father discovered that the gun was missing? He grew worried and pleaded with Sean to return the gun. He wrote notes to Sean in class urging him to please get the gun back. Desperate, he tried to negotiate a new deal with Sean, agreeing to give Sean one of his father's cigars for the gun. Sean kept making excuses and never returned the gun. Before he could figure out his next move, an incident occurred involving the gun that lcd to Arturo's suspension.

Several weeks after the gun exchange, an incident erupted on the school playground between Sean and several boys from a neighboring Catholic school. The Catholic school boys had come to Sean's school to continue a fight that had started the day before. During that fight, which was over a girl, Sean had pulled out the gun and waved it around at the boys. Tipped off by an administrator at the Catholic school that a fight was about to ensue, the school principal dispatched the school security officer to the playground and called the local police for backup. The security officer chased the boys away and Sean and the others were brought to the principal's office for questioning. During this round of questioning, Sean told police and the principal that Arturo had given him a gun. He also told them that Arturo had nothing to do with the conflict between Sean and the Catholic school boys.

Brought down to the principal's office, Arturo immediately admitted to authorities that he had given Sean the gun. Arturo's parents were called, he was immediately suspended for ten days, and his parents received a letter in the mail, notifying them of the date of his expulsion hearing. The letter outlined the charges, told the parents that Arturo could be expelled for up to two years, compelled the parents to attend the hearing, and, in a throwaway last line, informed the parents that they "may have an attorney or other representatives at the hearing for your child."

The Hearing

Hector called my office a few days before the hearing. He had tried to retain a private lawyer for his child but the price was too steep. That Hector even tried to find a lawyer showed great initiative. Parents are not encouraged to obtain counsel, and in my experience, in some circumstances, they are actively discouraged from getting attorneys. They are often told that being too adversarial in expulsion proceedings will backfire, causing the hearing officer or school board to mete out the heaviest possible punishment. They are also told that the best strategy is to confess wrongdoing, express remorse, and throw yourself on the mercy of the hearing officer.

We arrived at the Chicago Public Schools headquarters a half hour before our 9:30 A.M. hearing time. Soon the waiting area was filled with children and parents awaiting hearings. At approximately 10:15 A.M., our case was called and we were shown to a small conference room by the school board's attorney. The hearing officer, an employee of the Chicago Public School System, entered the room, turned on the tape recorder, and the hearing commenced.

Before the first witness was called, the board attorney, a wannabe prosecutor, started flexing his muscle. He objected that Arturo had too many attorneys and told me and my colleague that we had to go. He told us we had to make a choice—if my students were going to represent Arturo, then we had to leave; if we were going to represent him, then the students had to go. We explained to him that we were required by law and as clinical teachers to remain in the room with the students and supervise them. The students would handle the case but we would be close by in case they needed to consult. We weren't going anywhere. The hearing officer, bowing to the board attorney, said she had to leave the room to consult with her superiors before ruling on the motion. She returned, allowed us to stay, but asked us to keep our sidebar conversations as short as possible.

The prehearing antics only reinforced our impression that giving kids due process was not a high priority. Several other incidents during the hearing itself made this fact crystal clear. Repeatedly during the hearing, the board attorney reminded the hearing officer that there were several other families waiting, that they were falling behind, and that our case was taking up too much time. He took every chance to remind the hearing officer to keep the proceedings moving. The message from these objections was also crystal clear: "Keep the assembly line moving."

Our strategy in the expulsion hearing was simple. We wanted to tell our client's story—his narrative, his biography. Our goal was to give the hearing officer a picture of "who" Arturo was, "where" he came from, "how" he came to possess a gun, and "what" influences may have led him to bring the gun to school. If successful, we would paint the incident as a one-time isolated mistake in judgment, the result of peer pressure rather than malice, and draw Arturo as a good kid who made a bad decision, who was sorry for what he did, and who desperately wanted the chance to prove to himself, his parents, and his teachers, that he had learned from his mistake.

The board attorney's strategy was also simple—get out the fact that Arturo brought a gun to school, repeat it often, and, to the extent possible, try to tarnish Arturo by bringing up blemishes in his academic and behavior records and questioning the sincerity of his remorse. He would save most of his thunder for closing arguments, where he would rail about the dangers of guns in school, the need to punish children who bring them to school, and the need to impose the maximum two-year penalty on each child who brings a gun to school to teach them a lesson.

We knew that the most important witness called by the board would be the principal. We had talked to the school principal at length before the hearing. She had expressed serious misgivings about expelling Arturo but made it clear to us that she had no choice under the board's policy. She genuinely liked Arturo and his family and knew what a blow it would be to him to expel him from the school. She was torn. Somehow, we had to get her to show the hearing officer her angst.

During direct examination by the board attorney, she played the loyal soldier, citing the board's policy chapter and verse and talking about the primary need of protecting staff and students. Even during cross-examination, she held firm. She did say that Arturo was a good student with few disciplinary problems and expressed how shocked she was when she learned he had brought the gun to school. She admitted that this case had many mitigating circumstances that the board's chief executive officer, Paul Vallas, could take into account in deciding whether to make an exception to expulsion. But she would not agree that Arturo should not be expelled for anything less than the maximum period of two years.

After she was finished, the students and I took a break and made a special request of the hearing officer. We moved to allow the principal to remain in the hearing during the testimony of our witnesses. We told the hearing officer that it was important that she hear Arturo's account of what happened and that she evaluate the sincerity of his remorse. Both Arturo and his parents wanted her to hear his apology and needed her to know how heartbroken the whole family was by this incident. We wanted her there because we felt she had a right to hear what Arturo and his family had to say. We were also confident that she couldn't help but be moved by what she would hear and were hopeful that her reactions would lead her to plead Arturo's case to Mr. Vallas.

The board attorney objected. "She is my witness," he screamed. "She is finished with her testimony and has no right to stay in these proceedings." "She has every right," we countered. "Her recommendation to Mr. Vallas may be given great weight and she can't make an informed recommendation unless she is fully informed." The principal said she'd like to stay and the hearing officer, over the board attorney's objection, allowed her to stay.

By the end of the hearing, after Arturo's narrative was told, both the principal and the hearing officer were dabbing their eyes with Kleenex. The board attorney's closing argument, full of bluster about the evils of guns and the need to enforce zero tolerance laws, sounded silly in the context of Arturo's case. We knew we weren't going to win the hearing, but we felt like the hearing officer, the principal, and, most importantly, Arturo and his family, heard the story loud and clear. This was a good kid, from a good family, who made a stupid decision. If ever there was a case for mitigation, this was it.

Apparently, Mr. Vallas got the message too. Several months later we were notified that Arturo was expelled—not for the two years the board attorney had sought but for one year. It was a blow but not a crippling blow.

Lessons Learned

Much has been written about zero tolerance since I represented Arturo. There have been legions of stories about how schools have gone overboard in applying zero tolerance policies to students. Kids have been suspended or expelled for bringing toy guns to school, butter knives to cut bread or dish out cookies, nail files, Swiss army knife key chains, for shooting paper clips with rubber bands or for having two spent firecrackers in a coat pocket. Bringing Midol to school to alleviate menstrual cramps, sharing lemon cough drops or breath mints, tasting Alka-Seltzer, a swig of Scope, and possessing Tylenol have all run afoul of school zero tolerance policies against drug use. A student who wrote an essay for Halloween with violent overtones was not only expelled but jailed in Texas. Reportedly, he got an A on the paper. In a case in which our clinic was involved, a local school board suspended a ten-year-old for violating the school's sexual harassment policy. What did the boy do? He apparently told a friend that a girl in his class had "big boobs." A six-year-old North Carolina boy was suspended for a week for kissing a six-year-old girl on the cheek during recess.

In the latest absurd case, four kindergartners at a Sayreville, N.J., elementary school were suspended for pointing their fingers at other students on the playground and pretending to shoot them. This decision so outraged attorneys at the Rutherford Institute, the Virginia-based conservative non-profit group that represented Paula Jones in her sexual harassment lawsuit against President Clinton, that they agreed to represent the kids in trying to get the punishment removed from their records. Undaunted, the assistant superintendent of the school board responded to the threat of litigation by saying that the district would rather err by overreacting than by ignoring such behavior, especially in light of the recent shooting of a classmate by a six-year old in Michigan.

These cases clearly demonstrate that some schools have gone overboard in applying their zero tolerance policies. In the examples above, school authorities have completely abandoned their discretion, blindly applying broadly worded policies to innocuous conduct. Schools have simply stopped looking at the individual circumstances of each case. They are suspending or expelling kids, "no questions asked."

In defending their policies, some authorities insist that this is the only fair thing to do. When we exercised our discretion, they respond, we were criticized for abusing our discretion. It's true. Administrators were often criticized for being too lenient, too harsh, discriminatory, racist, preferential to athletes, etc., etc., etc. But the cure for abuses of discretion is not the abandonment of discretion. The cure is to demand that administrators use their discretion wisely—that's what we pay them for. It's requiring them to justify their exercise of discretion by providing a statement of reasons for their decisions. And it's having a system which allows for review of their decisions and a way to hold them accountable for gross abuses of discretion.

The abandonment of discretion has proved to be far more abusive than the previous system, which gave administrators wide discretion in disciplinary matters. And these abuses are starting to bother even conservative groups like the Rutherford Institute. Why are conservatives, who have long supported "mandatory minimum" sentencing, "three strikes and you're out" and other policies which rob "liberal" or "soft" judges of their discretion to take into account the individual circumstances of criminal defendants, now crying foul when school administrators are blindly applying zero tolerance policies? It's because these policies are starting to snag "good kids" as well as "bad kids," "rich kids" as well as "poor kids," "white kids" as well as "black kids." When their kids are ensnared by zero tolerance policies, suburban or wealthy parents are the first to argue for the exercise of reasoned discretion. I've fielded several desperate calls from such parents over the years. The calls always begin with the same line: "When I supported these policies, I never thought that they would be applied to my kids."

The pendulum appears to be shifting in the debate about zero tolerance policies, causing policymakers and the general public to rethink the wisdom of these trends. The outrageous cases are one reason for this shift. So is compelling evidence that zero tolerance policies, despite administrators' claims that they are applied uniformly, are taking a far more devastating toll on poor and minority students. Rev. Jesse Jackson's marches in Decatur brought a national focus on the racial disparities in the application of these policies and forced consensus on many issues, including the need to provide expelled students with quality alternative education options instead of simply casting them out on the streets.

When the dust clears, however, I suspect that children like Arturo will still get no relief. When reforms are proposed, few will cry for mercy for children who bring guns to school. Most will be expelled in assembly-line fashion. Most will not be represented by counsel at these hearings. Many will be referred to the juvenile or criminal court systems. Still more will find difficulty getting back into school. They may give up and drop out.

Their stories will not be told. No tears will be shed for them.

Arturo's case taught me a powerful lesson. While expulsion may be appropriate in many cases involving kids and guns, it is not necessarily appropriate in all cases. There is a difference between a child who brings a loaded gun to school to harm a student or a teacher and a child who gives in to peer pressure, brings an unloaded gun to a school, and loans it to another child to get him off his back. There's a difference between a child who cares little about school, is frequently truant, causes trouble when he does attend school, and has numerous police contacts and a child who is a good student, has near-perfect attendance, and who has had no disciplinary problems in school or in the community. Teachers and principals know that these differences matter and they should be encouraged to take them into account when deciding on appropriate punishments for students, not prevented from giving them consideration.

Arturo's case also reminded me of the pressing need—the obligation— to research and tell the stories of our clients. It reminded me not to give in to the inclination to give up on the Arturos of the world. If anything, this obligation is most pressing in the "hard" cases like Arturo's, when so many want simply to write kids like him off.

From the Jail Yard to the School Yard

TONY DEMARCO

Crime in the 1990s has actually been down about 13 percent while coverage on the news media has been up 240 percent.[1] You just need to turn on Fox and you would pick that up without any trouble. I am going to do something a little bit different here. What I am going to ask you to do is fantasize. I am going to ask you to close your eyes and I am going to describe something and hopefully, with your eyes closed, you will see it as it appears before you. You do not have to put your head back. You just need to close your eyes. I would like to take you to a State House, or a state capital, and I would like you to think about one of those bill-signing ceremonies that takes place. There is usually a long table with a very colorful skirt around the edge of it, and there is a whole sheaf of papers, maybe leather-bound, and maybe on that there is a stack of pens. Behind the table is the governor of the particular state, notable legislators, and perhaps even some community leaders that had something to do with that bill being signed. The governor starts to sign the bill in a sort of sporadic method, writing each letter, half letter, with a pen and handing a pen to a community leader or state legislator.

You have probably seen hundreds of these on the evening news. Now that you can picture that and the bill has been signed, the governor stops signing the bill, shakes a few hands, and walks to the podium, declaring, "This bill makes it possible for our law-abiding teachers and students to take back our schools. Now some weapon-toting punk can be permanently expelled from the mainstream public schools of . . ." Was that John Engler, the governor of Michigan? Was that Paris Glendening, the governor of Maryland?

Was it Tom Ridge, the governor of Pennsylvania? Was it Christine Whitman, the governor of New Jersey? Or was it all of the above?

In 1993, the American Bar Association Steering Committee on the Unmet Legal Needs of Children published a report on the state of this country's children, entitled *America's Children at Risk*. There was not one sentence in the 1993 version about suspension and expulsion. Not one sentence in a one-hundred-page document that dealt with children's issues across the country. It was surprising since 1993 was a watershed year. Things changed and they changed quickly.

America's courts and their schools are in disrepair, possibly because the only ones to use our urban courts and our urban schools are the poor. They are underfunded and they are understaffed. Massachusetts has been a leader in education. John Adams once said, "Education should not be for the rich alone. It should be for all the people." The first public school in America was established in Massachusetts. In 1842, Massachusetts enacted the first state compulsory school attendance law. A child eight to fourteen years old had to go to school for at least twelve weeks. They usually went to school from nine to one-thirty in the afternoon. The Education Reform Bill brought about a change in 1993, but not just in Massachusetts. Education reform has taken place in over twenty jurisdictions across the country. I am now going to discuss what these 1993 reforms brought about.

In 1993, I worked at the Children's Law Center of Massachusetts, a children's legal advocacy program. We had about one thousand intakes a year. Of those one thousand intakes, most are categorized as custody, special education, some delinquency, and a lot of child welfare. Three to four intakes were suspension/expulsion issues prior to 1993. In 1994, that number went to ninety intakes. In Massachusetts during the 1992–93 school year, ninety students were expelled statewide according to the Massachusetts Department of Education statistics. In 1993–94, that number went to nine hundred. In Minnesota in 1993, there were eighty students expelled.[2] In 1994, that went to 221 students.[3] Both Colorado and Tennessee had the same tenfold level of expansion.

There has always been a debate as to the meaning of expulsion. In Massachusetts, expulsion is forever. There is no right to alternative education. The statistics show that in Massachusetts, approximately fifteen hundred students have been expelled or excluded each school year from 1994 to 1998.[4] Some get alternative education, while others do not.

The watershed occurred when three events took place in 1993. The first event was a case called *McDuffey v. Secretary of the Executive Office of Education*.[5] *McDuffey* involved a suit by students in Massachusetts' cities and towns alleging that the state's school-financing system based on local property taxes denied them the opportunity to obtain a sufficient education in their respective public school systems.[6] School funding in Massachusetts historically comes from property taxes, and obviously the value of property to be taxed is going to be different in Lynn, Lawrence, Holyoke, or Chelsea than it is going to be in Wellesley, Weston, or Concord. Many states do not have this local reliance on property taxes and the state's share of the costs of education is considerably more. The *McDuffey* case lingered at the Supreme Judicial Court for about a year until Chief Justice Paul Liacos began writing the decision. The decision came down in June 1993[7] as one hundred pages of beautifully written prose by an extraordinary man. Chief Justice Liacos held that the Commonwealth has a constitutionally mandated obligation to provide an adequate or a real education for all the children.[8] The right is fundamental and belongs to every public school–aged child.[9] When the Commonwealth fails to make available to a child a public school education, it deprives that child of a right that is protected in our constitution.[10] The Commonwealth has an interest in insuring that all students receive education to become productive, contributing members of a democratic society.[11] It only took three days for the legislature to swing into action after that because the Supreme Judicial Court was threatening to do something about school funding. The Massachusetts Education Reform Act of 1993 became a reality.

Education reform had been undertaken in other states and it promised many progressive developments. First, it promised a lot of state money, particularly to the impoverished school systems. Money doesn't hurt—we all know that. Education reform promised to hold students accountable. The students were going to have to pass a comprehensive test to graduate. Students were going to have to show that they knew how to read, write, and do basic math. It was also going to hold teachers, principals, and building administrators accountable, to show that officials were paying proper attention to our kids' education. Part of the theory of education reform was that smaller is better. If we put the power in the principal, the principal can manage and administer that building with his or her staff and his or her people. This is a sound educational concept. The 1993 act gave the principals in Massachusetts expanded power under Chapter 71, Section 37H.[12] It gave principals the authority to expel students found on school premises with drugs or a weapon, or students who assault school staff.[13] No district was required to admit any student who was so expelled.[14]

Shortly thereafter, the Principal's Bill (the governor called it the Billerica Bill)[15] passed. This bill gave principals power to suspend any student who was charged with a delinquency felony complaint or adult felony as long as the principal or headmaster determines that the student's presence in the school would have a substantial detrimental effect on the welfare of the school.[16] Once the student has been found guilty, there is an admission of guilt, or a delinquency adjudication, the principal has the right to expel the student.[17]

The federal government attempted to ease the climate of fear with the passage in 1994 of the Gun-Free Schools Act.[18] This act provided that in order to receive federal education funds, each state must have a disciplinary policy that allows for the expulsion of a student for a year if a student possesses a firearm.[19] There was discretion in the act that allowed the student to return to school after one year.[20] In 1997, the act was further amended to include not only firearms but weapons and drugs as well.

Education is perhaps the most important function of local and state governments, and exclusion from the educational process is a serious watershed event in any child's life. The ramifications of being expelled last forever. Who are these kids? What are we consigning these kids to? The Commonwealth's zero tolerance policy is a basic one strike and you're out. You do not get a second chance.

I represented a student who used to carry a knife to school. He was afraid of walking home. He carried it for three years. Then he became afraid of what would happen should he have to use the knife, so he started to bring a crutch to school. He used the crutch at school for six weeks before he finally swung it at someone. At that point, he was taken into the principal's office where they emptied his pockets. They found the knife and he was expelled. Another student at Lynn English requested a hall pass to use the restroom, and while in the restroom he played with the pipes above the urinal. He played with them a tad too much, one popped, and water came spurting out. The water created a flooded bathroom and seeped through to the lower-floor classrooms. The fire alarm sounded. The school was evacuated in the middle of February. School officials were very irritated. Was it a foolish childhood prank? Absolutely! He was expelled and criminally charged with the felony of malicious destruction of public property. He was deemed a danger in that his presence constituted a detrimental effect on the welfare of the school. I don't know how he was a danger to the school unless he was going to personally drown them all. Zero tolerance doesn't mean zero thinking.

Since 1993, we have used repressive overkill to give the impression, if not the reality, that legislators have addressed the issue of violence and weapons in our schools. This authoritarian policy, it seems, is what American politicians do best. Lionel Trilling once said, "Our culture particularly honors the act of blaming someone." We take an academic pleasure in doing that. Punitive measures are used harshly and with very little long-term consideration of the potential effect.

The desire seemingly is to address the present issue, but the causes of the problem continue to go unattended. These are the same leaders that have brought us automatic transfer, minimum mandatory sentencing, unfettered prosecutorial discretion, and "blended" sentences. They now focus on our educational system. The same leaders that have created "disproportionate minority confinement" in our prison system and youth correctional facilities have used race as the defining factor in zero tolerance exclusions in our public schools. In Massachusetts, 9 percent of our public school population is African American. Eleven percent is Hispanic. Therefore, if my math is correct, approximately 20 percent of our school population is of Hispanic and African-American descent. However, 52 percent of the youths committed to the Commonwealth's Department of Youth Services (DYS) are of Hispanic or African-American heritage.[21] DYS is the Massachusetts youth correctional agency. When we shift to our schools, again, according to April 1999 Department of Education statistics, African Americans are 25 percent of the expulsions and have maintained that position for the last five years.[22] They are only 9 percent of the student body and yet 25 percent of those being excluded. Hispanics, who make up about 11 percent of the total student enrollment, account for one-third of the exclusions. Again, if you do the addition, you come up with one-fifth of the student body in Massachusetts that makes up almost 60 percent of the expulsions. We are disenfranchising more and more students, particularly the black and brown students, every single day.

I admit that I have some biases and what I would like to think are informed prejudices. However, what I have seen in the last six years is the militarization of our schools. There are a number of factors that have led to this trend. The first factor is low expectations. We do not expect much from our urban schools outside of Boston Latin. What these urban schools have in common is a disconnection from the students.

When I was at the Children's Law Center, I had a case where a parent was distraught over her thirteen-year-old son and how he was acting. She knew something was going on that was disturbing him and she felt powerless. She called the vice principal at the middle school and asked him to check on her son and find out what was going on. The vice principal got together with guidance and they called the student into the office. They started talking to him and learned that he had found a handgun. Not only had he found the firearm, but he had taken it on the bus from his home and brought it to school. He did not bring it into the school but had hidden it outside in a wooded area. What do you think they did? They "helped" him. He led them to the gun. He gave it to the vice principal. Soon after, he was expelled and charged with possession of a firearm, which at the time mandated a compulsory commitment to the DYS. The boy's mother was not happy with the response she received.

In the case of *Commonwealth v. Cass*,[23] a principal at a large high school in Erie, Pennsylvania, felt that something suspicious was going on in the student body.[24] He had seen notes passed.[25] He closed the high school down and ordered a lockdown.[26] The kids were kept in homeroom while police dogs were brought in and sniffed lockers.[27] The dogs sniffed three thousand lockers and pointed to six lockers. The police made a determination to search eighteen.[28] They made a decision to open each locker adjacent to the locker the dogs identified. In those eighteen lockers the police found one marijuana roach. One roach in three thousand lockers. The attorney filed a motion to suppress the marijuana charge based on an illegal search. The motion was denied and appealed. The case went up to the Pennsylvania Supreme Court and the principal's argument was that he had "reasonable cause to suspect" drug activity. First, there was increased student communication via the passing of notes in classes.[29] Second, the principal had noticed greater student traffic in the counseling center.[30] The trash barrels were full.[31] He thought this increased usage of the counseling center was due, perhaps, to drug use by the student body. Why, as a student, would you rely on adults who view things in that simplistic a manner? School officials are abdicating their responsibility to really counsel and discipline. They are abdicating that to the police.

Once a police officer is on the scene, school officials lose control completely. What we have is a policy of avoidance. It is an attitude that has driven the adult criminal justice system and the minimum/mandatory philosophy for years. Now that same policy, those same philosophies that are an anathema for the juvenile court and everything that the juvenile court stands for, are being taken not only into the juvenile justice system but into our educational system. It is a three strikes and you're out parallel.

Teachers should have an acceptance of the teachable moment. I am a teacher now for the first time in my life and, believe me, students make mistakes. We all make mistakes, and sometimes they are bad errors of judgment. But from that mistake we end up with something else. We end up with a teachable moment. Zero tolerance ends any discussion. When we lose that teachable moment, we lose something that we can all remember and learn from. Error and mistakes can be something that we can build on as individuals.

Who and what are our schools for? Principals in many of our urban areas receive their compensation according to the size of the school that they administer. They want as many kids as possible to enroll in September and October because it will enhance both responsibilities and salaries. Principals earn more pay, become better administrators, and achieve career advancement. But large schools create greater disconnection, while smaller schools, where teachers know students and are better informed about students, retain a more positive outlook.

The principal wants high enrollment of students before October, then he wants certain ones to leave before the testing in March. In Marblehead, they added one hour to the school day and teachers asked for a 12- to 15-percent raise because of that one hour. Schools are a business, just like prisons, and they are less concerned with who is sitting in those chairs than they should be.

When I was thinking about all this, I asked my son, a sophomore at Lynn Classical High School, "What are your subjects at school?" He responded with the standard—History, Science, Math, English, Foreign Language. And I said, "Well, that's five periods. What do you do in the others?" He said, "I have one period, 'study hall,' and the other is the MCAS."[32] I said, "What is MCAS?" He said, "I study for this test and I learn how to get a good mark on the test." How is that going to help him in life? It will not help him, but it is going to help the principal get a better job performance evaluation and a raise because more and more of the students in his school pass or attain high grades.

I end with a quote from a person normally not associated with higher education. Yogi Berra said, "You've got to be careful if you don't know where you're going, because you might not get there." I submit that we have decided to reform public education but we are not sure we know where we are going and what we want to accomplish with our reforms.

NOTES

1. "Network News in the Nineties: The Top Topics and Trends of the Decade." *Media Monitor* (Center for Media and Public Affairs). Jul./Aug. 1997.
2. Jennifer Vogel. "A Pound of Prevention." *City Pages*. Feb. 22, 1998.
3. *Ibid.*
4. See Massachusetts Department of Education. *Student Exclusions in Massachusetts Public Schools: 1997–98* (Apr. 1999).
5. 615 N.E.2d 516 (Mass. 1993).
6. *Ibid.*, at 517.
7. *Ibid.*, at 516.
8. *Ibid.*
9. *Ibid.*
10. See *McDuffey*, 615 N.E.2d at 516.
11. *Ibid.*
12. See *Mass. Gen. Laws*, ch. 71 sect. 37H (1996).
13. *Ibid.*
14. *Ibid.*
15. See *Mass. Gen. Laws*, ch. 71 sect. 37H1/2 (1996).
16. *Ibid.*
17. *Ibid.*
18. See 20 U.S.C. sect. 8931 (1994).
19. *Ibid.*
20. *Ibid.*
21. See Massachusetts Department of Education. *Student Exclusions in Massachusetts Public Schools: 1997–98* (Apr. 1999).
22. See Massachusetts Department of Youth Services. *Youth, Partnership, and Public Safety: The DYS Strategic Plan*. 6 (Nov. 1998).

23. 709 A.2d 350 (Pa. 1998).

24. *Ibid.*, at 357.

25. *Ibid.*

26. *Ibid.*, at 352.

27. *Ibid.*

28. See Cass. 709 2d at 352.

29. *Ibid.*, at 357.

30. *Ibid.*

31. *Ibid.*

32. Massachusetts Comprehensive Assessment System. The MCAS tests all public school students across the Commonwealth, including students with disabilities and students with limited English proficiency. It is administered annually in at least grades 4, 8, and 10. It measures performance based on the Massachusetts Curriculum Framework learning standards, reports on performance of individual students, schools, and districts, and serves as one basis of accountability for students, schools, and districts. See Massachusetts Department of Education at http://www.doe.mass.edu/meas/1098facts.html (visited Apr. 21, 2000).

Racial Profiling at School: The Politics of Race and Discipline at Berkeley High

Introduction

In recent years, a number of police homicides, beatings, and draggings have been widely publicized, but they represent only the tip of a giant iceberg. For the truth of the matter is that racial profiling, the practice of targeting behavioral problems on the basis of race, is routinely practiced, often unconsciously, by street cops, highway patrol officers, and drug enforcement agents throughout the country.

However, in the educational arena what is remarkable is that many teachers who protest against police brutality and senseless violence perhaps unknowingly practice racial profiling in the hallways and classrooms of their own schools. In other words, the seeming normativity and structured invisibility of racial profiling allows it to operate in educational space as unnoticed, unmarked, and unnamed. This is especially true in schools in which the majority of teachers are white and the majority of students are racial minorities (Sleeter 1993). Having taught in a number of urban public schools, I am familiar with the kinds of situations that students and teachers are facing, and recognize that cultural differences play a covert role in shaping school climate. However, the unwillingness of many educators and educational institutions to confront the continuing significance of race as it relates to growing gaps in discipline and achievement perpetuates ideas of difference as a priori and pathological, rather than as linked to processes of social and economic inequality at work in the broader society.

My purpose, then, is to offer some suggestive observations about the relationship between academic engagement, the transformation of urban educational space, and the changing meanings and practices of "discipline" for African-American youth. The approach I take challenges the ways in which discipline and achievement have been dichotomized in previous studies of black youth. In much of this literature, discipline is viewed primarily as a mechanism for social control as opposed to a strategy for creating a safer learning environment (Noguera 1995). What I am suggesting is that schools must seek ways to create more humane learning environments, both to counter escalating suspension and expulsion rates, and to transform social relationships within the school.

Accordingly, in the following pages I focus on the lives of several African-American youth whose discipline records indicate that they are in the midst of waging some kind of guerrilla battle with school officials, the police, and other representatives of the status quo.[1] By shifting my focus to what motivates these disenfranchised students to forge meaningful relationships with other students yet at the same time feel alienated from their teachers to the extent to where they underachieve in school, I hope to uncover and explore aspects of black culture and educational life that have been relegated to the margins.

Tales from the Field

S: School sucks!
AA: Why you say that?
S: 'Cause the shit is unfair. Straight up, unfair!

When I began working as the On-Campus Suspension (OCS) supervisor at Berkeley High School in 1994, many of my students would walk into my so-called "dungeon" and declare that school is "unfair." For many of them school was about fashion, folks, and fun, but the main objective was funds, that is, to eventually get paid. Don't get me wrong; not all of the students who came through the OCS program understood that the name of the game was to delay gratification, achieve academically, and eventually get paid. But most did. They just didn't believe in the system. That is, they didn't believe that the educational system was working for them. They knew it worked for white students. But they didn't think that it worked for them. And the numbers proved them right. African-American students at Berkeley High have been significantly over-represented in discipline data for years. In 1997–98, black students were over-represented in on-campus and off-campus suspension rates. More specifically, black students made up 68 percent of the off-campus suspensions but comprised only about 40 percent of the school population, and in terms of OCS, out of a total of 775 students sent during the fall 1998, 550 were black.[2]

Because most of the students were underprivileged (which is another word for underpaid), and because of the ways in which most of the students dress, talk, and generally carry themselves, confrontation with school officials and eventual punishment was almost expected, and to a degree accepted, though in hindsight this shouldn't have been the case (Anderson 1999). But the fact that many of my OCS students were part of the "educational under-class" and, according to the literature, responsible for their own educational failure because of the dysfunctional families and neighborhoods they came from, didn't really cross my mind, at least in the ways that it should have. It didn't in part because I was a poor, black, twenty-three-year-old male who came from a single-parent household myself. But more specifically, I didn't think of these students as part of the "educational underclass," and I don't think these students thought of themselves as part of the "educational un-derclass," because the battles that were most dear to them, and the strategies that they adapted to overcome the obstacles they faced, fell outside of the parameters of what most people think of as traditional "educational dis-putes"—grades and test scores. That is not to say that my students were not concerned about grades and test scores, because they were, but most of the psychic and emotional distancing that I witnessed had to do with students feeling a profound sense of alienation and boredom with the schooling process.

Mark Twain was once famously quoted as saying: "Don't let your school-ing get in the way of your education." At Berkeley High, most of the black students who came through the OCS program did not oppose education at all; what they opposed was schooling the content of their education and the way that it was delivered to them (Valenzuela 1999). Proof of this could be seen in interactions between teachers and students. In many of my daily conversations with teachers, very few indicated that they knew their students in a personal way. And conversations with students indicated that they felt so uncomfortable with their teachers that they weren't willing to go to them for help with a personal or even an academic problem. Further still, my observations of school administrators indicated that they routinely ignored the basic needs of students, teachers, as well as staff.

Thus, at Berkeley High, feelings of "unfairness" were (and still are) pervasive and corrosive. Real learning is difficult to sustain in such an environment. A mutual sense of alienation tends to emerge when teachers and students hold different understandings about the nature of schooling. Over short periods of time, such divisions and misunderstandings can exact a high cost in academic, social, and motivational currency (Valenzuela 1999). Worse yet, the school's obvious systemic problems, most evident in its racially skewed suspension and expulsion rates, have been continually brushed aside by district and on-site school administrators.[3] This lack of urgency concerning the relationship between race, discipline, and achievement is itself a sign that processes of racialization and normalization are alive and at work at Berkeley High.

Moreover, because of the invisible nature of these processes, students are often unable to articulate their frustrations and alienation effectively and, being inexperienced with the practice of collective action, most discipline-tracked students settle for individual resistance. That is, they engage in random acts of rebellion, posturing, psychic withdrawal, and physical withdrawal, and attend and participate in only those classes that interest them.

Such daily battles in educational space have enormous implications for the study of African-American opposition and resistance. For, contrary to the experiences of white students, for whom educational space has been a sort of democratic space, a place where people of different class backgrounds could come and share a common social and cultural assimilation experience as well as enjoy a modicum of social mobility, black students experience these white-dominated educational spaces as undemocratic, difficult to assimilate into, and more often than not, dangerous to negotiate.

Filthy and dilapidated educational facilities, white police officers, and racial epithets have been some of the visual reminders of the semicolonial status of black people in their quest for equal access to education since the *Brown v. Board of Education* decision. While the primary purpose of a great deal of civil rights scholarship has been to examine the effects of desegregation, the study of black resistance in multiracial, multicultural educational spaces has remained one of the least-developed areas of inquiry.

This is unfortunate, since examples of black resistance offer some of the richest insights into the ways in which race, gender, class, space, time, and collective memory shape both domination and resistance in educational space (Kelley 1994). In the following pages, then, I begin to remap black opposition to the "schooling" process by examining how the commingling of success and failure operates in the daily lives of individuals who see race (and sometimes gender) as perennial obstacles to social mobility and educational success.

Hidden Stories of Resistance

The militarization of educational space, the growing gap between black and white educational achievement, and the highly charged sociopolitical atmosphere caused by on-campus and off-campus police sweeps during the fall of 1994, turned OCS into a small war zone. OCS became a place where issues of race, class, and gender born in social spaces outside of the school (sidewalks, parks, and streets) raged into OCS, where the stories found a place in the public record.

But it is even more complicated than this. Because if the students thought that the OCS resembled a prison or a dungeon, then they could not help but notice that most of the "inmates" were black. And in some ways the design and function of OCS was, and still is, very similar to that of a prison.

Prisons basically operate in four ways. First, police, prosecutors, and judges have broad discretion to decide who gets arrested, who gets charged, and who gets sentenced to prison. This means that almost anyone who goes to prison knows of others who committed the same crime but who were either not arrested or were not charged or were not sentenced to prison. This means that a significant portion of the prison population experiences their confinement as arbitrary and unjust and may respond with anger which, if not managed properly, can make an individual increasingly antisocial rather than respond with remorse, which tends to have the effect of making a person feel more bound by social norms. Second, prison performs a punitive function. That is, the prison experience is supposed to be demeaning if not painful. The pain and loss of liberty, in theory, is supposed to deter future crime. Third, it goes almost without saying that most prisoners are not trained in marketable skills to the extent that securing a future job becomes difficult after release. And last, the prisoner's records stand as a stigma to discourage future employers from hiring the ex-offenders and mark them as "likely suspects" subject to perpetual harassment from law-enforcement officials.[4]

The OCS system parallels the prison system in these four ways. First, there is no clear expectation, consistent implementation, or widely followed policy concerning school discipline at Berkeley High. Interviews with teachers confirmed that Berkeley High lacks a uniform school discipline policy. According to one teacher: "There's nothing from the school or district. I mean, I just make up my own stuff based on things that other teachers do." The second commonality that OCS and the prison system share is that OCS is often demeaning. In my conversations with students, they reported feeling "bored to death because we do third-grade work in here," and others said, "This school just doesn't give a damn about us. They treat us more like animals than human beings." Third, when students are sent to OCS, they are losing time that could otherwise be devoted to class work. According to Linda Darling-Hammond (1997), repeatedly removing students from the learning environment has the cumulative effect of negatively impacting a student's education and further increasing the academic achievement gap.

Finally, OCS, like other forms of school discipline, has been shown to do long-term damage to students' educational aspirations. Studies have demonstrated that students who are suspended or expelled are more likely than their peers to drop out of school (Fine 1988). "The practice of cleansing the school of 'bad kids' is quite widely acknowledged and equally appreciated by administrators, teachers, and counselors," reports Fine (1988). "And for good reason," adds Wacquant (1997); otherwise, they would be faced with the impossible task of catering to tens of thousands of additional pupils for which the physical infrastructure is nonexistent due to the combination of political indifference and fiscal neglect that have turned public schools into warehouses for the children of today's urban outcasts.

Indeed, in 1994, I remember having hundreds of these so called "urban outcasts" brought into the old gym during one of the off-campus police sweeps (they call it "operation stay in school") and, because I was in charge of OCS (although not invited to participate in the actual planning phases of "operation stay in school"), I spoke with the students about the myriad inconsistencies of school discipline at Berkeley High. During these conversations, we talked about the ways in which the police department and school officials would "arrest black students in the street, but walk right by white students hangin' out in the park."[5] Students also spoke of being "harassed" and "disrespected" in the hallways, and teachers spoke of "hating the job of hallway supervision."

During these conversations, I put before my students an assignment designed to explore the ways in which race and racism operate beneath the surface, through systems, procedures, cultures, and language, in short, the institutional environment that shapes individual behavior. I began by asking them to imagine a crime, any crime. "Picture the first crime that comes to your mind," I said. "What do you see? What does the criminal look like? How old is the perpetrator? Where does that person live? Is the perpetrator rich or poor?" Nine times out of ten my students would identify the criminal as a *he*. Second, they would identify him as a *youth*, between the ages of fifteen and twenty-five. Third, they would identify him as *urban*. Fourth, they would identify him as *black*. Finally, he was almost always *poor*.

In a nation where blacks make up roughly 12 percent of the population, in 1994 they accounted for 56 percent of the nationwide arrests for murder, 42 percent of the arrests for rape, 61 percent of the arrests for robbery, 39 percent of the arrests for aggravated assault, 31 percent of the arrests for burglary, 33 percent of the arrests for larceny, and 40 percent of the arrests for motor vehicle theft.[6] In the educational arena, a recent study of high school disciplinary practices shows that in the two years since "zero tolerance" policies were popularized (in the wake of mass killings at schools), black students at the surveyed schools have been expelled or suspended three to five times more frequently than white students.[7]

Consequently, "racial profiling" in educational space is part of a larger struggle against inequalities of condition and treatment for black children and youth. At Berkeley High, profiling is responsible for many of the tensions I observed between students and teachers, especially in Berkeley High hallways. For example, in the following account, a black female student describes the differential treatment that black male and white male students receive in terms of negotiating hallway space:

S: I was walking down the hall this one time and I was a couple of steps behind a brotha and this white dude . . . and we all passed by this group of teachers (all white) and sure enough the only student the teachers asked for a pass from was the black man. And what was even more messed up . . . was the white boy had already told me he was cuttin' class. So I kept walkin' until I got down the hallway a bit and then I turned around

'cause I heard the brotha cussin' them out. He was sayin' 'Why you gotta stop me? Why not him?' And he was swearin' and actin' a fool and stuff.
AA: And then what happened?
S: Then I heard the teacher sayin' 'We're just tryin' to help you get to class. It's for your own good,' or some shit like that. And I'm tellin' you man, stuff like that happens here all the time.

The individual biographies and histories that students and teachers bring with them to their classroom experiences necessarily influence the chances for successful relationship-building at Berkeley High (Valenzuela 1999). Notwithstanding the teacher's expressed desire to "help" the student, her inability to see the ways in which racialization processes may have limited her and her colleagues' understanding of the ways cultural differences play a covert role in the communication process contribute to her making contradictory statements. On the one hand, she wants to help the student and cares about the student's future; on the other hand, she is oblivious to the ways in which the schooling context at Berkeley High more often than not privileges Euro-American identity over African-American or black identity.

The bias most mainstream teachers have toward black students arises from many sources, including popular culture and the media (Kochman 1981). However, at Berkeley High, an important factor is that most of the teachers are white, middle class, and come from more privileged backgrounds than the majority of black students.[8] Teachers' lack of knowledge of black culture and interactional styles makes them more likely to withhold social ties from these youth. As a result, as in the case above, what may appear to some teachers and administrators as aggressive behavior and opposition to schooling may feel like powerlessness and alienation from the black students' perspective.

To be fair, teachers occupy an uncomfortable middle ground. They are both victims of and collaborators with a system that structurally neglects African-American youth (Fordham 1996). Armed with limited professional development opportunities targeted at preventing racism in school discipline, and inculcated with the belief that if they do not suspend students who are "behavioral problems" schools will become violent, chaotic places where students do not learn, teachers experience a widening distance between themselves and students, and the possibility of alliance between the two diminishes.

Thus, at Berkeley High neither teachers nor students caught in the disciplinary track find much rewarding about everyday life.

Conclusion

School discipline at Berkeley High is like a mirror in which the whole school can see the darker outlines of its face. Our ideas of justice, good and bad, take visible form in it, and thus we see ourselves in deep relief. Because the system deals with some behavioral problems and ignores others, the image that we see is distorted like a carnival mirror. That is, the image reflected is not false, but the proportions are exaggerated and distorted. Like a carnival mirror, although nothing is reflected that does not exist, the image is more a creation of the mirror than a picture of the real world (Goffman 1963; Reiman 1990).

If the discipline system gives us a distorted image of "behavioral problems" at Berkeley High, we are doubly deceived. First, because it creates a particular image of discipline, that is, that behavioral problems are the work of the poor, urban, black males who are so well represented in suspension and expulsion rates. The second deception is the flip side of this: that academic success and upward mobility are the province of groups of Europeans and Asians.[9]

This is part of the powerful magic of school discipline at Berkeley High and, according to the data, at other urban schools across the country and the world (Wacquant 1997). That is, by virtue of its focus on individual responsibility, the discipline system at Berkeley High diverts our attention away from the ways in which the school itself may exploit and violate the rights of individuals, as well as of entire racioethnic groups. By virtue of its presumed neutrality, the discipline system transforms the established social order from one that is open to critical comparison with another into a supposedly *normal* social order immune to criticism. This is an extremely important bit of ideological alchemy. It stems from the fact that the same action can be labeled deviant or normal depending on the race of the individual who commits the act.

Schools wishing to reverse what often amounts to racist practices would do well to consider the ways in which current configurations of schooling limit the presence of academically oriented networks among African-American youth. For many of the social cleavages that develop between youth of different races emerge, in part, because of the major institutional cleavages already engendered by curricular and disciplinary tracking. At Berkeley High, for example, racial profiling is associated with "cultural tracking," whereby African-American youth are shuttled into the disciplinary track and away from honors and AP courses. The consequences of this form of "profiling" are evident in the marked differences between who completes required courses for admission to four-year colleges or universities (European-American students, 77 percent; Asian-American, 57 percent; Chicano/Latino, 53 percent; African-American, 33 percent; Filipino, 29 percent) and who receives a D or F in required courses (70 percent of African-American and 60 percent of Chicano/Latino students).[10]

This separation encourages and legitimates an academic hierarchy that relegates black youth to the bottom of the ladder. Once there, social distancing and deidentification with schooling further push African-American students who are not channeled into the more privileged tracks of the school toward the academic periphery, where they are deprived of access to the academic, social, and motivational currency available in the more academically rich and supportive environments of the school. The solution is not to continue to disproportionately place African-American students in the disciplinary track, but rather to restructure both disciplinary as well as academic tracks so that they encompass early intervention processes which enhance learning opportunities for all.[11]

Discipline tracking based on race, or racial profiling, which places students in the discipline system, not only reinforces students' misperceptions about each other, but also deprives African-American youth of potentially positive school experiences, including enhanced social ties and networks. The pervasive view among African-American youth that school is unfair underscores the extent to which many of them are alienated from school in general and from the most valued aspects of the curriculum specifically. Ironically, the stigmatized status of black youth enhances their peer group solidarity. With regard to this, one student made the following comment: "We may not control the classrooms, but we definitely control the hallways and the street." Vacillating between displays of aggressiveness and indifference, many black youth underachieve academically and suffer emotionally because of it. For teachers and administrators, rather than seeing the attitudes these youth display as aspects of agency, forms of critical thinking, or resisting the school's lack of concern about them, they offer negative appraisals of the students behavior. However, beneath the façade are black youth who want fairness to be an unconditional part of the teacher-student learning exchange.

Despite the evidence that black youth are underachieving in comparison to youth from other racial locations, the theoretical questions that emerge from this work involve the ways in which the discipline system subtracts resources from black youth and thus contributes to their academic decline. To the extent that I have illuminated these processes, this study provides an important framework toward reversing barriers to academic progress for African-American youth.

NOTES

1. The data used in this report are from follow-up in-depth individual interviews with a sub-sample of 30 students as well as direct participant observation with 12 students and 15 teachers, administrators, and counselors. Most of the student voices are from students who were repeatedly sent to OCS (repeatedly meaning more than seven times in a semester).

2. According to the most recent data the composition of the student body is: 38 percent European American, 38 percent African American, 10.5 percent Chicano/Latino, 11 percent Asian/Pacific Islander, and 0.6 percent Native American. An estimated 20 percent are non-native English speakers, and about 10 percent of students are enrolled in English as a Second Language classes. Although nearly one half of the students reside in areas of the city where the per capita income exceeds $60,000, approximately 37 percent of the students qualify for free or reduced lunch.

3. Currently, the Berkeley High School district purports to have a 0 percent dropout rate. However, diversity project data suggest that this claim is unfounded and the problems are a bit more complex.

4. This list, of course, is debatable. That is, some prison officials do try to treat their inmates with dignity and respect their privacy and self-determination to the greatest extent possible within an institution dedicated to involuntary confinement. But most don't. Some prisons do provide meaningful job train-

ing, and some parole officers are not only fair but go out of their way to help their "clients" find jobs and make it "legally." But most don't. And, of course, plenty of people are arrested for doing things that no society ought to condone. According to Reiman (1990), however, "On the whole most of the system's practices make more sense if we look at them as ingredients in an attempt to maintain rather than reduce crime!"

5. In this case the student is using arrest as a synonym for detain. Students caught in police sweeps were not charged by the Berkeley police department; however, they were suspended or given detention by Berkeley school officials.

6. Institute for Criminological Research, Rutgers University, 1994.

7. Applied Research Center, "Racial Disparity in School Discipline," 1999.

8. There is some degree of diversity among the adults employed at the school, but here too racial differences are manifested within the school's hierarchy. Whereas the majority of teachers are white (67 percent white, 19 percent African-American, 7 percent Asian/Pacific Islanders, 4 percent Chicano/Latino, and 3 percent mixed-race), the overwhelming majority of nonteaching staff is black. And though there is more diversity among the administrators and counselors (57 percent are white, 29 percent African-American, 7 percent Asian/Pacific Islander, 7 percent Chicano/Latino), minority parents are largely underrepresented on most decision-making bodies at the school (PTSA, Site Council, Berkeley High development group). It is also important to note that high turnover rates for teachers, and especially administrators, at Berkeley High make it difficult to sustain any progress in the efficiency with which the school is run.

9. A case in point: 90 percent of the students who received disciplinary referrals, on-campus suspensions, or expulsions are African-American or Chicano/Latino, in juxtaposition to SAT scores, where white and Asian students consistently exceed state and national averages and go on to graduate from top universities.

10. At Berkeley High they now have inflated GPAs in the ninth grade because the school no longer gives out Ds in the core courses.

11. For example, at Berkeley High, OCS works in isolation from other student support services like the health center, conflict resolution, and the student learning center. There is no reason these resources shouldn't be linked in a way which maximizes the academic and emotional resources available to the student.

REFERENCES

Anderson, E. 1999. *Code of the Street: Decency, Violence, and the Moral Life of the Inner City.* New York: Norton.

Darling-Hammond, L. 1997. *The Right to Learn: A Blueprint for Creating Schools That Work.* San Francisco: Jossey-Bass.

Fine, M. 1988. *Framing Dropouts.* Albany: State University of New York Press.

Fordham, S. 1996. *Blacked Out: Dilemmas of Race, Identity, and Success at Capital High.* Chicago: University of Chicago Press.

Goffman, E. 1963. *Stigma: Notes on the Management of Spoiled Identity.* New York: Simon and Schuster.

Kelley, R. 1994. *Race Rebels: Culture, Politics, and the Black Working Class.* New York: Free Press.

Kochman, T. 1981. *Black and White Styles in Conflict.* Chicago: University of Chicago Press.

Noguera, P. 1995. "Preventing and Producing Violence: A Critical Analysis of Responses to School Violence." *Harvard Educational Review* 65(2): 189–212.

Reiman, J. 1990. *The Rich Get Richer and the Poor Get Prison.* New York: Macmillan.

Sleeter, C. 1993. "How White Teachers Construct Race." In C. McCarthy and W. Crichlow (eds.), *Race, Identity, and Representation in Education.* New York: Routledge.

Valenzuela, A. 1999. *Subtractive Schooling : U.S.-Mexican Youth and the Politics of Caring.* Albany: State University of New York Press.

Wacquant, L. J. D. 1997. "Three Pernicious Premises in the Study of the American Ghetto." *International Journal of Urban and Regional Research* 21(2): 342–50.

Decatur: A Story of Intolerance

VALERIE JOHNSON

Between October 1 and 4, 1999, six African-American male students were expelled from the Decatur, Illinois, public schools for two years for allegedly participating in a fistfight at a football game on September 17, 1999.[1] On October 2, Rainbow/PUSH Coalition (R/PC) Decatur chapter vice president Keith Anderson arrived at the R/PC national headquarters in Chicago seeking assistance with the case. Chief among Anderson's concerns was a quote that had appeared in the local Decatur newspaper in which a Board of Education member claimed that the expulsion decision was "in line with the board's zero tolerance policy toward violence." As far as Anderson knew, the district had not publicized such a policy in its manual of Student Discipline Policy and Procedures.

At first glance the issue appeared to be an isolated case of injustice. But after I traveled to Decatur and met with school officials as the R/PC's national education spokesperson, and over the course of several months, it became clear to me that the case of the Decatur Six was symptomatic of a larger national trend in the use of zero tolerance policies. Indeed, the Decatur expulsion case speaks volumes about our national educational priorities and the way we treat our youth.

Although zero tolerance school discipline policies are not new, the involvement of the Reverend Jesse L. Jackson, Sr., and the Rainbow/PUSH Coalition in the Decatur, Illinois, expulsion case gave the issue national prominence. Proponents of the expulsions viewed Reverend Jackson's involvement in the case as interference in the local affairs of the Decatur school board.

Opponents, on the other hand, raised questions regarding the equity and efficacy of school discipline policies. Although contentious, the debate has grave implications for the policies and practices of local school boards as well as for the fortunes of African-American students, who are disproportionately impacted by school discipline policies.

When, in August 1999, the Decatur, Illinois, Board of Education unanimously adopted and passed a joint resolution on school violence, it joined a growing national movement. The resolution read:

> Be it resolved that the Board of Education for the following School Districts support and join Macon County . . . the law enforcement and mental health agencies in declaring a no-tolerance position on school violence, and encourages all citizens to make a commitment to violence-free schools.

The resolution and the national trend ultimately led to the crisis in Decatur, Illinois. Absent a growing national concern about school safety or subsequent legislation, the fistfight that occurred on September 17, 1999, in Decatur would have been punishable by a ten-day suspension at most.

Although the fight involved no weapons and resulted in no sustained injuries, the school board contended that it constituted an extreme act of violence, and charged the boys with "gang-like activities" and two counts of "physical violence with staff or students." On October 7, 1999, joined by concerned ministers and community leaders, I met with Decatur Board of Education president Jackie Goetter and other Decatur public school officials to set forth objections to the expulsions.

The first was that the district's zero tolerance resolution had been arbitrarily applied. Having examined the district's school discipline code, I found no mention of any zero tolerance resolution. We felt that it was an undue burden that the youth were subject to penalties resulting from an infraction that had not been clearly set forth and disseminated in the district's school discipline code.

Second, although the youth had varying levels of participation in the fight, ranging from victim to perpetrator, and all had different school records, all received the same punishment. This suggested that the board viewed the youth as a group rather than as individuals, and points to one reason why zero tolerance policies are so objectionable. Rather than considering mitigating circumstances, zero tolerance policies are absolute—regardless of the context or consequences, minimal involvement results in the same punishment as maximum involvement.

After the fistfight, even the victim was subject to a two-year expulsion. Although he was subsequently given the opportunity to withdraw pending expulsion, his withdrawal carried the same weight as an expulsion because he was not allowed to enroll in any public or private school in Decatur. When later asked why even the victim of the fight was subject to expulsion, school board attorney Jeffrey Taylor indicated that the victim had also thrown some punches. In response to Reverend Jackson's query as to whether the punches might have been defensive in nature, Taylor indicated that they were disturbing nonetheless. There was also evidence that at least one of the expelled students had not actually thrown any punches in the fight but had, like other youth, run toward the fight. According to district representatives, the student was expelled because he had reportedly pushed past a principal when he was asked to stop.

Third, the punishment of a two-year expulsion from school did not fit the infraction. A record search turned up no prior example of an expulsion solely on the basis of a fistfight. Other two-year expulsions in Decatur had resulted from weapon or drug violations, bomb threats, and a case in which there had been sustained injuries resulting from a fight in which karate was used.

Fourth, the youth were denied due process in their expulsion hearings. Although two student eyewitnesses to the youths' involvement were allowed to enter written statements into the record, they were not present at the hearings and therefore were not subject to examination. Equally problematic, witnesses who were present at the hearing to testify against the six youth were essentially giving second-hand information reportedly handed down through an investigation of the fight.

At the October 7 meeting, I also appealed to district officials on the basis of morality and ethics. My argument and that of others who were present was that there was no educational or societal value in expelling the youth for two years. In a later meeting between Reverend Jackson and district officials, Superintendent of Schools Kenneth Arndt confirmed the basis of this concern. Arndt explained that approximately 80 percent of youth expelled for extended periods did not return to finish their education, but instead typically dropped out and became involved in more serious offenses. Several ministers and community leaders made passionate appeals to school officials, vowing that they would personally insure that the youth would not get into further trouble if allowed to return to school. District officials concluded the meeting promising to take our concerns under consideration.

On October 11, 1999, Decatur R/PC representatives attended a regularly scheduled meeting of the board of education to inquire about the status of the case, and were met with silence from the board. After consistent inquiries were not addressed, Keith Anderson, vice president of the local chapter, sought the advice of longtime friend and vice president of the National R/PC, Reverend James T. Meeks. Reverend Meeks advised Anderson to bring the youth and their parents to R/PC headquarters for a meeting with Reverend Jackson on Saturday, October 30, 1999. Upon meeting with Reverend Jackson it was decided that he would seek to meet with board officials in Decatur on Wednesday, November 3, 1999.

On November 2, 1999, Reverend Jackson arrived in Decatur to hold a community rally at one of the local churches. The rally was a resounding success, with approximately 1,500 in attendance. Reverend Jackson told the audience that the district "should be in the business of educating rather than punishing youth, and in lifting them up rather than locking them out of educational opportunities." And he added, "God has zero tolerance for sin, but because of mercy and grace, we are all saved."

Reverend Jackson also strongly admonished the expelled students, telling them that he did not condone violence in any form. After allowing the boys their request to apologize to the community and to appeal for mercy, Reverend Jackson further stated that "youthful indiscretions of this nature should not warrant a death sentence and the denial of educational opportunity."

The response from Decatur Board of Education president Goetter was chilling. In news reports Ms. Goetter revealed considerable angst about Reverend Jackson's involvement in the issue. She said that the expulsions were a local issue and that she did not understand why a man of Reverend Jackson's prominence would become involved with the case. She saw it as an attempt to meddle in local issues and emphatically insisted that the board's decisions regarding the boys were a closed matter.

The response from the media was also troubling. Rather than focusing on the merits of the issue, reporters repeatedly asked Reverend Jackson whether he would have become involved if the youth were white. Reverend Jackson emphatically denied their suggestions, indicating that "the expulsions were not a matter of black or white, but rather, a matter of wrong or right."

And he reminded them that he had gone to Kosovo to negotiate the release of three hostages, none of whom were African American.

The following morning, Reverend Jackson and R/PC representatives met with Ms. Goetter and other Decatur school officials. Ms. Goetter again strongly reiterated her objections to Reverend Jackson's involvement. She did, however, indicate that the board would be willing to review the youths' records after the 1999–2000 school year to determine whether they could return to school for the fall 2000–01 school term, but, as it stood, the two-year expulsions would remain in effect.

Reverend Jackson pointed out that the boys had already been out of school far longer than the typical ten-day suspension for a fistfight. Reverend Jackson also argued that the system should be concerned with the boys' futures and in insuring that they continued their education. As Reverend Jackson saw it, the social and economic costs to the community would be far greater if the boys were not returned to school. Still, Reverend Jackson's numerous appeals were rejected. So he met afterward with representatives from the local media and announced his intention to hold a march and rally on the upcoming Sunday in Decatur, and to take the boys back to school on the following Monday.

The march and rally on November 7 attracted more than 6,000 participants. Before the rally, we received hundreds of telephone calls, faxes, and e-mails from across the nation, reporting similar incidents of unfair expulsions and suspensions. It became exceedingly clear that the issue was bigger than Decatur and had national implications.

Prior to the march and rally it also became clear that the Decatur public schools had a history of excessive expulsions and suspensions. During the 1998–99 school year, Decatur public schools had suspended more than 15 percent of its student population. And it was also apparent that African-American youth in Decatur were disproportionately impacted by the system's discipline policies. Although African-American youth represented 39 percent of the district's student population, they represented 60 percent of the suspensions and 71 percent of the expulsions during the 1998–99 school year. Between the 1994–95 school year and the end of the fall term of the 1999–2000 school year, African-American youth represented 83 percent of the district's expulsions.

These trends are consistent across Illinois and the nation. While African-American youth represented 21 percent of the total student population in

Illinois during the 1997–98 school year, they represented 43 percent of the state's 2,744 expulsions. During the 1996–97 school year, African Americans represented 17 percent of the nation's public school population and 32 percent of the nation's suspensions. Whether the subject is school discipline in Illinois or across the nation, the result is the same—African-American youth bear the brunt of school punishment. And contrary to the claims of Decatur school officials, the issue is both local and national.

The national media descended on Decatur for the Sunday march and rally. That night, Illinois governor George Ryan telephoned Reverend Jackson with concerns about his vow to take the boys back to school the following day. Reverend Jackson attempted to assuage the governor's concerns, but informed him that he had no intentions of altering his plans.

But the next day, Monday, November 8, the Decatur Board of Education cancelled classes in the district's three high schools, having received threats from white supremacist groups vowing to retaliate if the youth were allowed to return to school. At 10:00 A.M., Governor Ryan arrived in Decatur to meet with school and R/PC representatives in an attempt to mediate a solution to the escalating crisis. After several hours, the situation remained deadlocked. The chief concern of Decatur officials was the appearance that they had caved in to R/PC demands. Unfortunately, the youths' futures were not their primary concern; rather, the board feared the loss of confidence by the community.

So, the governor issued an executive order allowing the expelled youth to enroll in an alternative education program. In many respects, this solution appeased district officials' concerns. The governor's intervention allowed the district to save face while simultaneously allowing the youth an educational option—one of many options that district officials had never considered.

Finally, the Decatur Board of Education allowed Reverend Jackson to make an appeal to the full board for the first time. After hearing Reverend Jackson's remarks, the body met in closed session and decided to modify the term of the expulsions to the end of the school year. Thus, the students would be allowed to reenroll in school as early as the summer of 2000.

Although many viewed the day's events as a triumph, they had not considered Reverend Jackson's dogged tenacity for justice. The governor had successfully brokered a compromise to send the youth to alternative schools immediately, and the board had modified the expulsions to one year. Reverend Jackson, however, remained bent on seeing the boys return to their respective schools immediately. Much to the chagrin of the media and local school officials, the youth decided not to enroll in the alternative programs. Reverend Jackson argued that the time that the youth had already been out of school had been more than enough punishment for a fistfight at a football game. He strongly felt that to compromise on the issue would make a mockery of the injustice that had occurred.

The following day, Decatur officials decided to escalate the conflict. In the meeting with the governor and Reverend Jackson, district officials had made claims that the fight was the worst they had ever seen in Decatur and bordered on criminal offense. On Tuesday, November 9—almost two months after the September 17 fight—the state's attorney brought criminal charges against the students and other youth for their involvement in the fight. Then, district officials released the youths' confidential school records to the national media. Although releasing school records can be a criminal offense, the board acted to sway public opinion in the case and deflect attention away from its own actions.

When the media received the records, they reported only on those students who had previously been suspended and who had poor grades. It was widely reported that one of the youth was a third-year freshman. The expulsions, however, had not been related to previous offenses or academic standing, a fact highlighted by the board on numerous occasions. By releasing the records, school officials waged an outright campaign to mischaracterize the boys as delinquents who had little to no regard for education. Indeed, later that day a video depicting the fight at the football game was released to the national media. Prior to the release of the tape, district officials had shielded it from public viewing. With public attention mounting, it became a weapon in the war to regain their reputation and to deflect attention away from the larger issue of the unwarranted expulsions.

In a glaring omission, the media failed to report that two of the expelled youth were within a few credits of graduating. Also underreported was the fact that one of the seniors was the cocaptain of his school's basketball team, had received a 3.5 grade point average in the previous school term, and was also a peer mediator at his school. The other senior was captain of the school's track team, and both had received numerous inquiries from colleges and universities.

Meanwhile, R/PC attorney Lewis Myers, Jr. filed charges in U.S. Federal Court in Champaign, Illinois, on behalf of the boys and their parents, seeking the boys' return to school. The four counts presented in the motion pertained to the district's zero tolerance policy, the district's characterization of the youth as gang members (ganglike activity), disproportionate punishment, and improper notice. A subsequent amendment to the motion added counts alleging racial discrimination and violation of equal protection.

The Decatur school district also began to face pressure from the office of the State Board of Education. Indeed, Illinois superintendent of education Glen "Max" McGee had indicated that he believed the Decatur board should have held the students' expulsions in abeyance in order to allow them to transfer to alternative schools.

The night of November 9, McGee met with Reverend Jackson and R/PC representatives to seek Reverend Jackson's agreement *not* to take the students back to school the next day. R/PC representatives responded with a "ten-point plan."

Of chief concern to Reverend Jackson and R/PC representatives was the ability of the two seniors to complete the credits that they needed to graduate on time. Another goal was to assure the two seniors would have the opportunity to enroll in school in time to play their respective sports and thereby be eligible for sport scholarships to college. Other key components of the ten-point plan were:

- That Superintendent McGee actively seek dismissal of the criminal charges against the youth;
- That Superintendent McGee seek the support of the chair of the House Elementary and Secondary Education Committee to convene hearings on suspensions and expulsions across the state; and
- That the Decatur school board review and clarify its zero tolerance policy and establish a committee comprised of education experts, clergy, and other community leaders to review disciplinary decisions and make recommendations for improvement.

But the Decatur board refused to meet with Reverend Jackson and Rainbow/ PUSH officials.

So, on Sunday, November 14, Reverend Jackson led another march and rally, and approximately 10,000 participated. Speaking before the crowd, Reverend Jackson vowed to take the youth back to school on Tuesday, November 16.

Reverend Jackson decided to cross police lines at Eisenhower High School with the parents of the expelled students. In a last-minute decision, Reverend

Jackson also decided that the youth should not accompany them, given the fact that they faced criminal charges. Reminiscent of the 1957 placement of National Guard troops at Central High School in Little Rock, Arkansas, Decatur police blocked the entryway to the school. Reverend Jackson, R/PC Illinois field director Mark Allen, and two other demonstrators were arrested and charged with felony mob action, contributing to the delinquency of a minor, and solicitation to commit a crime.

After Reverend Jackson's arrest, the demonstrators grew increasingly hostile. Reverend James Meeks climbed atop a car and appealed to the crowd to maintain calm and reason. Later that evening Reverend Meeks was allowed to make an impassioned appeal to Decatur board members to consider the R/PC ten-point plan. After deliberating, however, board members issued a statement indicating that they would hold firm to their decision.

On the following day, Thursday, November 17, 1999, Attorney Lewis Myers, accompanied by Reverend Jackson and R/PC representatives, filed a court case for damages resulting from the release of the students' private school records. As Reverend Jackson entered the court building he was served with a notice to appear in court the following day for a preliminary hearing on the Decatur Board's attempt to bar Reverend Jackson, R/PC representatives, and the youth and their parents from Decatur Public School property.

The next day, the youths' parents, along with other R/PC representatives, were served with court documents to appear in court with Reverend Jackson later on that afternoon. Ironically, in their attempt to block all demonstrations on school property, the Decatur Board also named white supremacist leader Matt Hale as a defendant in the trespass case.

Before appearing in court, Reverend Jackson and R/PC representatives accompanied the youth and their parents to the regional superintendent's office to enroll the youth in alternative education programs. Upon arriving, Reverend Jackson was met with a bevy of media, white supremacist Matt Hale, and parents protesting R/PC efforts to enroll the youth in alternative programs. Although the governor authorized the youth to enroll in the programs, these parents believed the governor's intervention to be unfair, because they had been on waiting lists for months seeking to enroll their children in alternative programs. For Reverend Jackson and R/PC representatives, the protests pointed to yet another flaw in the provision of education—youth are routinely expelled without any option for alternative educational opportunities. Despite passage of the Safe Schools Act in 1995, which established a system of alternative schools across the state, adequate provisions had not been made to accommodate all students who had been expelled.

On November 22, 1999 a hearing was held in Federal Court in Champaign, Illinois. Wishing to resolve the matter as soon as possible, Judge Michael McCuskey set the trial date for December 27–29, 1999, thereby maintaining the possibility that the boys would have the opportunity to return to their schools in January.

Between November 22, 1999 and the beginning of the December trial, the youth faced preliminary/probable cause hearings for the criminal charges against them. Attorney Lewis Myers assembled a team of dedicated lawyers who were willing to volunteer their time and resources to defend the boys. In addition to assistance with the criminal charges, Myers sought and received significant assistance from prominent attorneys across the nation for the civil cases.

On December 8, 1999 Reverend Jackson, R/PC representatives and several education activists met with U.S. Secretary Richard Riley to discuss the proliferation of zero tolerance policies and their disproportionate impact on African-American youth. Although Secretary Riley declined Reverend Jackson's request to join him in speaking out against recalcitrant districts, he indicated that he had recently introduced legislation in the U.S. Congress that directly addressed the issues raised by the Decatur expulsions.

The Department's legislation proposes that all school discipline policies should be sound and equitable, and that all students should be provided with an education even if suspended or expelled. The proposed legislation also provides that due process should be afforded students who are facing suspension or expulsion, and that changes in discipline policy should require the input of parents, teachers and administrators.

On December 27, 1999, the case originally brought on behalf of the Decatur Six against the Decatur school board began in U.S. District Court. The parents gave impassioned testimony about their impression that the board had already made a decision to expel the boys prior to any hearings. Mr. Jeffrey Perkins, an African American who was on the board during the youths' expulsion hearings and the only board member who had voted against their expulsion, testified that several board members had characterized the boys as gang members and a pack of dogs prior to making their decisions.

Another witness for the plaintiffs, Dr. Walter Amprey, former superintendent of the Baltimore public schools, testified on zero tolerance policies and the importance of establishing uniform discipline policies. Amprey testified that in reviewing the documents, he did not recall ever seeing the term "zero tolerance." When asked specifically about the district's zero tolerance policy, Jeffrey Perkins testified that the zero tolerance resolution that the board had adopted did not carry the same weight as policy, and that he could not recall any discussion by the school board about the resolution during any expulsion hearing.

Witnesses for the defense included Decatur schools superintendent Kenneth Arndt; board president Jackie Goetter; Gary Hunt, director of Decatur public schools' human resource department; and Walt Scott and Ed Boehm, two principals who were present at the football game when the fight occurred. Defense witness testimony suggested that Board of Education members had rubber-stamped the hearing officer's recommendation to expel the youth without reading the records pertaining to the case. Upon questioning principal Ed Boehm, it also became apparent that board officials had exaggerated the length of the fight and the extent to which it had disrupted the football game. When initially asked how long the game was interrupted by the fight, Mr. Boehm testified that the fight interrupted the game for fifteen to twenty minutes. After plaintiffs' attorneys played the tape, it was revealed that the game had been interrupted a total of two minutes and one second, and that the fight itself had lasted less than twenty seconds.

However, on January 11, 2000, Judge Michael McCuskey ruled in favor of the defendants, indicating that plaintiffs had not met their burden of proof. In the opening statement of his order against the plaintiffs, Judge McCuskey characterized the fight as a violent confrontation. He also indicated that the absence of weapons did not mean that "innocent bystanders were not harmed, frightened, and forced to flee the stands to avoid serious injury." The videotape of the fight had proven to be a double-edged sword from the beginning. Public opinion regarding the severity of the fight had been split. For some, the fight was reminiscent of fights that routinely occur among spectators at sporting events across the nation, or brawls that they themselves were involved in as youth. For others, however, the fight was the worst that they had ever seen, and far beyond the pale of a routine brawl on the playground. Unfortunately for the plaintiffs, the judge was of the latter opinion.

And although Judge McCuskey acknowledged that the district had in fact passed a zero tolerance resolution in August 1999, he concluded that the plaintiffs had failed to establish that the school board had actually utilized it in the expulsion case. Judge McCuskey gave considerable weight to Jeffrey Perkins's testimony that the resolution had not carried the weight of a policy.

As for the disproportionate number of expulsions of African-American students, Judge McCuskey acknowledged them but ruled that "a claim of racial discrimination and violation of equal protection cannot be based upon mere statistics standing alone." He further cited U.S. Supreme Court rulings that to "establish a discriminatory effect in a race case, the claimant must show that similarly situated individuals of a different race were not prosecuted."

Evidence indicated that the range of expulsion time for white students for their participation in fights had been from five months to a period of one year, three months. However, Judge McCuskey considered the modified term of expulsion. With the modified calculation, the plaintiffs' term of expulsion did not exceed the average term of white students who had been expelled. Judge McCuskey gave considerable weight to the defendant testimony that the fight far exceeded the magnitude of other fights in the district.

Judge McCuskey, seemingly discounting the testimony from the mothers of the youths, ruled that the district had adequately notified the parents of the significance and importance of the expulsion hearings, and that the district did not have the burden of due process typically afforded in non-school-related hearings. According to Judge McCuskey, "due process requires an opportunity to be heard in a meaningful manner. Accordingly, an expulsion hearing is sufficient to meet procedural due process requirements if the plaintiff knew the charges against him, received notice of the expulsion hearing, and was given a full opportunity to explain his position in an evidentiary hearing."

Reverend Jackson voiced disappointment over the decision but said that R/PC had achieved victories prior to the court hearing. On October 7, 1999, the youth had faced two-year expulsions without the option for alternative education. As a result of the R/PC's involvement and tremendous community intervention, the board's original two-year expulsion was modified to the end of the school year, with the opportunity to attend alternative schools. This indeed was a victory, albeit incomplete. The two seniors graduated in May 2000 with their respective classes, and the other four youth are receiving credit for their work in the alternative programs. At the press conference after the ruling, Reverend Jackson vowed to continue the quest for justice in Decatur, stating his intentions to appeal the court's decision.

The Decatur expulsions were ultimately modified because of the efforts of the Reverend Jackson and the Rainbow/PUSH Coalition, Decatur ministers and community leaders, a team of dedicated attorneys led by attorney Lewis Myers, and government officials such as Governor George Ryan and Illinois Secretary of Education Glen "Max" McGee. Without these combined efforts, the expelled youth would have had no opportunity to continue their education until 2001. Equally important, the effort served to galvanize the Decatur community like no other issue had previously, and empowered the expelled youth and their parents to seek justice.

As a result of Reverend Jackson's intervention in the Decatur cases, four pieces of legislation were introduced in the 2000 term of the Illinois state legislature pertaining to expulsions. One bill, introduced by Representative Monique Davis, sought to establish a uniform list of infractions by which a student could be expelled and limit the maximum term of expulsion to one year, but it was defeated in committee.[2] The chief criticism of the bill was that it encroached on the prerogatives of local school boards. The committee established a subcommittee to investigate suspensions and expulsions across the state; however, their allegiance to local control points to the limitations of challenging school discipline policies on a statewide basis. Instead, it is imperative that citizens across the state act locally through the election process and hold board of education members accountable to the larger community concern of educating all children in order that they may become productive members of our society. Ultimately, all power resides within the citizenry, and abdicating this responsibility undermines government's capacity for corrective action and the realization of our fundamental goals for all youth.

NOTES

1. Although seven Decatur public school students were originally implicated, one student was allowed to withdraw pending expulsion. He was, however, included in all negotiations to return the youth to school.
2. H. B. 3991, introduced to the House Committee on Elementary and Secondary Education on February 9, 2000.

America Still Eats Her Young

GLORIA LADSON-BILLINGS

I realized there is this tremendous anger toward America's youth. . . .
[We] are gutting the education infrastructure and
replacing it with the police.

—JESSE JACKSON[1]

During the 1970s, protest singer–poet Gil Scott Heron released an album entitled *Winter in America*. On the album was a song with an even more provocative title—"America Eats Her Young." The essence of the song was that America has a callous disregard for the health and welfare of its children. It sent them to fight an unjust war in Vietnam. It shot them down on the university campuses of Kent State and Jackson State. It pursued them with attack dogs and fire hoses when they tried to attend schools and be served at lunch counters or bus station waiting rooms. Unfortunately, this disregard for the health and welfare for the young in the society has worsened. The targets of our scorn are even younger and the social policy of "zero tolerance" indicates that America still eats her young.

When I was a kid growing up in West Philadelphia in the late 1950s and early 1960s, the major form of entertainment was the Saturday matinee at the local movie theater. We didn't have Little League or Pop Warner or any other "organized youth activities." We played plenty of sports and other playground games, but the real community fun happened every Saturday at the Leader Theater. First, the price was right—10 cents before 5:00—and we could stay all day. The theater showed a double feature, cartoons, and a serial. What we saw at the movies typically became the hot topic on Monday morning in the schoolyard. I was introduced to Frankenstein, Dracula, and the Mummy at the Saturday matinee.

One Saturday we saw a movie entitled *Rumble on the Docks.* I remember it as a B-film about street gangs on the waterfront. However, something about the movie struck a chord with a number of the boys in the community. By Monday, two brothers—a fifth grader and a sixth grader—decided that it would be fun to simulate the two film gangs at our school. Before anyone knew anything, a sizable number of the fifth- and sixth-grade boys had divided themselves into the "diggers" and the "stompers," just as in the movie. Each day at recess, lunchtime, and before and after school, the two groups were engaged in full-fledged battles. Fights broke out all over the school. The girls decided that they, too, should join the "fun," and so they aligned themselves with the undersized fifth-grade diggers. They called themselves the "coverers" to signify their role in covering for the diggers.

Students were identified as members of one of the gangs by chalk-lettered symbols written on their coats or jackets. To increase our numbers, a few of us stole pieces of chalk and surreptitiously wrote our gang symbol on the backs of the coats of some unsuspecting classmates. Once out on the playground with a freshly written "D" on their backs, our unknowing "new recruits" generally learned of their membership because someone from the rival gang would slug them in the back. Shocked by the assault, people would defend themselves. In an instant, a full-fledged fight would ensue. They were in the gang.

Our school administration was used to kids fighting on occasion, but this everyday—at every break—violence was unprecedented. Understandably, the principal, the teachers, and the parents wanted it stopped. As I recall, no one got seriously hurt during these melees and it was starting to be fun. It was dangerous and seductive and it created a sense of affiliation for some students that they had never experienced.

Within a couple of weeks the principal had ferreted out the leaders of the gangs, and, in typical elementary-school fashion, they "ratted out" their gang members. To teach them a lesson, the school took the tiny gangsters to the local police station. There, a police officer took the group through the lineup room (almost no one reached the five-foot line) and gave them a stern lecture about engaging in behavior that would land them in jail. Everyone was terrified and before long we all promised to walk the straight and narrow. Our careers as gang members ended abruptly.

Now I am not naïve enough to believe that a brief trip to the police station would solve the social ills of today's schools. The children of this present era have seen, heard, and experienced too much to be fooled by the staging of an arrest. They have become hardened by the realities of a society that tries eleven-year-olds as adults and offers the death penalty as the only solution to what ails us. However, what I learned from my elementary school experience was that adults have a responsibility to protect children—all children. And that protection needs to be in the form of care and support, not punishment and recrimination. My classmates were marched to the police station as a form of "second chance"—not as zero tolerance. We were kids. We did something stupid. But we were not considered unsalvageable. The adults in our school and community understood that we were their future and they were not about to throw that future away lightly.

During my high school years we engaged in another kind of foolish violence. We thought of it as "school pride," but it was more likely a dangerous form of bravado. Whenever our football team played certain rivals, we expected a fight to erupt at the end. In fact, a common expression was, "We lost the game, but we won the fight!" This situation became so commonplace that school authorities started banning student spectators from the games. The games were reassigned to neutral, unannounced sites. The team members were taken to the game, the game was played, and we learned about the results the following day. After three or four of these "no fans allowed" contests, we changed our behavior. Once again, the adults in our school community demonstrated a concern that told us that there were rules and boundaries, not that we were unredeemable.

My personal examples are not offered to suggest either a romantic nostalgia or ignorance about our present-day circumstances. Are our children more violent? Indeed they are, because *we* are more violent. Our children are just that—our children. They did not arrive from some other planet. They are the products of the world we created. They have seen more assaults, murders, and rapes than any previous generation. Should we lock them up and throw away the key to solve the problems we thrust them into? Zero tolerance is a simplistic and cruel response to a complex problem that requires careful thought and action.

How did we get to this place? How did we become enemies of our own children? When did we start hating them? I would argue that we became alienated from our children when we ceased to consider them *our* children. Lisa Delpit[2] talks about teaching "other people's children" because she recognized the gulf that has grown between teachers and the children they teach. Not surprisingly, this gulf replicates the racial/cultural chasm that exists in the society. Today, our urban classrooms are comprised mainly of low-income children of color. Their teachers are mostly white, middle-class, monolingual females. These facts do not mean that teachers do not care about the children they teach. However, we are witnessing earlier and earlier demonization and criminalization of young children of color, particular young African-American and Latino male children.

The suspension and expulsion rates, special education designations, and school drop-out rates for African-American and Latino students are more than twice those of white students. These numbers mirror the statistics of our adult prison population. In too many instances, African-American and Latino children (particularly male children) are seen as "prisoners in training," and zero tolerance serves to speed up that eventuality.

Although the rhetoric of zero tolerance (along with mandatory sentencing and three strikes) makes for good political talk, it ignores the realities of life in a democratic society. Zero tolerance doesn't solve a problem—it shifts it. When we say students will be expelled for one incidence of violence, we seem to forget that making them "disappear" from school does not make them disappear from the society. They go somewhere, and that somewhere is typically the street. Their time on the street is rarely productive and serves to introduce them to a pattern of behaviors that too often leads to incarceration. The school cannot construct itself as an entity separate from the rest of the community. It cannot say, "Well, he's not here anymore. We took care of the problem." Indeed, the school may have exacerbated the problem. Now we have a young person who may not be under any adult supervision. His alienation from the school can create an even more volatile situation.

Zero tolerance is a policy that essentially writes off the individual in an attempt to intimidate the group. The school's responsibility to the individual ends once he violates a zero tolerance policy rule. The school uses the policy to send a message to the rest of the student body that they too will be excluded if they violate the policy. Schools suggest that zero tolerance policies function as a deterrent to dangerous behavior in the same way that the death penalty supposedly serves as a deterrent to capital crimes. Unfortunately, this reasoning fails to recognize that the states with the greatest application of the death penalty also have the highest level of crime. Where is the deterrence?

These extreme policies of reprimand tend to assuage our need to punish people. They are the simple, Band-Aid-type responses that are being applied to a moral and ethical hemorrhaging that plagues our society. We know they don't work. If they did, we would not experience the level of recidivism that we do in our prisons. We want to put people in jail and throw away the key and we want to start the process earlier and earlier.

One of the scariest aspects of the zero tolerance policies is the potential for abuse. Davis[3] tells of a parent in Providence, Rhode Island, whose son was asked by his teacher to remove a diskette from a defective computer. The boy used a small utility knife to remove it and was expelled for violating the zero tolerance policy a few months short of graduation. In an interview conducted by Wing and Keleher,[4] the Reverend Jesse Jackson commented on additional examples of abuses: a child with a rubber hammer as a part of a Halloween costume, a child with a butter knife cutting her birthday cake to share with classmates, and a child who gave another classmate two cough drops—all were sanctioned for violating their school's zero tolerance policies. Have we become so draconian in our approach to student behavior that we cannot apply reason and common sense to discipline and classroom management?

The understandable question that remains is "What are we to do?" No, we cannot permit students to bring weapons to school where they will be a threat to other students as well as to themselves. We cannot allow students to use the school as a place to traffic in drugs. We cannot endorse violence and other sorts of antisocial behavior. But the shortsightedness of zero tolerance policies cannot become our default position. I would argue that there are at least three things that we can do that will better serve everyone's interests. We must remember that our children are children. We must remember that our children are students. And, we must remember that schools are sites for the creation and maintenance of the public good.

Our children are children. This seems such a simple (perhaps simplistic) statement, but it bears repeating. Our society forces the poorest children to grow up very quickly. They do not have much of a childhood. Limited resources such as child care, decent paying jobs, and poor housing force children growing up in poor families to take on adult responsibilities earlier than their middle-class counterparts. Poor children take on child-care responsibilities for younger siblings at an early age. They have to do things like cook and clean because their parents and other caregivers may have to work multiple jobs at odd hours. They live in neighborhoods where playing outside is not possible or safe. Being a child is not much fun for poor children. But, they are children.

At this writing, the nation is just recovering from the shock of the first-grade boy who brought a gun to school and killed a six-year-old classmate. How did a six-year-old get a gun? What would make him think that it made sense to try to solve a conflict by shooting someone? Once the news media dug into his background, we learned that this little fellow was enduring a living hell. His father was incarcerated. His mother had been evicted from her home, and he was left to live in a crack house with some relatives. What chance did the child have to be a child? School has to be a place where our children get to live out their childhoods.

The school cannot be a place that tells some children that they are not children. Even teenagers (who are described by a colleague as bigger than us, faster than us, and more plentiful than us, in the school setting) are still children. They do not have the same rights and responsibilities as adults. The United States is one of the few modern nations that does not expressly provide for children in its Constitution, and so we must take the moral and ethical leadership to protect them.

We must remember that our children are students. While remembering that our children are children who are entitled to their childhoods, we must also remember that in school, our children are students. The primary reason for sending them to school is so they can achieve the knowledge and skills that will serve them well as citizens in a democracy. We cannot think of school as a place to baby-sit children or keep adolescents out of the labor market.

The road to disengagement from school and antisocial behavior starts early for poor children of color. These children relinquish their childhood early in schools. As early as third grade, African-American and Latino boys are characterized as dangerous. On the other hand, white middle-class people have prolonged childhoods that extend sometimes into their thirties. White college students who go on to graduate school often are still seen as "children." They may not be held to the same standard of decorum as poor children of color because of their dependent status (their parents may subsidize their expenses).

We must remember that children, as smart, creative, and imaginative as they can be, are still children. And when they are of school age, they are students. Our responsibility is to protect them and their status as students.

My colleague told me about an encounter she had at her elementary school with a first grader, whom she met in the corridor. "Where are you going?" she asked. "I'm going to the restitution room because I was talking in class," he replied. "Restitution room? Do you know what restitution is?" she asked. "A place for bad people?" he queried. My colleague and I later talked about the way that schools create policies and structures that separate children from their childhood. Restitution is a concept tied to our legal system. It refers to paying back and making something right. What kind of restitution can be made for talking out of turn? The boy was being placed in a holding room where he was unlikely to learn very much that would support his academic achievement.

This language and structure of the penal system has invaded our schools at every level. Low-performing schools are placed on "probation." Administrators spend increasing proportions of their budgets on security and safety equipment. At urban schools, principals buy metal detectors instead of books and brag about decreased incidents of violence. The entire purpose of schools is obscured by the press to manage bodies. I heard one encouraging word at a conference where a principal of a New York City high school reported on how he increased the safety in his building. He said that he removed the metal detectors, fired the security guards, and brought an elementary school into his building. He told his high school students that they had to take responsibility for looking after their younger "brothers and sisters" in the building. Immediately, instances of violence decreased. The principal had remembered that he presided over a place where children/adolescents were students. He decided to *teach* them how to be more responsible and safe. The students rose to the occasion.

Schools are sites for the creation and maintenance of the public good. In a consumer-driven society in which those with the most toys are considered winners, it is difficult to continue to trumpet the need for an investment in the public good. Our current retreat from the public sphere is appalling. We are enamored of all things private. We want private, gated communities. We want private transportation. We want private health care. And, we want our children to attend private schools. But we are a huge nation—the only remaining superpower in the world. We argue that democracy is precious and citizen participation is vital. Where in the society can we insure that that message is constantly and consistently spread? The public school!

Our public schools represent one of the boldest experiments in real democracy ever undertaken. Its premise is that, regardless of race, class, gender, ability, language, or national origin, students can learn the work of democratic citizenship that is vital to preserving the democracy.

My own professional life was profoundly shaped by my public school experiences. My working-class parents had minimal education. My mother completed high school but my father went no further than the fourth grade in a one-room segregated school in the South. When we were young children, my father took my older brother and me to work with him one day to experience the backbreaking labor he did each day. It did not take us more than that one day to figure out that going to school was a lot better than not. The two admonitions regularly offered by my dad were, first, go to school, and second, when you're old enough, make sure you vote. I thought they were a strange pairing, given that my mother's admonitions were to always make your bed and wear clean underwear. (You wore clean underwear in case you were in an accident, and you made your bed in case you had to be brought home by strangers.)

My father had a deeper insight into what the society demanded. To him, school could be a place of radical transformation. You could go in ignorant and disenfranchised and emerge knowledgeable and prepared to participate in the hard work of nation building—in the community, among the races, and throughout the world. Despite the many injustices perpetrated against African Americans, my father thought that the nation continued to have an opportunity for redemption. At eighty-five years old, my dad now suffers from dementia. He spends his time quietly sitting in his room at a nursing home. He does have lucid moments and can carry on a limited conversation, particularly a conversation about the past. But, try as I might, I cannot imagine being able to explain the idea of zero tolerance to him. All I can tell him is that, despite all of the efforts of hardworking, decent people like him, America still eats its young.

NOTES

1. B. Wing and T. Keleher, "Zero Tolerance and Racial Bias: An Interview with Jesse Jackson," *Colorlines* 3(1) (2000): 31–33.

2. L. Delpit, *Other People's Children: Cultural Conflict in the Classroom.* New York: The New Press, 1995.

3. N. Davis, "CD-ROM Helps Organizers Confront Institutional Racism." *Color-lines* 3(1) (2000): 33.

4. Wing and Keleher, "Zero Tolerance."

PART TWO

Social Contexts

The right to a free, appropriate public education for all children has been at the heart of struggles for civil and human rights for a century and a half. Brilliant and defiant African Americans like Mary McLeod Bethune; abolitionists like Angelina and Sarah Grimke, who taught literacy; the Ida B. Wells Barnett antilynching campaign newsletters; the courageous nine students of Little Rock nurtured by Daisy Bates; the freedom schools inspired by the teaching of Septima Clark; and the massive, contemporary, parent-led urban movements for schools which will teach their children—this legacy is now confronted by zero tolerance. Punishing kids by depriving them of an education, zero tolerance has become the current tool to restrict education only to the "deserving." Resisting zero tolerance is today's fundamental civil rights issue. It is a struggle for the right to an equal and relevant education.

The connection between schools and civil rights is primal. In our lifetime, *Brown v. Board of Education* and its progeny illustrate the many strategies employed to seek education as the pathway to equality and opportunity. Yet the relationship between the schools and the courts is also historically intertwined; schools have been a referral source for juvenile and criminal courts. Often different children, challenging or misbehaving children, were removed from school by being referred to the court and law enforcement: for truancy, for fighting, for theft, for being disruptive. In the past decade, this process of excluding children from school has accelerated. With the pressures of test scores, school probation, sensationalized school shootings, police presence in schools, and parent anxieties, many educators seized the opportunity to transform school discipline into law enforcement and expulsion.

In a way, it should be no surprise that the criminalization of youth has extended into the schools. The popular vilification of children as criminals, as superpredators, as diseases has convinced many parents and educators that children are to be feared and that the greatest danger is among us. If teachers can only teach *your* child if they expel *that* child, if someone else's son is the disruptive threat to an otherwise docile classroom, then the one child can be exiled for the good of the whole. The fact that the offender is most likely to be African American and male, or a disabled boy, or a challenging adolescent with an attitude—these can be overlooked in the rush for law and order or an illusive sense of safety.

The fundamental right to an education, the civil rights of equal protection and social justice, the due process rights of fair procedures, and the first amendment rights of free speech are trampled by zero tolerance codes and practices. Youth, parents, teachers, school boards, and attorneys for the youngsters being expelled are concerned. Their voices are part of a growing civil rights cry to resist zero tolerance.

"Look Out Kid / It's Something You Did": Zero Tolerance for Children

BERNARDINE DOHRN

A seismic change has taken place. Youngsters are to be feared. Our worst enemy is among us. Children must be punished, held accountable, expelled. We have developed zero tolerance for children.

Urban gang shootings catapulted juvenile homicide rates to three times their previous rate in the decade 1985 to 1994. This terrifying, tragic, and lethal homicide spike by children involved saturated media coverage, popular panic, and political "get tough" legislative and prosecutorial responses.

The Columbine school shooting tragedy expanded the previous national, racially coded pandemonium about youth violence. To some extent, the criminalization of children was qualitatively transformed, temporarily recasting the examination of youth violence into a white, upper-middle-class discourse on alienation and isolation. School shootings became a trope—an inspiration for politicians, funding streams, educational abdication, and law enforcement expansion. Yet, perhaps most significantly, "normal," *nonviolent* youth behavior and misbehavior became further criminalized, all in the name of safety. The daily discourse about children shifted from innocence to guilt, from possibility to punishment, from protection to fear. This sinister vilification of childhood now permeates basic life: the schools, the parks and neighborhoods, child protection, health and mental health care. Children bear the brunt of the national soul-searching into the conditions of childhood in America at the dawn of the twenty-first century.

Public Perceptions of Children

Casting children as fearsome makes full use of racial, ethnic, and gender stereotyping, resulting in dramatic, disproportionate impact on arrests (Poe-Yamagata and Jones 2000; Bell 1998; Chesney-Lind 1999) and on school exclusion (Skiba and Michael 2000), as well as in broad brush strokes impacting all youth. Columbine's murder of children by children presented an inescapable contrast to the language and conceptual framework of juvenile "superpredators," which characterized much of the reporting of and political response to urban youth violence in the '90s. In fact, the sensationalized school shootings of 1997–99, all of which involved young, white male accuseds and young, white (and often female) victims, represented something of a "chickens coming home to roost" (attributed to Malcolm X 1963) for the '90s. Now, in Pearl, Mississippi, in Jonesboro, Arkansas, in Springfield, Oregon, in West Paducah, Kentucky, in Edinboro, Pennsylvania, it was suburban or small-town religious white boys with guns killing their fellow students (Schiraldi, Donohue, and Ziedenberg 1998).

Researchers know that there is less than a one in a million chance of suffering a violent school death (including both homicides and suicides) (Centers for Disease Control 1996). The out-of-school rate of death for children is approximately forty times greater (Sickmund, Snyder, and Poe-Yamagata 1997). Put another way, 99 percent of the violent deaths of children occurred outside of school grounds between 1992 and 1994. School shootings are not a trend; in the '90s, there were some 20–50 school shooting deaths per year (National School Safety Center 1998). Finally, 90 percent of all childhood deaths occur in or near *home*, not in school, and they take place *after* school (Schiraldi, Donohue, and Ziedenberg 1998).

The media response far outstripped the earlier dramatic epidemic of gun-involved youth homicides; between 1990 and 1995, while juvenile homicides dropped 13 percent, related coverage on network evening news programs increased by 240 percent (Center for Media and Public Affairs 1997). Homicides by children have further declined—down 56 percent between 1995 and 1999, and youth crime was down 30 percent, yet public opinion polls indicated in 1999 that 62 percent of the public believed that youth crime was on the increase (Dorfman and Schiraldi 2001).

Children shooting children also crystallized a pervasive racialized language to describe *some* children in trouble with the law (Canada 1995). Urban African-American, Latino, and Asian children were regularly referred to as animals (wolves, beasts of prey, vermin) or as diseases (plague, pestilence, scourge, cancer, virus, infestation, parasite) (Conquergood 1997). Prominent academics joined the fray, calling youth "fatherless, jobless, and godless" and predicting the coming of "the tens of thousands of severely morally impoverished juvenile superpredators. So long as their youthful energies hold out, they will do what comes 'naturally': murder, rape, rob, assault, burglarize, deal deadly drugs, and get high" (Dilulio 1995); youth are people who "show the blank, unremorseful stare of a feral, pre-social being" (Wilson 1996). This dehumanizing and demonizing language became a commonplace means of describing adolescent children, particularly African-American and Latino young men. Furthermore, these children were ritually described as "remorseless" (Drizin 1998); news stories depicting youth as remorseless jumped from 25 percent in 1993 to 67 percent in 1994 (Squires and Ettema 1997).

In contrast, white schoolboys who murder are described as alienated, victimized, and isolated (Rush 1999; "Tragedy in Colorado" 1999). Just three months before the Columbine massacre, Eric Harris was characterized in court documents as "a bright young man who is likely to succeed in life," and Dylan Klebold was described as a person with "a great deal of potential" (National Public Radio 1999). In fact, there was support for those rural and suburban children who went to trial for murder in Paducah from the Rev. Jerry Falwell (Drizin 1999) and the very politicians who capitalized on the urban youth homicide epidemic to repudiate the underpinnings of juvenile justice and a separate justice system for children (Zimring 1998; Zierdt 1999; Ayers 1997).

No one can ignore the shocking fact that in the decade of 1985–94, 25,000 children were murdered in the United States (Sickmund, Snyder, and Poe-Yamagata 1997). In fact, there is the equivalent of a Columbine virtually every day in America. The proliferation of lethal handguns to children (83 percent of victims aged 12–18 were killed by handguns: Zimring 1998; Sickmund, Snyder, and Poe-Yamagata 1997), the syndication of territorial youth gangs into illegal drug cartels (Blumstein 1995), the flourishing of youth violence reported on local TV news stations (Gilliam and Iyengar 1997), and the resulting public fear, the pandering of politicians and law enforcement officials (Males 1996), and the popularization of youth demonization by noted academics (Zimring 1996) are the elements that reinforce and strengthen one another, spiraling into a qualitative change in how society perceives, and even thinks about, its adolescents.

The tangled interplay of youth homicides, public fear, media frenzy, politicians' pandering, and law enforcement's escalated power have reinforced each other and created an overlapping system of causes and consequences (Polakow 2000). As each relatively rare incident of youth violence is seized upon and amplified, public fear mounts, and prosecutors and legislators vow action. Within this climate, a less visible, less sensational shift has quietly been executed. It has become acceptable—even mandatory—to punish children by depriving them of an education. This change profoundly impacts millions of children, their classmates and families, and our common future.

Today, behaviors which were once punished or sanctioned by the school vice principal, by family members, or by a neighbor or a coach are more likely to lead to an adolescent being arrested, referred to juvenile or criminal court, formally adjudicated, incarcerated in a detention center, waived or transferred to adult criminal court for trial, sentenced under mandatory sentencing guidelines, and incarcerated with adults (Sickmund, Snyder, and Poe-Yamagata 1997). The discretionary decision of what to charge for a given offense ("charging inflation" by prosecutors and police) has transformed what was yesterday's battery into assault, simple assault into aggravated assault, a schoolyard fight into multiple felony charges. The arrest of multiple juvenile defendants for each incident further escalates youth crime statistics.

This decade of relentless reconditioning of how children are perceived—by law enforcement, legislators, professionals, academics, media and film, and frightened neighborhood residents—has shifted the paradigm. Through the catalyst of changes in criminal and juvenile law, much adolescent behavior has been criminalized and youngsters themselves vilified. The massive shift to demonize youngsters is evident in the increasing numbers of court cases (Stahl 1999), detained and incarcerated youth in overcrowded facilities (Puritz and Scali 1998; Sickmund, Snyder, and Poe-Yamagata 1997), and legislative crackdowns on juvenile crime (Geraghty 1999; Sickmund, Snyder, and Poe-Yamagata 1997). In the past decade, the number of formally processed delinquency cases increased 78 percent (Stahl 1999).

The transformation in how we comprehend ourselves and discern our children has taken an incalculable toll on adults and children alike (Hart 1998). As a result, in the 1990s, fiscal priorities shifted from education, child

protection, and scholarships to punishment, prison construction, law enforcement growth, and expanded mechanisms for the social control and exile of
sectors of youth. Correctional spending nationally exceeds $40 billion per
year, to pay for a 500 percent rise in the prison population since 1972 (Mauer
1999). In two short decades, budgets for prisons grew twice as fast as spending
on colleges and universities nationwide; prison spending increased 823 percent between 1988 and 1995, while education expenditures grew only 374 percent (Macallair, Taqi-Eddin, and Schiraldi 1998; Ambosia and Schiraldi 1997).
More sobering, the vast majority of states spend at least one and a half times
as much on prisons as they do on education (Phinney 1999).

New York state spent over $700 million on new prison construction in
the '90s while slashing state and city college budgets by $600 million, one
result being that the number of people of color enrolled in New York's state
colleges and universities is substantially lower than the number currently
incarcerated there (Gangi, Schiraldi, and Ziedenberg 1998). Not only are more
children seeing the inside of prison walls rather than classrooms, there is a
new movement to place more, and younger, children in the adult criminal
justice system (Juskiewicz 2000).

One hundred years ago in Chicago, the world's first juvenile court for
children was premised on the removal of children from adult jails and adult
poorhouses (Tanenhaus 1998–99); at the centennial, children are being rein-
carcerated with adults, tried as adults in adult criminal court, and subjected
to imputation of adult *mens rea* with mandatory sentencing statutes that
repudiate rehabilitation as a goal.

Criminalizing Youth Behaviors

"I would that there were no age between ten and three-and-twenty,
or that youth would sleep out the rest; for there is nothing in
the between but getting wenches with child, wronging
the ancestry, stealing, fighting."

—WILLIAM SHAKESPEARE, *THE WINTER'S TALE*

A major consequence of the tidal wave of fear, violence, and terror associated
with children has been adult legislative and policy decisions to criminalize

vast sectors of youth behavior. In part, this tendency is fueled by an organized drive on the part of certain political forces to "get tough on youth violence"; in part, the changes have resulted from an accumulation of legislative reactions to a particular sensationalized case, the hackneyed mantra to "do something."

The sum total of a decade's *legal* responses is the transformation of the *social* landscape which children inhabit. Schools have become military fortresses. Hanging out becomes illegal. Fewer systems want to work with adolescents in need. Youngsters who have themselves been neglected or abused by adults pose too many challenges and have too many problems (Armstrong 1998; Fagnoni 1999; Courtney and Piliavin 1998). Health care and mental health services are rarely organized for adolescents. Schools want to get rid of the troublemakers and the kids who bring down the test scores. Minor offenses are no longer handled by retail stores, school disciplinarians, parents, or youth workers, but the police are called, arrests are made, petitions are filed.

Six of seven juvenile arrests are for a nonviolent offense. Of the 2.7 million arrests of young people under eighteen years of age, property offenses (particularly larceny/theft), drug offenses, disorderly conduct, running away, curfew violations, loitering, and liquor law violations account for the vast majority of the arrests (Sickmund, Snyder, and Poe-Yamagata 1997). Ironically, if Shakespeare had his way and if all male children aged 10–23 were captured and incarcerated, eliminating youth crime tomorrow, 90 percent of the violent crimes would still take place—because of the adult offenders (Snyder and Sickmund 1995, 48). The intense focus on a youth crime epidemic, thus, is a social choice rather than a strategic response to crime and public safety.

The criminalizing of adolescent behavior takes place in multiple ways. Major social institutions for youth have constricted eligibility and access and eased methods for expulsion. Schools, child welfare systems, and probation, health, and mental health services have all made it easier to violate, terminate, exclude, and expel youngsters. Where they go for survival, help, socialization, development, care, and attention is unclear. One door which always remains open is the gateway to juvenile and criminal justice. Overcrowded juvenile correctional institutions, deficient, abusive facilities, and disproportionate minority confinement are among the consequences (Puritz and Scali 1998).

Policing Schools:
School-Based Arrests and Exclusion

Schools have become a major feeder of children into juvenile and adult criminal courts; simultaneously, schools themselves are becoming more prison-like. Closed campuses, metal detectors, locker and backpack searches, contraband, interrogations and informers, heavily armed tactical police patrols, surveillance cameras, uniforms (Harrigan 1998)—these are elements of public and even private or parochial high school life today. It is paradoxical but fundamental that a handful of high-profile school shootings mask a broader and deeper criminalization of school life, accompanied by the policing of schools, which has transformed public schools across America into a principal referral source for juvenile justice prosecution.

Two policies contribute to this dramatic new role for schools: first, the increased policing of schools and the simultaneous abdication of educators leads to a significant increase in school-based arrests; and second, school exclusions increase, including substantial suspensions/expulsions of students, propelled by the legislative green light which mandated "zero tolerance" policies as a condition of federal funding. Rather than insisting on the pedagogic possibility arising from adolescent misbehavior—for both the miscreant and the other students—rather than seizing the "teachable moment," rather than keeping an educational perspective on sanctioning and social accountability, principals and teachers, admittedly under pressure from frightened parents, have ceded their authority to law enforcement personnel, particularly to police and prosecutors, and have willingly participated in excluding trouble-makers, difficult kids, and children in trouble from the very education that is their primary hope. These so-called "zero tolerance" and security policies were escalating even before the high-profile school shootings of 1997–98 and the Columbine High School tragedy. Since then, the policies, the dollars, and the hardware for policing and militarizing schools have only increased.

School-Based Arrests

How grave is the school crime problem? Serious violent crime is extremely rare within schools and constitutes a small percentage of the total amount of school offending (*Annual Report on School Safety* 1998). In 1997, there were over 180,000 school fights leading to arrests, almost 120,000 thefts in schools resulting in arrests, nearly 110,000 incidents of school vandalism provoking arrests, and under 20,000 violent crimes (National Center for Education Statistics 1996–97).

In the 1996–97 school year, 47 percent of public schools reported at least one nonviolent or less serious crime to police, 10 percent reported at least one serious violent crime (generally assault), and 43 percent reported no crime to police (*Annual Report on School Safety* 1998). Ninety percent of principals surveyed reported no major serious, violent crime in their schools (National Center for Education Statistics 1996–97). In fact, victim self-reports indicate that actual school crime numbers have not changed significantly during the past twenty years (*Annual Report on School Safety* 1998).

The first three categories (some 400,000 arrests) are noteworthy. Most school crime is theft, some 62 percent (*Annual Report on School Safety* 1998). School-based incidents such as fighting, theft, and vandalism have traditionally been handled within a school disciplinary system. Forty years ago, an offender would be sent to the office of the vice principal, a parent might be called, detentions (remaining for an hour after school) might be mandated, a letter of apology might be required. It would have been difficult to imagine police being called, arrests and handcuffs employed, criminal complaints filed, and incarceration demanded.

In today's Chicago Public Schools, and increasingly in suburban and rural school districts, police are routinely employed as school employees. Some schools employ police officers using teacher salary budgets and encourage uniformed police, armed tactical-unit police, or plainclothes police to patrol their schools. Police officers may make half again their salary by contracting with the public schools. School-assigned police may be evaluated based on their numbers of arrests. Police may be under no obligation to consult with the school principal about how to respond to a particular youth's misbehavior or to a particular incident. In certain locations, police fail to inform principals or school officials that a student has been arrested during school hours, on school grounds. One authority has replaced another.

At Paul Robeson High School in Chicago, for example, local police precinct data indicate that 158 students were arrested at Robeson in 1996–97. Arrest charges that year at this major urban high school are revealing: 61 arrests for pager possession; 21 arrests for disorderly conduct; 14 for mob action; 16 for non-firearm weapon possession. In 1998, after Robeson adopted a strategy of small school reform, arrests plummeted to 28, 22 of those for pager violations (Chicago Police Department 1998; Klonsky 1998)!

Massive locker searches resulted in student arrests across Chicago: 40 students at Westinghouse High School, 46 at Kenwood High School, and 50 at Roosevelt High School. In each case, the substantial majority of teens were charged with possession of beepers ("Search Ends" 1995; "Kenwood Reaps" 1994; "Teens Arrested" 1994). Possession of pagers appears to be an offense which is both a status offense (for which adults would not be arrested) and an expansion of drug laws by labeling a pager as "drug paraphernalia," or contraband, thus transforming a technological convenience into a crime. School-based arrests for possession of pagers are a classic example of the criminalization of youth.

Additional school-based arrests include offenses such as disorderly conduct or mob action, discretionary prosecutorial choices which could involve significant disruption or merely minor incidents. That decision to call a shouting match a crime, to arrest rather than intervene and instruct, to prosecute rather than resolve the dispute—is turning schools into policed territory. Researchers suggest that the expectation of school crime in fact creates it (Devine 1996).

This pattern of accelerating school incidents into delinquency offenses or criminal acts further exaggerates the statistics of disproportionate minority confinement and involvement in juvenile justice. In the 1990s, the large public urban high schools became sites of substantial police presence, under pressure to control youth misbehavior, and without influential parents with resources to buffer their children from the juvenile justice system. Since Jonesboro and Littleton, both suburban and rural high schools have also become fortresses, and arrests and mandatory expulsions are mushrooming. This bleeding of urban responses into middle-class life has its own dynamic and momentum, focusing more, perhaps, on drugs, tobacco, dress, and culture, with more private institutionalization of youth as a consequence (Chesney-Lind 1999).

The increasing regimentation of school time results in few breaks, little time for lunch, and closed campuses in high schools. Closed campuses result from neighborhood residents' and parents' complaints about the mobile presence of children during the day. Teachers monitor student lunch periods and move their own lunchtime to the end of the day, shortening the school day. In fact, schools are increasingly simulating prisons, as if preparing students for their likely future: locked in, regimented, searched, uniformed, and observed with suspicion (Pardo 1999; Foucault 1995).

Search and seizure of student lockers, backpacks, and persons is legitimized (Scheft and Abramson 1993). A culture of informing on fellow students is encouraged and mandated by school officials, without exploration of the ethical considerations and conflicting values involved. The blurring of school discipline and delinquency accelerates (Pressman 1995).

Perhaps most significantly, the policing of schools is eroding the relationship of educator to student by replacing the role of teachers with police and prosecutors and substituting the function of school discipline with criminal punishment (Devine 1996). Law enforcement rather than education becomes a prime vehicle of socialization for adolescents. Teachers and principals are abdicating their historic role to educate through experience, to seize the moments of transgressions, mistakes, adolescent blunders, and poor judgment and to reimagine another form of behavior. Indeed, serious and threatening offending has no place in school, or in the environment of youth. Yet misbehavior and malfeasance goes with the territory of high school. When school sanctioning is handed over to law enforcement *in the first instance* for the vast majority of minor school infractions, not only the offender and the victim fail to learn from the incident, and not only is the consequence more likely to be crushing rather than illuminating, but the entire community fails to take hold of the problem as a school community matter.

The failure to place serious reliance on peer juries, teen courts, or restorative community justice alternatives and to rely instead on armed police for school safety has startling and profound consequences. It is an abdication of adult responsibility to engage with youngsters (Centennial Poll 1999). It creates a juvenile delinquency record for vast numbers of youth who might otherwise not be in trouble with the law. Having any delinquency or criminal record has increasing consequences for obtaining scholarships, access to higher education, job eligibility, and the likelihood of escalated sanctions if there is a subsequent police investigation or arrest.

School Exclusion: Suspensions and Expulsions

Suspensions and expulsions from schools have simultaneously exploded as a new national trend. Fueled initially by federal legislation mandating a one-year "exclusion" for possession of a firearm on school property (Gun Free Schools Act 1994), state legislatures rushed to comply. Within a five-month period, legislation was passed in every state placing schools in compliance with the Safe School Act mandates, the quickest-ever state compliance to maintain federal funding eligibility.

One year later, the Safe School Act revised and expanded the prohibition to "dangerous weapon" rather than "firearm," and the door was open for a stampede—and for wide discretion which fell disproportionately on African-American and Latino students. A dangerous weapon was defined as "a weapon, device, instrument, material, or substance, animate or inanimate, that is used for, *or is readily capable of,* causing death or serious bodily injury" (18 USCA 930(g)(2) 1998).

In Massachusetts, for example, the number of school expulsions or exclusions under state law rose to over 1,500 per year, for the state added additional grounds for expulsion, including assault on school staff and possession of drugs or drug paraphernalia. The disproportionate racial impact is crystal clear. In Massachusetts, statewide, although African-American students comprised 8.4 percent of the school population in 1996–97, they suffered 23 percent of the expulsions; Latinos, who were 10 percent of the school population, made up 33.8 percent of the expelled students (Massachusetts Department of Education 1996–97).

These numbers are the result of the Massachusetts Reform Act of 1993, which provided sweeping changes to permit principals to expel students for possession of weapons, drugs, or assaulting school personnel (Mass. Gen. Laws, ch. 71 (1996), Sec. 37H). Further, Massachusetts, like other states (Lewis 1997), added a Felony Conviction Law or Principal's Bill (Sec. 37H1/2), authorizing principals, at their discretion, to suspend any student charged with a felony and expel any student convicted of a felony if "the student's continued presence in school would have a substantial detrimental effect on the general welfare of the school." This permits school principals to pick and choose.

The one-year expulsion of a high school girl who brought a novelty lipstick knife to school was upheld on appeal; the court found that there was no fundamental right to a public education under the state constitution, no statutory vagueness, no violation of due process, and no abuse of discretion (*Doe v. Superintendent* 1995). This pattern is doubly troubling in states where there is no mandatory alternative education (Mulligan 1997). Further, it is rare to find students with legal representation at the administrative hearings (Children's Law Center 1999).

This synergistic relationship between police and principals goes further in Chicago, where law permits schools to suspend or expel students who have been charged or convicted of violating the law, even when the alleged delinquent or criminal behavior did not occur on school property or during school hours (Chicago Public Schools 1998–99; Ferkenhoff 1997). These laws presume that principals will find out about non-school-based felony arrests and convictions of students from their closer relationship with police and prosecutors. This permeability between systems of education and criminal justice is codified in a series of laws recently passed by the Illinois legislature which facilitate more record sharing between law enforcement personnel and school and child welfare personnel (Illinois School Records Act 2000). The United States House of Representatives seeks to offer incentives to states to accommodate even greater exchange of individual files between schools and law enforcement by including in a proposed juvenile justice bill a provision that gives states additional funds if they make juvenile records available to schools (Juvenile Justice Bill 1999).

This wholesale relaxation of confidentiality protections for youth, a fundamental principle of the juvenile court founders, has further increased the incidence of suspensions/expulsions and of school-based arrests. Schools are routinely notified of a student's non-school-site arrests, probation, or detention. The knowledge that a student is in trouble or is a troublemaker may be a factor in his being more intensely scrutinized or being seen as a "bad kid."

The Hull House women, a century ago, were proponents of compulsory education, an end to child labor, and the creation of a separate court for children (Dohrn 1999). These innovations were interrelated, for the primary goal was education and opportunity for children, not the exploitation of hazardous labor or incarceration with adults in prisons or adult poorhouses. Grace Abbott and her colleagues documented school attendance as a bellwether for the well-being of children (Abbott 1938). What irony that 100 years later, schools and courts have again partnered, but this time to exclude, arrest, expel, and suspend *from* school and to punish, prosecute, and imprison in the criminal justice system.

Reviving Status Offenses: Truancy and Beyond

Offenses committed by youth that would not be crimes were they perpetrated by an adult are known as status offenses. They include truancy, running away, liquor law violations, and incorrigible or ungovernable offenses (Steinhart 1996; Rosenheim 1976). Girls, historically and continuing today, constitute a substantial proportion of status offenders. In 1995, status offenses comprised 23.4 percent of girls' arrests; in 1996, over half of those arrested for running away from home (a single status offense) were girls (Chesney-Lind 1999).

With the passage of the Juvenile Justice and Delinquency Prevention (JJDP) Act in 1974, there was a national commitment in the form of a mandate to remove status offenders from the definition of delinquency, as a result of persistent efforts to get troubled youth or minor offenders out of youth prisons because of the harmful effects of incarceration. Removal or deinstitutionalization of status offenders from juvenile correctional facilities became one of four mandates under the act (Snyder and Sickmund 1995; Coalition for Juvenile Justice 1998). Illinois, for example, abolished status offender categories in 1975 (*Illinois Trends and Issues* 1998). By the early 1990s, large numbers of status offenders had been successfully deinstitutionalized. What happened to them is another matter for inquiry, but at least they were no longer incarcerated with delinquent and criminal offenders.

In jurisdictions which continued to adjudicate status offenders in juvenile court, such as Massachusetts, categories or charges such as "stubborn children" or "unruly" are frequently used for children who are truants or have special needs. Although there is a reasonable doubt standard for adjudication of these children, they most frequently plead guilty to the status offense; advocates and caseworkers see it as a tool to obtain services (Catherine Krebs, personal communication, June 1999).

Now, however, many children identical to those once considered status offenders are being relabeled and reenter the juvenile justice system under new, trivial categories. Beginning in the decade 1987–96, the expansion of drug offenses resulted in an increased likelihood of formal handling (arrests and court filings), rising from 54 percent to 62 percent. "Public order" offenses, including disorderly conduct, liquor law violations, and weapons offenses, increased from 46 percent to 60 percent. The single largest increase in the likelihood of formal handling was in the generic category of "other public order offenses," where the likelihood of formal processing increased from 29 percent to 54 percent (Stahl 1999)!

Pending federal legislation would permit the incarceration of runaways and encourage the uses of contempt violations against status offenders as a path to detention and delinquency. This backlash against the once successful effort to abolish the incarceration of status offenders is an example of the continual pressure to unravel the progress of the federal Juvenile Justice and Delinquency Prevention Act mandates.

While the public and political focus has been fixed on youth homicides and violent offenses, there has been substantial growth in expanded versions of status offenses. This new wave of legal adjudications of common youth misbehaviors is largely invisible but impacts hundreds of thousands of youth, and their families, each year. In part, the attrition of informal, community, and civic methods of responding to the needs of youth—school attendance, youth centers, children's SSI disability insurance, job apprenticeships—has created a vacuum. The abolition of truancy as a status offense in many jurisdictions, for example, was not accompanied by constructive programs for truants—in general, there were no additional resources for adolescents in crisis. Into that space, law enforcement, legal adjudication, and punishment stepped forward, in the name of "accountability" and "services." But the consequences for youth are dire.

Loitering, Curfew, and Association Offenses

Local municipalities, frequently authorized by state legislatures, rushed to enact new curfew ordinances, some 1,000 since 1990 (Coalition for Juvenile Justice 1998). Curfew laws, directed at youth to prevent youth crime in the late evening, fail to address the peak juvenile crime times, between 2 P.M. and 5 P.M. during the school year. Gang offending is similarly concentrated in mid to late afternoon (Sickmund, Snyder, and Poe-Yamagata 1997).

In 1992, the Chicago City Council enacted the Gang Congregation Ordinance, which prohibited criminal street gang members from loitering with one another or with others in any public place (*City of Chicago v. Morales* 1999). The ordinance created a criminal offense punishable by a fine of up to $500, imprisonment for not more than six months, and a requirement to perform up to 120 hours of community service. During the three years of its enforcement, police arrested over 42,000 and issued over 89,000 dispersal orders. The ordinance was overturned by an appellate court, the Illinois Supreme Court, and the U.S. Supreme Court, as unconstitutionally vague, failing to provide notice to the public about what conduct was illegal. The Chicago City Council subsequently passed a revised loitering ordinance.

Curfew ordinances are notorious for being subject to racial and ethnic disparities in enforcement (Macallair and Males 1998). Furthermore, arrests of girls for curfew violations increased by 155.2 percent between 1987 and 1996 (Chesney-Lind 1999). Curfew violations have vastly widened the net of criminal involvement for youth, particularly youth of color and young women.

Young Women in Juvenile Justice

Each year, girls account for one in four arrests of youth in America, yet their presence in the juvenile system remains largely invisible. Traditionally they were arrested and incarcerated in large numbers for status offenses and sexual activity (Meis Kopfner 2001), but arrests and prosecutions of young women declined after the 1974 JJDP mandate to deinstitutionalize and divert youth charged with status offenses into program alternatives to legal adjudication. But the past decade of criminalizing youth has resulted in increasing arrests of girls, once again, for status offenses or other minor violations of law.

Fully one-quarter of all female delinquency arrests are for status offenses (as compared to less than 10 percent for boys), while another quarter of girls arrested are charged with larceny theft (basically, shoplifting!). Girls arrested for running away from home increased by 20.7 percent and, as noted above, curfew arrests of girls mushroomed an astonishing 155.2 percent between 1987 and 1996 (Chesney-Lind 1999). Although media reports suggest that girls, as well as male delinquents, have become violent predators, the facts again belie this violent characterization.

Arrests of girls for violent crime offenses during the decade 1987 to 1996 did skyrocket, up 118.1 percent. Female delinquency charges for "other assault" increased 142.6 percent in the same period (American Bar Association 2000). Assault charges can range from conduct involving simple verbal aggression and threats to minor school conflicts, nonserious disputes, and harmless fights; increasingly, girls have been arrested for simple assault (Steffensmeier and Steffensmeier 1980). Analysis suggests that much of the "tyranny of small numbers" (attributed to Barry Krisberg, coined in public speeches and conversation 1994) results from relabeling or bootstrapping—the practice by police, prosecutors, or judges which transforms a nondelinquency, noncriminal offense into an offense subject to incarceration (Chesney-Lind 1997). Girls, for example, are more likely to be arrested for noninjury assaults (Currie 1998, 40) or as bystanders or companions to males involved in fighting. Virtually every person-to-person offense among girls in the Maryland juvenile justice system (97.9 percent) involved assault, and half of those were a fight with a family member, generally a parent (Mayer 1994). This form of escalated charging is most pronounced against African-American girls (Bartollas 1993; Chesney-Lind 1997).

Legislative erosion and organized opposition to the JJDP mandate against incarcerating children charged with status offenses has taken multiple forms, resulting in greater reincarceration of young women. In 1980, the definition of status offender in the federal law was amended to exclude children "who violated a court order" (Chesney-Lind 1999; Pub. L. 96-509). Girls in foster care placements or group homes, for example, who run away, can be classified as delinquents and incarcerated rather than characterized as status offenders who could be diverted away from court adjudication into specified programs for youth. This subversion of the original intent and purpose of JJDP falls most heavily on female delinquents; the gender double standard results in judges sentencing girls to detention for contempt citations (violations of court orders) in far greater numbers than boys—apparently in an attempt to control and contain young women to protect them from themselves in a manner which would not occur with young men. The 4.3 percent likelihood of incarceration for girls in the juvenile justice system accelerates to 29.9 percent when they are held in contempt (Bishop and Frazier 1992; Chesney-Lind 1999).

One consequence of the combination of traditional and contemporary juvenile justice pressures on young women is a racial, two-track system of justice, where white girls are institutionalized in private facilities and young women of color are detained in public facilities (Moone 1997). In fact, well over half of the youth populations in private institutions are white (Chesney-Lind 1999, 194).

The number of girls held in private institutions has dramatically increased; 62 percent of incarcerated girls are being held in private facilities, and 85 percent of those are detained for "nondelinquent" offenses (such as violations of court orders, or status offenses) (Chesney-Lind 1999). The number of young women detained in public detention facilities has remained steady (Krisberg et al. 1991, 43; Moone 1997, 2). Translated bluntly, this means that white girls are recommended for "treatment" while African-American and Latina girls are detained (Chesney-Lind 1999; Miller 1994, 18).

Pending federal legislation would encourage the use of contempt violations as a path to detention, and once again would permit the holding of children in adult jails. It is girls, frequently held in rural and small-town jails for minor infractions, who become most subject to violent abuse and suicide in such confinement (Chesney-Lind 1988; Ziedenberg and Schiraldi 1997).

Women have become the fastest growing sector of people in prison in the past decade; similarly, detentions of girls increased 23 percent between 1989 and 1993 (Poe-Yamagata and Butts 1995, 12). Girls remain in detention longer, awaiting placement in private facilities or correctional institutions, and are generally disliked by those working in the overwhelmingly male system of juvenile justice (Chesney-Lind 1999). The failure to take into account past or current physical or sexual abuse and the lack of appropriate gender and cultural programming to address the needs of young women delinquents are pervasive.

Transgressions by girls have historically been treated differently than male misbehavior. It is profoundly disturbing that the combined invisibility and double-standard paternalism/harshness against young females result in increasing loss of freedom for young women and inequality of response in programming. The women of Hull House would be dismayed and enraged by this backtracking on fundamental justice for children.

Erosion of Civic Responsibility for Children

Addressing the needs of both public safety and positive youth development requires an active and participating public. If the only popular cry is for short-term fixes—"Expel them so teachers can teach," "Get them out of the neighborhood," "Lock them up and throw away the key," and "Something must be done"—society will continue on its current course of escalating punishment for children and increasing adult abdication of responsibility. If schools are not for learning from mistakes, if child welfare is not for protecting children who have been harmed, if health systems are not geared to healing youth, further reliance on exclusion, incarceration, and prison becomes the likely option. Tens of thousands of productive adults who passed through the juvenile justice system in their youth are witnesses to the healing and redemptive effect of getting a second chance—of the program, the judge, the probation officer who made a difference and allowed them to turn their lives around (*Second Chances* 1999).

"Time Out" from Zero Tolerance: What Can We Do?

Zero tolerance has become an epidemic. We need a "time out" from school zero tolerance policies and applications, locally and nationally, and from all *mandatory* school expulsions except possession of guns. We can use the temporary moratorium to promote debate, discussion, education, and alternatives in communities and schools across the nation.

Two basic principles can provide unity and guidance in the volatile discussion of school discipline and juvenile justice: (1) No child should be punished by being deprived of an education; and (2) all school disciplinary measures must be fair, equitable, and individualized. Indeed, the American Bar Association House of Delegates voted to oppose mandatory zero tolerance policies in schools because they replace individualized, equitable adjudications with dangerous, one-size-fits-all sentences of school expulsion (American Bar Association 2000).

With those two principles as common ground, seven practical recommendations are offered to shift the current paradigm away from criminalization of youth and toward a primary focus on education and learning:

1. Small schools are safer schools. Kids need schools where everyone is known, with daily, strong parent and community presence inside the schools. Relationships and trust, rather than hardware and militarization, lead to safety and learning opportunities.
2. Open all schools after school, with rich programming and activity by

youth and family serving agencies. Most youth crime occurs in the 3 P.M.–6 P.M. time immediately after school.

3. Employ community justice sanctions within schools for school offending, such as peer juries, teen court, restorative justice, and mediation. Involve youth themselves in sanctioning misbehavior.

4. Transparency requires schools to track and report all school suspensions and expulsions annually, by school, including race, age, gender, and reason for exclusion.

5. Offer excellent alternative education *only* as a last resort for every child expelled from school, with opportunities to return to the home school at the earliest possible moment.

6. Remove guns from the environment of children. This is an adult responsibility.

7. It is a human rights obligation to provide children with an education, to encourage child participation, and to utilize a standard of "best interest of the child" in child sanctioning. Schools can teach the *Convention on the Rights of the Child* (1989), and schools and parents can advocate for United States ratification of an international treaty which has been adopted by every other nation in the world.

The adult problem is masked by our social focus on the "youth problem." In scapegoating kids, we reveal that as a society, we don't like adolescents very much. Youth, being the intelligent people they are, are vividly aware of the angry popular backlash directed against them. Their voices, their opinions, and their interests are ignored except in their role as a consumer market for products. Increasingly, youth themselves are demanding "Books, Not Bars" (Youth Force Coalition 2001). Adults neglect children both in public fiscal policy and in a commitment of our own precious time. At stake here is a question of the civic will to invest in our common future by seeing other people's children as our own.

REFERENCES

Abbott, Grace. 1938. *The Child and the State*, Vols. 1 and 2. Chicago: University of Chicago Press.

Ambosia, Tera-Jen, and Vincent Schiraldi. 1997. *From Classrooms to Cellblocks: A National Perspective*. February.

American Bar Association. 2000. *Final Report: Bi-partisan Working Groups on Youth Violence*, 106th Congress.

Annual Report on School Safety. 1998. U.S. Department of Education and U.S. Department of Justice. Washington, DC.

Armstrong, M. L. 1998. *Adolescent Pathways: Exploring the Intersections Between Child Welfare and Juvenile Justice, PINS, and Mental Health*. Vera Institute of Justice, May.

Ayers, William. 1997. *A Kind and Just Parent: The Children of Juvenile Court*. Boston: Beacon Press, 1997.

Bartollas, Clemens. 1993. "Little Girls Grown Up: The Perils of Institutionalization," in *Female Criminality: The State of the Art*, Concetta Culliver, ed. New York: Garland Press.

Bell, James. 1998. "Shadowboxing with the Apocalypse: Race and Juvenile Justice." *Youth Law News*.

Bishop, Donna, and Charles Frazier. 1992. "Gender Bias in the Juvenile Justice System: Implications of the JJDP Act." *Journal of Criminal Law and Criminology* 82(4): 1162–86.

Blumstein, Alfred. 1995. "Youth Violence, Guns, and the Illicit Drug Industry." *Journal of Criminal Law and Criminology* 86(10).

Canada, Geoffrey. 1995. *Fist, Stick, Knife, Gun: A Personal History of Violence in America*. Boston: Beacon Press.

Center for Media and Public Affairs. 1997. "Network News in the Nineties: The Top Topics and Trends of the Decade." *Media Monitor* 11 (July/August).

Chesney-Lind, Meda. 1988. "Girls in Jail," *Crime and Delinquency* 34(2): 150–68.

———. 1997. *The Female Offender: Girls, Women and Crime*. Thousand Oaks, CA: Sage Publications.

———. 1999. "Challenging Girls' Invisibility in Juvenile Court." *Annals for the American Academy*, AAPSS (July): 185.

Chicago Police Department. 1998. Statistics, 1996–97. Paul Robeson High School.

Chicago Public Schools. 1998–99. *Uniform Discipline Code*, 14–20.

Children's Law Center. 1999. Interview with Catherine Krebs, attorney, Lynn MA. June.

City of Chicago v. Morales. 1999. 537 v.s. 41.

Coalition for Juvenile Justice. 1998. *A Celebration or a Wake? The Juvenile Court after 100 Years.* 1998 Annual Report, Washington, DC.

Convention on the Rights of the Child. 1989. G.A. Res. 44/25, U.C. GAOR, 44th Sess., U.N. Doc. A/RES/44/25 (1989).

Conquergood, Dwight. 1997. *The Power of Symbols.* A Report to the Human Relations Foundation of Chicago. Northwestern University.

Courtney, Mark E., and Irving Piliavin. 1998. "Foster Youth Transitions to Adulthood: Outcomes 12 to 18 Months After Leaving Out-of-Home Care." July.

Currie, Elliot. 1998. *Crime and Punishment in America.* New York: Metropolitan Books.

Devine, John Francis. 1996. *Maximum Security: The Culture of Violence in Inner-City Schools.* Chicago: University of Chicago Press.

Dilulio, John J., Jr. 1995. "Moral Poverty." *Chicago Tribune,* December 15, sect. 1, p. 31.

Doe v. Superintendent of Schools of Worcester. 653 N.E.2d 1088 (Mass 1995).

Dohrn, Bernardine. 1999. "Justice for Children: The Second Century." In Gwen Hoerr McNamee, ed. *A Noble Social Experiment? The First 100 Years of the Cook County Juvenile Court 1899–1999.* Chicago: Chicago Bar Association.

Dorfman, Lori, and Vincent Schiraldi. 2001. *Off-Balance: Youth, Race and Crime in the News.* Building Blocks for Youth.

Drizin, Steven. 1998. "Should We Demand Juveniles to Cry Us a River?" *Chicago Tribune,* Commentary, April 27, p. 15.

———. 1999. "Race, Class, Religion, Politics Cloud Juvenile Justice." *Chicago Sun Times,* May 24.

Fagnoni, Cynthia M. 1999. *Challenges in Helping Youths Live Independently.* U.S. General Accounting Office. Testimony before the Subcommittee on Human Resources, Committee on Ways and Means, House of Representatives, May 13, p. 1.

Ferkenhoff, Eric. 1997. "City Schools Clamp Down on Violence by Students." *Chicago Tribune,* May 1.

Gangi, Robert, Vincent Schiraldi, and Jason Ziedenberg. 1998. *New York State of Mind?: Higher Education vs. Prison Spending in the Empire State: 1988–1998.*

Geraghty, Thomas F. 1999. "The Centennial of the Juvenile Court: What Would Jane Addams Think?" *CBA Record* (January): 50.

Gilliam, Frank D., Jr., and Shanto Iyengar. 1997. *Super-Predators or Wayward Youth? Framing Effects in Crime News Coverage.*

Gun-Free School Act. 1994. 20 U.S.C.A. Sec. 8921.

Harrigan, Margaret. 1998. Conversation with Margaret M. Harrigan, Ed.D.

Hart, Peter D. 1998. *Children's Court Centennial: Attitudes Toward Youth and Juvenile Justice.* Research Associates. December.

Illinois Public Aid Code, 305 ILCS 5/11–9 (permitting law enforcement access to certain public aid records without subpoena or notice requirements).

Illinois School Records Act. 2000. 105 ILCS 10/6 (effective 1/1/00) (permitting state's attorneys and police officers unrestricted access to student records and further requiring the school to make law enforcement requests part of the child's permanent record); 705 ILCS 405/5–325 (requiring school officials to provide to the State's Attorney upon request information or a written report relating to alleged commission of an offense).

Illinois Trends and Issues. 1998. Illinois Criminal Justice Information Authority, Chicago.

Juvenile Court Act of 1987, Abused, Neglected and Dependent Minors (as amended), 705 ILCS 405/2–31. Originally P.A. 85–601, Art. II, sec. 2–31, eff. 1/1/88. Relevant portion amended by P.A. 87/14, Art 2, sec 2–6, effective 7/24/91.

Juvenile Justice Bill. 1999. H.R. 1501, reauthorizing H.R. 1150 Juvenile Justice and Delinquency Prevention Act.

"Kenwood Reaps Beepers in Sweeps." 1994. *Chicago Tribune*, November 1.

Klonsky, Michael. 1998. "Small Schools: The Numbers Tell a Story, A Review of the Research and Current Experiences." The Small Schools Workshop at the University of Illinois at Chicago.

Krisberg, Barry, Robert DeComo, Norma C. Herrera, Martha Steketee, and Sharon Roberts. 1991. *Juveniles Taken into Custody: Fiscal Year 1990 Report.* San Francisco: National Council on Crime and Delinquency.

Lewis, Tamar. 1997. "School Codes Without Mercy Snare Pupils Without Malice." *The New York Times*, Education, March 12, pp. A1, A24.

Macallair, Dan, and Mike Males. 1998. *The Impact of Juvenile Curfew Laws in California.* San Francisco: Justice Policy Institute.

Macallair, Dan, Khaled Taqi-Eddin, and Vincent Schiraldi. 1998. *Class Dismissed: Higher Education vs. Corrections During the Wilson Years.* Washington, DC: Justice Policy Institute.

Males, Michael. 1996. *The Scapegoat Generation: America's War on Adolescents.* Monroe, ME: Common Courage Press.

Massachusetts Department of Education. 1996–97. Data sheet: *Student Characteristics.*

Mauer, Marc. 1999. *Race to Incarcerate.* The Sentencing Project. New York: The New Press.

Mayer, Judith. 1994. *Girls in the Maryland Juvenile Justice System: Findings of the Female Population Task Force.* Cited in Chesney-Lind 1999.

Miller, Jody. 1994. "Race, Gender and Juvenile Justice: an Examination of Disposition Decision-Making for Delinquent Girls." In *The Intersection of Race, Gender and Class in Criminology,* Martin D. Schwartz and Dragan Milovanovic, eds. New York: Garland Press.

Moone, Joseph. 1997. *Juveniles in Private Facilities, 1991–1995.* Washington, DC: Department of Justice, 1997.

Mulligan, Amy E. 1997. "Alternative Education in Massachusetts: Giving Every Student a Chance to Succeed." *The Boston University Public Interest Law Journal,* 6:2 (Winter): 629.

National Center for Education Statistics. 1996–97. *Violence and Discipline Problems in U.S. Public Schools.* Washington, DC: U.S. Department of Justice. NCES 98–030.

National Republic Radio. 1999. www.npr.org/news/national/1999/Apr/990423.shooting.html.

Phinney, David. 1999. *Prison Funding Explodes in Growth.* ABCNews.com. July.

Poe-Yamagata, Eileen, and Jeffrey A. Butts. 1995. *Female Offenders in the Juvenile Justice System.* Pittsburgh: National Center for Juvenile Justice.

Poe-Yamagata, Eileen, and Michael Jones. 2000. *And Justice for Some: Differential Treatment of Youth in the Justice System.* Washington, DC: Building Blocks for Youth.

Polakow, Valerie. 2000. *The Public Assault on America's Children: Poverty, Violence and Juvenile Injustice.* New York: Teachers College Press.

Pressman, Robert. 1995. *State Law Challenges to School Discipline: An Outline of Claims and Case Summaries.* 3d ed. Boston, MA, and Washington, DC: Center for Law and Education. October.

Puritz, Patricia, and Mary Ann Scali. 1998. *Beyond the Walls: Improving Conditions of Confinement for Youth in Custody.* American Bar Association Juvenile Justice Center, OJJDP, Washington, DC.

Rosenheim, Margaret K. 1976. *Pursuing Justice for the Child.* Chicago: University of Chicago Press.

Rush, Adam. 1999. "Troubled Teens Share Traits, Suffering from Alienation, Anger." *Portland Oregonian*, May 2.

S. 254. 1999. Violent and Repeat Juvenile Offender Accountability and Rehabilitation Act, 5/20/99; H.R. 1501, Juvenile Justice Bill, 6/17/99.

Schiraldi, Vincent, Elizabeth Donohue, and Jason Ziedenberg. 1998. *School House Hype: School Shootings and the Real Risks Kids Face in America.* Washington, DC: The Justice Policy Institute.

"Search Ends in Arrest of 66 Students." 1995. *Chicago Tribune*, May 3.

Second Chances: Giving Kids a Chance to Make Better Choices: 100 Years of Children's Court. 1999. Criminal Justice Institute and Children and Family Justice Center.

Sickmund, Melissa, Howard N. Synder, and Eileen Poe-Yamagata. 1997. *Juvenile Offenders and Victims: 1997 Update on Vilence, Statistics Summary.* Washington, DC: Office of Juvenile Justice and Delinquency Prevention.

Skiba, Russell J., and Robert S. Michael. 2000. *The Color of Discipline: Source of Racial and Gender Disproportionality in School Punishment.* The Indiana Education Policy Center, Policy Research Report #SRSI, June.

Snyder, Howard N., and Melissa Sickmund. 1995. *Juvenile Offenders and Victims: A National Report.* Washington, DC: Office of Juvenile Justice and Delinquency Prevention.

Squires, Catherine R., and James S. Ettema. 1997. *Superpredators in the News and Public Policy.* A Report to the Human Relations Foundation of Chicago. February 19.

Stahl, Anne L. 1987–1996. 1999. *Juvenile Court Processing of Delinquency Cases.* OJJDP Fact Sheet, # 104, U.S. Department of Justice, Washington, DC.

Steffensmeier, Darrell J., and Renee Hoffman Steffensmeier. 1980. *Criminology* 18 (1980): 62–85.

Steinhart, David J. 1996. "Status Offenders." *The Future of the Juvenile Court*, David and Lucille Packard Foundation, vol. 6, no. 3 (Winter).

Tanenhaus, David S. 1998–99. "Justice for the Child: The Beginning of the Juvenile Court in Chicago." *Chicago History* (Winter): 4–19.

"Teens Arrested at Roosevelt High." 1994. *Chicago Tribune*, December 14.

"Tragedy in Colorado: Growing Gap Between Teens, Adults Creating a Cultural Divide in Relationships." 1999. *Los Angeles Times*, April 22.

Wilson, James Q. 1996. As quoted in John J. DiPulio, Jr., "Should Society Punish or Rescue Teen Predators?" *The Plain Dealer*, Cleveland, OH, August 2.

Youth Force Coalition. Books Not Bars. 2001. Communication with Robin Templeton, June.

Ziedenberg, Jason, and Vincent Schiraldi. 1997. *The Risks Juveniles Face When They Are Incarcerated with Adults.* Washington, DC: Justice Policy Institute.

Zierdt, Candace. 1999. "The Little Engine That Arrived at the Wrong Stations: How to Get Juvenile Justice Back on the Right Track." *University of San Francisco Law Review* 33 (Spring): 401.

Zimring, Franklin E. 1996. "Crying Wolf over Teen Demons." *Los Angeles Times,* August 19, B6.

———. 1998. *American Youth Violence.* New York and Oxford: Oxford University Press.

How Distorted Coverage of
Juvenile Crime Affects Public Policy

VINCENT SCHIRALDI AND
JASON ZIEDENBERG

Coverage of juvenile crime is badly skewed toward hyperviolent, idiosyncratic acts, presented out of context with social forces that foster delinquency. This noncontextual, exaggerated coverage negatively affects both public opinion and policy making in the field of juvenile justice, resulting in a populace badly misinformed about the behavior of its own children and a body politic responding in increasingly punitive ways. Ironically, in this the 100th anniversary of the founding of America's juvenile court, this phenomenon has America racing away from the core tenets of the juvenile court it invented—individualization, rehabilitation, confidentiality, and treating kids differently from the way we treat adults—and doing so faster than any nation on earth.

A good example of this distorted crime coverage presented itself in the fall of 1997. In the same week, the nation was rocked by two shocking killings by juveniles. In one, a fifteen-year-old boy from Ocean County, New Jersey, who himself had been sexually molested by an adult he had met over the Internet, molested and killed an eleven-year-old boy who had been attempting to sell candy door to door. Later that same week, Luke Woodham stabbed his mother to death in Pearl, Mississippi, and then went and shot two students to death in his high school. That same week, Attorney General Janet Reno announced juvenile crime data for the year, showing a significant 30 percent decline in juvenile homicides over the previous three years.[1]

Most Americans probably heard of the former and not of the latter: the killings in New Jersey and Mississippi garnered prominent coverage, the

Mississippi killing becoming the first of a "trend," not of school shootings, but of media coverage of school shootings, that has lasted to the present day. The attorney general's press conference, while arguably far more significant from the standpoint of setting public policy, failed to even get coverage in her hometown paper, the *Washington Post.*

Around the same time, the Justice Policy Institute in Washington, D.C., received a call from an eager producer at Fox News, looking to do a "thematic" story on Luke Woodham. Apparently Woodham had a very high IQ and had written a letter which one of his high-IQ friends subsequently read on national TV, a sort of "we-smart-kids-aren't-going-to-take-it-any-more" letter. The producer was looking for stories of other smart kids who had killed—a preposterous theme woven out of the extraordinarily complex and highly individualistic factors which led Woodham to embark on his killing spree. When I told her that I had a high IQ, a lousy jump shot, grew up in a blue-collar neighborhood in Brooklyn, was constantly teased because of all of the above, and never even raised my voice to my mother, she pretended like she had another call and moved off in search of other cases to bolster her predetermined theme.

The disconnect between research and data about juvenile crime and the setting of public policy on juvenile crime is becoming increasingly acute. If you asked most doctors, politicians, and regular citizens, for example, if it was a good idea to start every day with a plate of fried eggs, home-fried potatoes, and bacon and toast with lots of butter, there would be pretty good consensus that that would be bad for one's health and generally a bad public policy. If you asked researchers or policy experts across the political spectrum if they thought that in order to reduce juvenile crime, America should imprison even larger numbers of kids with adults, abolish confidentiality protections across the board, and cease paying attention to whether minority kids are disparately treated by the juvenile justice system, there would be broad consensus that those were not good ideas. These proposals would never be on the list of the vast majority of the nation's criminologists or crime policy experts. These are the types of policies being enacted from coast to coast.

A more current example of the disconnect is seen in the debate over school violence. Despite a 72 percent decline in the number of school-associated violent deaths between the 1992–93 school year and the 1999–2000 term—matching the general decline in juvenile crime—polls show that seven out of ten Americans fear that a school shooting is likely to happen in their community.[2] Because of their fears, principals and teachers, egged on by some parents, are grappling with ways to make their schools safer. According to a recent study, the best way to ensure safe schools is to develop institutions with peer mediation and anger management programs, and to have schools enforce rules in a nonaggressive way. In contrast, kids in schools that have metal detectors, school police officers, and random locker searches reported that they are more afraid and more likely to be victimized than students in schools that choose the rules-based strategy.[3] Nevertheless, schools across America, many of which will never experience a serious violent incident, are installing video cameras, hiring officers, and expelling and suspending upwards of 3.1 million students a year. We're turning our schools into virtual prisons, even though a recent report by the president and a study produced by the Republican Congress urged that we set aside metal detectors and zero tolerance policies for a more balanced, "best practices" approach.

The main reason there is a profound disconnect between researchers and policy analysts and the process by which this nation decides crime policies is that media coverage of crime obscures our understanding of what is happening and what the nation needs to do about it. The media is the enemy of rational thought on the crime issue.

Coverage of crime, be it juvenile or adult, fixates on the titillating, idiosyncratic cases which, while they sell soap, tell us little about actual crime trends. Bad enough, but typical crime coverage is presented in such a fashion as to tell little in a meaningful way *even* about the idiosyncratic events in question, offering the rarest of glimpses into the context of what motivated or contributed to the actions of high-notoriety offenders. Such offenders are presented as monstrous beings that are unaffected by conditions around them and therefore unfixable by either individual solutions designed to ameliorate their specific behavior or by social policy designed to cure or prevent similar offending by similarly situated offenders. Stories about kids who were helped by the rehabilitative aspects of the juvenile court to turn their lives around are relegated to the end of the evening news, right behind births of bears at the local zoo.

The "cure," therefore, very much fits with the dominant American fixation on the citizen as individual actor, rigidly fixed to a social contract, unaffected by changes in economic or social conditions. The best solution is to get government off of the backs of citizens, reward the good, and punish the bad. These solutions are most neatly summed up in the inmate saying, "If you do the crime, you do the time," or the National Rifle Association saying, "Guns don't kill people, people kill people." Crime occurs not because of poverty, racism, inadequate education, unequal opportunities, access to guns, childhood abuse and neglect, familial mental health problems, or any other of a host of social ills which we could address through a public health approach to violence. If you cannot find the truth by deadline, these root causes simply don't exist in the public discourse. The easiest reporting and the easiest public policy solutions miraculously coincide, thereby creating "sound bites instead of sound policy."

The problem with all of this is that the policies arising from such a belief system do not work, have huge fiscal and human costs, have turned America into a nation with the highest rates of incarceration, executions, *and* violent crime in the Western world, and are administered in a manner which has virtually hobbled our nation's young black and Latino men.

The media's role in all of this has, with few exceptions, been either unwitting dupe or deliberate coconspirator. Either the media simply do not know better and do not take the time to find out, or, more crassly, they do know, do not care, and focus on the blood and gore because it is more profitable to titillate than to inform and bore.

Although the aforementioned analysis is a bit simplistic, it is an important framework around which to discuss media coverage of juvenile crime and is a theory to which much of the criminological community subscribes, if in less vitriolic terms. And, unfortunately, there's a lot of data to back it up.

The majority of times kids are depicted on the evening news, it is in connection with violence, even though less than one half of 1 percent of juveniles were arrested for a violent crime last year. Between 1992 and 1996, while homicides in America were declining by 20 percent,[4] coverage of homicides on the ABC, NBC, and CBS evening news increased by 721 percent.[5] Not surprisingly, six times as many people ranked crime as the number one problem in 1993 as in 1992, and fear of crime has been at or near the top of the polls every year since.[6]

It's impossible to talk about this subject and not discuss the coverage school shootings have been receiving and the impact that coverage is having on both public policy and public perceptions. There were about 55 school-associated violent deaths in the 1992–93 school year, and about 16 in the 1999–2000 school year.[7] By comparison, about 100 people are killed by lightning each year.[8] Which is sort of the gold standard for all idiosyncratic events. In 99.4 percent of the times a kid is killed in America, it is not inside a school, where kids have less than a one in three million chance of being killed.[9] Twelve kids died in the shooting at Columbine High School, and 11 kids die at the hands of their parents or guardians every two days in America.[10]

None of the rural communities in which these kids were killed had experienced a juvenile homicide inside or outside of a school in the previous year; most had not had one in the previous three years. There were 90 homicides in rural communities in 1997, and 1,800 in America's cities.[11] Ninety-four percent of the counties in America had one or no juvenile homicides in 1996.[12] So kids are not killing one another at increasing or alarming rates, and kids rarely kill one another at all. Less than 3 percent of the homicides in America involved someone under age eighteen killing someone else under eighteen.[13] Killings by kids under thirteen are at their lowest rate since that statistic first was calculated in the mid-1960s.[14] It's no more fair to stereotype America's 20 million high school students as Luke Woodham than it would be to taint all adults with the sins of Timothy McVeigh. If there are any lessons to draw from the data, it is that the children of America are not some media-created image of a school shooter. Rather, they are the kids on the other side of the yellow tape, weeping over the deaths of their classmates, just like all the rest of us.

Failure to put this kind of context into coverage of juvenile crime has resulted in a public which is not just misinformed but *profoundly* misinformed about juvenile crime. Americans now think juveniles are responsible for 43 percent of homicides, when they are actually responsible for about 9 percent of homicides.[15] Two-thirds of Americans think juvenile crime is on the increase, while there has been a 68 percent decline in violent juvenile crime since 1993.[16] Although there was less than a one in three million chance of being killed in a school last year, 71 percent of respondents to a *Wall Street Journal* poll believed that such a killing was likely in their school.[17]

In research conducted by Frank Gilliam, Ph.D., of the University of California at Los Angeles, three randomly assigned groups viewed a 15-minute video clip of the evening news which included, among other stories, a segment about a robbery at an automated teller machine. Using computer technology to "morph" the race of the alleged perpetrator, Gilliam presented his groups with a white suspect, a black suspect, or no suspect at all. Regardless of the race of the viewer, all groups "remembered" the suspect as black regardless of his race, and those who actually viewed a black suspect were significantly more fearful than those who actually viewed a white suspect.[18] As politicians run for office and conduct focus groups of likely voters, they are fed back these fears and misconceptions, closing the "media–public opinion–policy making" loop. They then begin legislating and talking about crime, churning up the media to again cover crime, whether crime is on the increase or not. This serves to escalate punishment for youth whether (a) it is the best policy or not, or (b) youth crime is increasing or not.

Between 1992 and 1997, 47 states made it easier to try juveniles as adults.[19] In supporting his Violent Youth Predator Act of 1996, Florida congressman Bill McCollum stated on National Public Radio that, "they're the predators out there. They're not children any more. They're the most violent criminals on the face of the earth."[20] In 1999, Senator Orrin Hatch succeeded in passing a bill through the United States Senate which eliminated an 11-year-old provision requiring states to address the disproportionate confinement of minorities. In defending his bill, Senator Hatch stated, "I haven't heard one shred of information that proves there is discrimination here. When you prove that, I will be right there, side-by-side with you."[21] More divisively, he asked, "Should they not be convicted when they sell drugs to our kids? Everybody knows that it happens."

In offering the "sense" of Congress in the preamble to his juvenile crime bill, Hatch summed up nicely how media-promulgated misinformation can work its way insidiously into public policy when he wrote:

> Congress finds that (1) juveniles between the ages of 10 and 14 are committing an increasing number of murders and other serious crimes; (2) on March 24, 1998, 11-year-old Andrew Golden and 13-year-old Mitchell Johnson shot and killed 4 fellow students and a teacher and injured 10 additional students in Jonesboro, AK; (3) under Arkansas state law, neither of the *gunmen* [emphasis mine] could be charged as an adult despite the viciousness of the crimes and the clear and well-planned intent demonstrated by the *gunmen* [again, emphasis mine] in carrying out their scheme; (4) the tragedy in Jonesboro is, unfortunately, an all-too-common occurrence in the United States.

The changing structure of the media has played a direct role in developing this loop of fear and hype, and has allowed us to believe crime is up when it isn't and that juveniles commit much more crime than they actually do. With the noted exception of daily newspapers, most media have grown by leaps and bounds throughout the 1990s, especially cable television and the new Internet media. As a result of new technologies, the time with which breaking news can be reported to the nation has been cut to minutes, and the space between communities seems smaller. So, where a crime story was once something reported on locally, with the daily newspaper giving one the local scale to measure how often tragic events happened in one's community, the new media have created a crime context in which Americans are now part of a national community. Suddenly, viewers are concerned about crimes that happen both down the street and 5,000 miles away. As a result, viewers who watch more minutes of the evening news report being more fearful than those who watch less frequently.[22] People consistently report more fear of crime than generally exists in their own communities, where they are personally able to test the chance of crime.

Even before the new media took hold, there have always been more entrenched structural reasons why crime coverage is so bad. For one thing, covering a crime scene in a noncontextual way is easy work. You go to the scene and there is drama, a knowledgeable spokesperson—the police officer—available for comment, crime scene tape, and flashing lights. It is a situation made for tight TV deadlines. By contrast, getting context is difficult. Some of the people with information, like the defendants, their attorneys, and their families, are bound to keep silent because it is either perceived to be or actually is in their interest to do so, or because the suspect is contesting the charges.

Another reason it is difficult to give a balanced picture of crime is that violent crime is less common than other types of crime and is, therefore, more likely to receive coverage under the "man bites dog" rule. Almost half of the time kids are depicted on the evening news,[23] it is in connection with some form of violence, even though less than one-half of 1 percent of juveniles in America were arrested for a violent offense in 1996.[24] At the same time, there were 130 times as many kids arrested for running away from home and truancy—acts which aren't even a crime if you're an adult—than for murder. As such, the tiny sliver of unusual stories making it onto the evening news which shape Americans' views of typical juvenile crimes are wildly out of step with typical juvenile offense patterns. Policies driven by such coverage are equally unlikely to strike at the causes and solutions to juvenile crime.

Despite these challenges, there are some effective steps legal professionals, criminologists, researchers and citizens can take to bridge the gap between good policy and politics. First of all, teachers, parents, students, and citizens have to view the media lens with a skeptical eye. Though TV and the print media will likely continue to be the primary ways in which we get information, we have to train ourselves to look for more context and to seek out the best ideas when trying to deal with the real challenges of youth violence and juvenile crime. That means that if we want to know both what works and what's promising with respect to enhancing school safety and the school experience, we need to reach beyond the daily newscast to the research and policy community for ideas on how to improve our schools.

Next, journalists need to take the high road and either not cover or not cover prominently those stories that have no value beyond entertainment. Some have already begun to do so, such as television station KVUE in Austin, which does not cover crime cases unless they meet certain criteria,[25] or the *Chicago Sun-Times*, which refused to cover out-of-state school shootings on its front page. Furthermore, as difficult as it can sometimes be, more context must be added to juvenile crime coverage from a personal and statistical point of view. If a crime occurs in an environment where crime does not typically occur, it is the media's responsibility to prominently feature in the story that this crime is *not* part of a growing trend, if that is indeed the case. The media must develop more skepticism about themselves and an awareness that just because something is receiving more coverage, this doesn't mean it's happening more frequently. In those debates that my colleagues and I have had with some of the top reporters in the country, it is clear that they simply could not believe—despite the data—that there was not an increase in school shootings.

Finally, legal advocates and journalists need to ensure that the right story is airing about juvenile crime. More context also means telling the truth about the systems we design and what they say about ourselves. Despite the volumes of coverage we have seen over the last two years about school shootings and the alleged "broken" juvenile justice system that produced the shootings, the problem has been portrayed as a youth crime epidemic that is a white suburban concern. The way the story has been framed, one would think we need to reconfigure the juvenile justice system to better serve the communities of Littleton and Jonesboro. Thankfully, both these predominately white middle-class communities are relatively safe. There is already a functional juvenile justice system and network of community and family supports that is now serving these children. When kids in the "right" neighborhood get arrested, psychiatrists, priests, coaches, and mentors come to court. Their parents take the day off. Resources are brought to bear to help turn the young person around. Most importantly, the young person is treated like an individual whose life is worth redeeming.

But that isn't the standard that is applied to predominately African-American and Latino youth. The kids of West Baltimore, Southeast Washington, East L.A., and East St. Louis find that there is a different set of rules at play in their "rehabilitation," and this is a truth we rarely portray on the 24-hour news cycle. White kids get the treatment and African-American kids get prison, and learn the hard lessons that come with that environment. African Americans make up 15 percent of the age ten to seventeen youth population but represent 26 percent of all arrests, 32 percent of delinquency referrals to juvenile court, 46 percent of all juveniles in long-term institutions, and more than half of all tried as adults.[26] More generally, while minority youth, including Latinos, make up one third of America's adolescent population, they comprise over two thirds of the 100,000 youth confined in local and state detention facilities.[27] In 1997, three out of four of the new admissions to adult prison were minority youth.[28]

Some would argue that minority children are treated this way because they just commit more crime. But as Frank Gilliam's research has shown[29] there is a real and growing divide between the images we see, the biases we bring to the consideration of crime, and what is actually happening in kids' lives. Delbert Elliott at the Center for the Study and Prevention of Violence at the University of Colorado has done some groundbreaking research using self-reported data from several thousand youth.[30] What his research found is that black and white kids admit to committing violent crime at rates more similar than folks would think. African-American adolescents self-report committing about one and a half times as much violent crime as white youth do. But blacks are arrested for violent crime four times more frequently and incarcerated in either adult or juvenile institutions at about seven times the rate of white kids. As Elliott followed these young people into young adulthood, he found that African-Americans maintained a relatively high level of violent offending, while white kids "matured out" of violent offending. When Elliott controlled for employment, or a meaningful, long-term relationship, he found that African-American kids matured out of violent behavior at the same rate as whites. African-American children generally turn out the same way white kids do, if granted the same opportunities.

So, here is a real juvenile justice system story that is made for TV news: it is the story of race, crime, and the differing treatment of kids before the courts. It is a socially profound story that is both moving and dramatic. Unlike the school-shooting script, we know that statistically it affects hundreds of thousands of kids every year. It is the real story of how the nation has two juvenile justice systems, but it is something we rarely hear over the drone of hyperbolic crime coverage.

The next generation of youth advocates and juvenile justice and public interest lawyers must stop howling at the moon of bad media coverage and instead try to do something about the images we are projecting of our children. The media are not some untamable beast to which only the right wing and schoolhouse assassins have access. Rather, they should be viewed as amoral carnivores, willing to snap up whatever bit of meat is tossed in their direction. The other side just has a better set of butchers.

We now need to learn from the well-organized, well-funded conservative movement, and tell our stories and the stories of our kids in a way that maximizes their chances of being covered. That means that, while assuring that important confidentiality protections are not violated, we must proffer both usable data and real-life case stories to the media. As Aristotle once said, the soul cannot think without a picture. Youth advocates and attorneys have access to the real pictures of what young people's lives are like and why they became involved in crime in the first place. Advocates are learning that when they aggressively market stories to the media that actually fit with emerging crime or policy trends, the media are willing to cover them, and cover them prominently.

Advocates also need to become more aggressive critics of the media, to shame them and set a context of skepticism in the minds of the public. The media do not own the airwaves, but that they are licensed out to them by the government, involving a routine process of applying for renewal every year. What a great class project it would be for some group of law and journalism students to conduct a content analysis of the big four networks' coverage of juvenile crime in a community, and then file a brief opposing the renewal of the license of the network whose disconnect between coverage of juvenile crime and actual juvenile crime was most egregious. While it is unlikely that a license renewal would actually be prevented, just the attempt would get you on page one and on the top of the evening news—at least on the other three networks.

None of this is to say that the deck isn't stacked against the reforming of the media's coverage of youth crime. But in the wake of Watergate, a group of conservative leaders decided that the Left held a tight control over both the media and academia, and set out a deliberate—and successful—plan to increase their control in both arenas. That phenomenon is now way out of whack and needs to be redressed. So, if you don't like the news, go out and make some of your own.

NOTES

1. Reno, Janet. "Press Conference of the Attorney General of the United States." Thursday, October 2, 1997.
2. Brooks, Kim, Vincent Schiraldi, and Jason Ziedenberg. *School House Hype: Two Years Later.* Washington, D.C.: Justice Policy Institute, 2000.
3. Mayer, Matthew J., and Peter E. Leone, "A Structural Analysis of School Violence and Disruption: Implications for Creating Safer Schools." *Education and Treatment of Children* 22(3) (August 1999).
4. *Crime in the United States: Uniform Crime Report* (1996; 1994). Washington, D.C.: Department of Justice [1997; 1995].
5. *Media Monitor: August 1997.* Washington, D.C.: Center for Media and Public Affairs, 1997.
6. Donziger, Stephen, ed. *The Real War on Crime.* Washington, D.C.: National Center on Institutional Alternatives, 1996.
7. *School-Associated Violent Deaths Report: 1999–2000.* Westlake Village, Calif.: National School Safety Center, 1999.
8. *1996 Annual Summaries.* Asheville, N.C.: National Climatic Data Center, 1997.
9. Brener, Nancy D., et al. "Recent Trends in Violence-Related Behaviors Among High School Students in the United States." *Journal of the American Medical Association,* 1999.
10. A conservative figure of the number of children killed by abuse and neglect is 2,000 per year. *A Nation's Shame: Fatal Child Abuse and Neglect in the United States.* Washington, D.C.: U.S. Department of Health and Human Services, 1995.

11. Fields, Gary, and Paul Overberg. "Juvenile Homicide Arrest Rate on the Rise in Rural America." *USA Today*, March 25, 1998.

12. Snyder, Howard N., and Melissa Sickmund. *Juvenile Offenders and Victims: 1999 National Report.* Washington, D.C.: Office of Juvenile Justice and Delinquency Prevention, 1999.

13. *Crime in the United States, 1998: Uniform Crime Reports.* Washington, D.C.: U.S. Department of Justice, 1999.

14. *Ibid.*

15. Results of Sept. 1994 Gallup poll, in Melissa Sickmund, Howard N. Snyder, and Eileen Poe-Yamagata, *Juvenile Offenders and Victims: 1997 Update on Violence.* Washington, D.C.: Office of Juvenile Justice and Delinquency Prevention, 1997.

16. *Crime in the United States* (1999).

17. Question 009—Public Opinion On-Line. The Roper Center at the University of Connecticut, December 10, 1998.

18. Gilliam, Frank D., Jr., et al. "Crime in Black and White: The Violent, Scary World of Local News." *Harvard International Journal of Press and Politics.* 1996.

19. *Juvenile Offenders and Victims.* (1999).

20. McCollum Interview, *Morning Edition* (National Public Radio broadcast, June 25, 1996. Transcript 1897–3).

21. Rivera, Ray. "Hatch: No Proof of Bias." *Salt Lake Tribune*, November 11, 1999.

22. Farkas, Steve, and Anne Duffett. *Crime, Fears and Video Tape: A Public Opinion Study of Baltimore Area Residents.* New York: Public Agenda, 1998.

23. Dorfman, Lori, Katie Woodruff, Vivian Chavez, and Lawrence Wallack. "Youth and Violence on Local Television News in California." *American Journal of Public Health* 87(8) (August 1997): 1311–16.

24. Uniform Crime Report, 1996.

25. Holly, Joe. "Should the Coverage Fit the Crime?" *Columbia Journalism Review*, May/June 1996.

26. *Juvenile Offenders and Victims,* 1997.

27. Jones, Michael, and Eileen Poe-Yamagata. *Justice for Some.* Washington, D.C.: Building Blocks for Youth, 2000.

28. *Ibid.*

29. Gilliam, "Crime in Black and White."

30. Elliott, Delbert S. "Serious Violent Offenders: Onset, Developmental Course, and Termination." *Criminology* 32(1) (February 1994).

Zero Tolerance as Mandatory Sentencing

ROBERT SCHWARTZ AND LEN RIESER

merica's schools have always had the ability to discipline students for misbehavior. Discipline was administered swiftly and, in many instances, arbitrarily. In the 1970s, building on the "due process revolution" of the prior decade, advocates for children and parents challenged unfair discipline as well as discipline of students with disabilities.

In 1975, the United States Supreme Court in *Goss v. Lopez* required public schools to act fairly when they disciplined students.[1] "Fairness" was a relative term. In order to expel a student, school boards would be required to hold a formal hearing. Suspension of a student for a few days, however, required little more of the school administrator than giving the student an explanation and an opportunity to be heard. In the two decades after *Goss*, suspensions were common, but expulsions were rarer, in part because of the procedural burdens placed on school officials.

Beginning in the early seventies, federal courts also prevented wholesale exclusion of children with disabilities from the public schools. Congress codified the early judicial rulings in 1974, when it passed the Education for All Handicapped Children Act, which is now known as the Individuals with Disabilities Education Act (IDEA). IDEA required, among other things, that a child with a disability receive appropriate educational services; for a child with an emotional disability, this was interpreted to mean that the school must help the child improve his or her behavior, typically through the use of positive supports rather than solely punishments. Courts also prohibited schools from excluding a child for misconduct if it could be shown that the

misconduct was a "manifestation" of his or her disability. In practice, however, these guarantees turned out to mean less than might have been expected
by advocates for children.

Ironically, the due process revolution has turned out to serve the state's
interest much more than it has served individual children. School administrators learned that, so long as they complied with certain simple procedural
requirements, they could successfully expel a child for almost any conduct.
Even the more complex procedures for children with disabilities, moreover,
turned out to provide relatively little practical protection, since most parents
could not navigate those procedures on their own and few had the money to
hire lawyers. In addition, recent amendments to the law have tended to favor
school districts. In 1997, for example, Congress made clear that IDEA does
not restrict a school's right to ask police to arrest a misbehaving child, regardless of whether the school has done its part to design an adequate program for the youngster.

With procedural obstacles cut down to size, Congress and the states addressed
when children should be expelled. This substantive issue has two parts. One
is the question of school exclusion. The second is the question of which kind
of misbehavior will warrant not only exclusion but also referral to juvenile
or criminal court.

In 1994, Congress amended the Elementary and Secondary Education
Act (ESEA) by requiring states to expel for at least one year students who
possessed a gun on school grounds. In order to avoid losing billions of dollars
in federal aid to education, states had one year in which to amend their laws
to conform with the new ESEA requirement. A year later, "gun" was amended
to read "weapon."

States varied in the laws they passed. Some mimicked the original federal law, only requiring expulsion in gun cases, but many went much further. Most states, for example, require expulsion not only for guns but for
any weapon or anything that can be used as a weapon. States rarely differentiate disciplinary policies by the age of the offender or the nature of the
weapon.

Thus, in our work as lawyers for children and families, we have received
reports of a North Carolina high school student expelled for having a card-
board cutout of a rifle in his car window—he was expelled for having a

"replica" of a weapon. There was the thirteen-year-old Massachusetts girl expelled for having a lipstick container *sans* lipstick—the pin that held the lipstick could be used as a weapon. There was the six-year-old boy in western Pennsylvania who was suspended for having a plastic axe (a weapon!) attached to his fireman's costume at the first-grade Halloween party. And another six-year-old's proposed expulsion was reduced to a lengthy suspension after press and public objected. This child had brought to school a nail clipper with a two-inch nail file that, the school maintained, "could" be used as a weapon.

School districts began developing their own "zero tolerance" rules, going well beyond the ESEA or state law mandates, in the wake of highly publicized school shootings in the late 1990s. Even though there was no evidence of an increase in school violence—merely an increase in reporting of school violence, both in the press and to newly created state registries—the new policies went beyond banning guns, which were already prohibited. As we have noted, the new zero tolerance policies also extended to any item that "could be used" as a weapon, as well as (in many cases) any drug, sometimes including medications. The new policies went after minor fights, heat-of-the-moment threats, and other incidents that represented little risk to school safety.[2]

These recent zero tolerance policies do not take into account whether a student knew he or she had the object that is deemed to be a weapon, or intended to do any harm. Some policies now also prohibit threatening language or writings—and it is relatively easy for a statement to qualify as "threatening." We have seen a child disciplined for writing "bomb" on a roll of toilet paper, and another child removed from school for writing, in a private journal that his teacher somehow obtained, that he wished the teacher was dead.

Examined closely, "zero tolerance" turns out to have very little to do with zero tolerance, and everything to do with one-size-fits-all mandatory punishment. Indeed, few could quarrel with a policy of zero tolerance toward children who misbehave. Adults who raise, teach or supervise children *should* react to misbehavior, but their responses should be appropriate to the age, history and circumstances of the child as well as to the nature of the "offense."[3]

Let us examine how the new zero tolerance policies have been fortified by the trends mentioned earlier.

1. Public policy toward school children increasingly relies on theories of criminal law, on the criminal law itself, and on penal-like sanctions in school settings, to respond to normal developmental behavior.

In the last two decades of the twentieth century, the criminal justice world argued about the best way to get tough on crime. The adult criminal justice system focused on several highly connected goals of punishment: deterrence (both of the individual and of society in general), incapacitation, and retribution.[4] Rehabilitation, once the leading rationale for incarcerating offenders, was abandoned as a goal of punishment, although society was willing to have it happen if it could, but only as a by-product of the other reasons society punishes offenders.

The premise of adult punishment is that adults, as rational decision makers, are capable of making cost-benefit analyses that deter them from misbehaving because of the impact of criminal sanctions. Deterrence also works because individual adult offenders who are punished modify their behavior accordingly and are deterred from misbehaving again. Retribution is appropriate because society feels comfortable "getting even" with its most serious offenders. (Latter-day proponents of capital punishment recognize that it has no deterrent value, but they place a premium on its retributive qualities.)

When we examine mandatory expulsion rules—and their companion policies requiring referral of children and youth to the criminal justice system—we see that they endorse theories of punishments developed in the adult criminal justice system. Thus, students are expected to be deterred—either in general, or in individual cases—because of a school's rules. Students are "incapacitated" by being segregated from the school community through expulsion and referral to juvenile court and to disciplinary schools. And there is a notion of retribution as well, since modern school discipline policies care little for the well-being of the student (which might be considered "rehabilitation") and operate much more along the "let the punishment fit the crime" model of the adult criminal justice system.

Two related but different policies buttress the general "toughening" of American criminal justice policy at the end of the century. One policy is grounded in sentencing guidelines. The theory behind guidelines is that as a matter of fairness, similarly situated defendants should receive similar sentences. In practice, sentencing guidelines have erred on the side of "toughness," and they have made a major contribution to the quadrupling of America's prison population since 1980.

The second policy goes beyond "guidelines" to requiring mandatory sentences. Mandatory sentences are actually mandatory minimum sentences. They are usually imposed for gun or drug offenses, or, more recently, for sentencing enhancement (such as "three strikes" legislation that mandates minimum sentences upon conviction of a third felony).

Despite the obvious harshness of mandatory sentencing and sentencing guidelines, which reduce judicial discretion, they at least have the benefit of being related to the perceived seriousness of the offense, or tied to the criminal history of the defendant. America's criminal justice system has yet to embrace a single sentence for all crimes—indeed, we moved beyond single draconian sentences for minor offenses two hundred years ago.[5]

In contrast, zero tolerance policies for students adopt a theory of mandatory punishment that has been rejected by the adult criminal justice system because it is too harsh! Rather than having a variety of mandatory sanctions for a range of school-based offenses, state laws apply the same expulsion rules to the six-year-old as to the seventeen-year-old, to the first-time offender as to the chronic troublemaker, to the child with a gun as to the child with a nail file.

To the extent that zero tolerance policies purport to increase fairness (adopting a theory of sentencing guidelines), they fail at that goal as well. First, unlike sentencing guidelines, state and local zero tolerance polices do not give school administrators discretion to select among a range of punishments. Instead, administrators believe that they are mandated to expel students. Second, to the extent that zero tolerance policies were designed to eliminate racial disparities in school discipline (though we hypothesize this aim, there is no evidence in any legislative history that this is one of the goals of zero tolerance), zero tolerance polices turn out in practice to be racially biased.[6]

2. Zero tolerance polices are part of a trend to treat younger children as though they reason and behave like adults.

Through the 1990s, we saw younger and younger children being prosecuted as adults. Pennsylvania has no lower age limit for trying a child as an adult for murder. In the mid-nineties, the state's General Assembly legislated by slogan ("Adult time for adult crime"), changing the juvenile code to require more automatic treatment of youth as adults. The national press began calling to ask whether "children were different today." Pennsylvania, like many other states, began constructing new adult prisons for youth who are sentenced as adults.

There is nothing in what we know about child and adolescent development to suggest that adult penal theories have relevance to children. Deterrence has limited applicability to them, and its relevance diminishes the younger the child. Does anyone seriously believe that six-year-olds in general are deterred from bringing nail clippers to school because one of their classmates was expelled for doing so?

Similarly, retributive punishments by definition are not tailored to the developmental status of the child, but tailored to their offense. The same is true of incapacitation by expulsion. We know of no mandatory expulsion policy that has even a surface claim of being grounded in theories of child development. Zero tolerance polices are not designed to benefit the misbehaving child. Rather, they are intended to allow the remaining students to benefit by the expulsion of their classmates.

Zero tolerance policies are thus grounded on adult penal theories that are divorced from knowledge of child development.

3. Inappropriate penal theories that support zero tolerance are nurtured in schools that look increasingly like correctional institutions.

Consider the modern urban American schoolhouse. Students wait in long lines to pass through metal detectors staffed by security guards. Increasingly they are asked to wear uniforms. They find police or probation officers who are as much a part of the school staff as guidance counselors. Schools are approaching the ambience of "total institutions" like the military, prisons, or mental hospitals described by Erving Goffman.[7]

There comes a point when schools move from valuing discipline because it enhances learning to exalting discipline *over* learning. The more that children appear as fungible parts of a system and less as individuals with different histories, capacities, and offenses, the more education will suffer.

4. Zero tolerance policies that require referral to the juvenile justice system are abetted by sophistic arguments that the justice system is the only way to get help for children who misbehave.

It is easy to refer a child to the justice system if the referral seems benign. Indeed, there are many caring juvenile court judges in the country, and many programs that serve children well.

On the other hand, few parents would want their children unnecessarily labeled as a delinquent or criminal merely because a school administrator thinks that the child needs help. Labels come with a cost, one of which is a 50-percent chance that a child who is placed in a public juvenile justice facility in this country will be in an institution that fails to comply with minimum national standards of care.[8]

There are many in law enforcement who overlook the risks to children that come with labeling them as adults or criminals. A prosecutor in Florida insists that transferring children to adult court is his way of helping them, because he has services in his county jail. A Tennessee police detective charges an eight-year-old boy with murder—after he stabbed his mother's abusive boyfriend following years of domestic violence—"more to get [the boy] into the system, get him counseling and away from the mother."

5. Most juvenile courts acquiesce to zero tolerance policies that send students to juvenile court.

Our modern version of "zero tolerance" is not only about expulsion. More insidiously, it involves the referral of misbehaving youth to juvenile or criminal court. Few would quarrel with a school that sent a gun-toting high school student to the justice system. But gun referrals are a small percentage of those students who end up in the nation's juvenile and criminal courts. School quarrels that once ended in after-school detention now result in referrals to juvenile detention centers.

Some few juvenile court judges are rejecting referrals of emotionally disturbed children who behave precisely as they are expected to behave. One juvenile court judge in central Pennsylvania chastised a school district for referring a fourteen-year-old girl with serious emotional problems to juvenile court for making threats to a teacher. The court dismissed the case, which should have been handled through the student's IEP. The court wrote, "While this decision is not intended to effectively cut off all access to the criminal court system by school authorities, the instances where it is appropriate should be rare indeed."[8]

Unfortunately, examples of juvenile courts dismissing inappropriate referrals are rare. Most judges tolerate the referrals, while some even encourage them.

Juvenile courts lost a part of their caseload to the adult criminal courts as a result of get-tough policies of the 1990s. As thousands of youth were transferred to adult courts, juvenile courts had room for the new referrals, and showed little inclination to turn them away.

In Pennsylvania we've seen juvenile court judges in two counties order—without apparent authority—school districts to refer to the court any child who threatened violence or was violent. Judges ordered mandatory detention for those students, so they could be "assessed" in some way. It is unclear what kind of assessment the judges had in mind. We received a call from a psychiatrist of a twelve-year-old boy with emotional problems. The boy brought a toy pistol to school. The psychiatrist didn't object to the boy being disciplined. She didn't understand, though, why he had been arrested and had spent the prior two months in a maximum security detention facility being "assessed." All the detention did was interrupt his treatment.

Thus, even when schools might decline to refer troublesome students to juvenile court, they often receive pressure from the courts to make the referral anyway in service of the judge's notion of "zero tolerance." Sadly, the worldview of too many judges is seen through a lens of law enforcement, not one of lessons or lectures.

It is easy to imagine school discipline polices that are grounded in common sense, and that are sensitive to student safety and the educational needs of all students. Such policies are the kind that most parents would want if their own children were being disciplined. Then children would be treated less like criminals and more like children who struggle with the demands of growing up. They would be taught how to behave, not treated like criminals for misbehaving. They would be part of their society, not excluded from it.

NOTES

1. 419 U.S. 565 (1975).

2. Brooks, K., Schiraldi, V., and Ziedenberg, J. 2000. *School House Hype: Two Years Later.* Washington, D.C.: Justice Policy Institute.

3. The American Bar Association, the largest voluntary professional organization in the world, agrees with this view. At its midyear meeting in February 2001, the ABA adopted the following as policy:

> RESOLVED, that the American Bar Association supports the following principles concerning school discipline:
>
> 1) schools should have strong policies against gun possession and be safe places for students to learn and develop;
> 2) in cases involving alleged student misbehavior, school officials should exercise sound discretion that is consistent with principles of due process and considers the individual student and the particular circumstances of misconduct; and
> 3) alternatives to expulsion or referral for prosecution should be developed that will improve student behavior and school climate without making schools dangerous; and
>
> FURTHER RESOLVED, that the ABA opposes, in principle, "zero tolerance" policies that have a discriminatory effect, or mandate either expulsion or referral of students to juvenile or criminal court, without regard to the circumstances or nature of the offense or the student's history.

4. Packer, H. L. 1968. *The Limits of the Criminal Sanction.* Stanford: Stanford University Press.

5. Meranze, M. 1996. *Laboratories of Virtue: Punishment, Revolution, and Authority in Philadelphia, 1760–1835.* Chapel Hill: University of North Carolina Press.

6. "Blacks Likely to Lose Out in School Crackdown." *San Francisco Chronicle,* December 18, 1999, p. A21.

7. Goffman, E. 1961. *Asylums: Essays on the Social Situation of Mental Patients and Other Inmates.* New York: Doubleday.

8. Parent, D. G., Lieter, V., Kennedy, S., Livens, L., Wentworth, D., and Wilcox, S. 1994. *Conditions of Confinement: Juvenile Detention and Corrections Facilities.* Washington, D.C.: Office of Juvenile Justice and Delinquency Prevention.

9. *In re J.G.,* Court of Common Please of Northumberland County, PA, JU-98-119, 120, 121, 122 (August 6, 1998).

Education, Delinquency, and Incarceration

JAMES BELL

Just over 100 years ago the first juvenile court was established in Chicago. Shortly after, W. E. B. Du Bois wrote in his seminal work *The Souls of Black Folk* that "the problem of the 20th Century is the problem of the color line." Around that same time, psychologist G. Stanley Hall coined the term "adolescence." Today, color, adolescence, and incarceration have converged in a way that would probably shock and dismay both of those forward-thinking gentlemen.

That nexus has resulted in the disproportionate representation of young people leaving the educational system and checking into the juvenile justice system. Young people do not forfeit their rights to education because of their involvement in juvenile justice, but my litigation experience—and I have litigated dozens of cases throughout the United States on behalf of young people caught up in the system—has shown that most juvenile justice facilities have poor education programs and that young people are being denied their fundamental right to education.

Education for Youth in Confinement

Secure confinement facilities are required to provide services for young people that are rehabilitative in nature, and an essential part of rehabilitation is education. Clearly, it is important for children currently attending school to keep up with their classmates while incarcerated. And young people who have stopped attending school must begin the process of catching up.

Indeed, incarcerated juveniles have a constitutional right to an adequate educational program.[1] This means that any young person being held in any type of juvenile facility is entitled to attend school in the facility before and after his or her adjudication hearing—and this right includes special education services when they are needed.[2] Courts have held that state compulsory education laws require the provision of a program of education for juveniles in detention awaiting adjudication. Further, such a program is supposed to be provided to young people "within a few days of detention."[3] And yet, facilities will often not begin a school program for young people until they have been there at least a week. Facility administrators seem to believe that leaving a child in his or her room for a week somehow makes the child better-prepared to attend the school program. For juveniles in long-term detention—meaning 30 days or longer—the courts have held that the Eighth Amendment prohibition against cruel and unusual punishment requires states to provide "treatment."[4] This treatment must include appropriate educational services.

While courts have been reluctant to specify what form educational programs should take, they have suggested guidelines. Courts have recommended prompt evaluation of children to determine whether, and in what areas, they may be academically deficient. After assessment, children who need remediation should be placed in programs to learn basic reading, spelling, and math skills. And vocational training should be available to help young people learn skills they can use once out of detention.

In a landmark case, *Morgan v. Sprout*,[5] the court went further, ordering a state institution to implement an educational plan that would achieve the following:

(1) Provide a complete educational assessment of each incoming student.
(2) Provide special education services and programs to all students who are diagnosed as needing such services.
(3) Establish an in-service training program for all teaching staff.
(4) Hire a teaching staff certified to teach in the fields to which they are assigned.
(5) Bring high school programs into compliance with state requirements for public high schools.

(6) Institute a periodic testing program to determine the educational progress made by individual students.

(7) Obtain sufficient instructional materials to run an individualized program that provides rewards for academic progress.

Special Education in Confinement

Children may be eligible for special education services if they suffer from severe vision or hearing problems, orthopedic impairments, chronic illness, mental retardation, speech or language impairment, attention deficit disorder, serious emotional disturbance, or learning disabilities.[6] Research indicates that anywhere from 20 percent to 60 percent of detained children are eligible for special education.[7] Some of these children come into detention with a well-documented history of special education services, and others have disabilities that have gone undetected or unaddressed by the school system.

Federal timelines for assessment and implementation of special education programs apply, even though a child may be in "temporary" detention. Institutions confining children must also refrain from discriminating against educationally handicapped children under the Rehabilitation Act of 1973.[8] Indeed, the requirements of federal law are quite explicit regarding services to be provided to youth with special needs in secure confinement. The court in the 1995 *Boyd* case held that "the purpose of the Individuals with Disabilities Education Act is to assure that all children with disabilities have available to them a free and appropriate education. The regulations make clear that the reference includes state correctional facilities."[9] Nonetheless, children in confinement often go without identification of their special education needs and the related services mandated by law.

As an advocate for youth in detention, I have found this issue problematic and controversial. Increasingly, parents are reluctant to have their children labeled as needing special education. They believe the labeling itself reduces their children's chances for success. But as an advocate for the child in detention, I have seen that special education diagnoses often help a child receive more attention and more services. Special education–eligible children are entitled to a broad range of assessment, evaluation, educational, and related services (including transition services) under the IDEA.[10] Even though parents often do not want the diagnosis, these services can be tremendously helpful in discovering if and why young people are underperforming and uninterested in school. So two forces that want to improve the situation for young people in detention can be at odds.

Types of Youth Confinement

Young people are detained in several types of facilities, all of which are required to provide education to them. It is important to know the difference between each type of facility so that the educational requirements for each are clearly understood.

Adult Jails

Adult jails hold adults for a maximum of one year. These facilities are commonly referred to as "county jails" and are characterized by multiple-occupancy cells, small recreational yards, and some form of commissary. Adult jails usually confine both male and female adults. They have a small section for isolation and one or more cells that are used for detoxification from alcohol or drugs. Most juveniles detained in adult jails are awaiting adjudication.

One of the major problems with confining children in adult jails is that since these jails were not originally constructed with the intention of holding children, there are usually no classrooms. One of my cases in Kentucky is representative of this problem. There, the classroom and the recreation room were in the same space—a weight machine and an antiquated exercise bike shared a room with six chairs for classroom instruction. The facility routinely housed at least 30 youth.

Unfortunately, it is routine for children to be given old worksheets with no supervision as "education"—or to be denied any educational programming at all. The public should know that often institutions are violating the law by not providing basic educational services, and that young people who have not been charged with a crime—let alone a "delinquent act"—are being denied their basic rights. And without schooling, there rarely are any other activities for children to participate in while incarcerated. They become bored and may continually demand attention or destroy property, which lands them in isolation for long periods of time.

Detention Centers

Juvenile detention centers are the most appropriate place for children who must be confined. They have classrooms, day rooms, and a gymnasium or some other type of indoor recreation space. Staff at detention centers is supposed to be specifically trained to deal with the unique needs of detained youth.

The conditions of detention centers are usually substantially better than those in adult jails, although most are chronically overcrowded and services provided to youth are being reduced. The chronic crowding puts pressure on the education program, because there are often too many young people to accommodate in classrooms. Crowding makes it almost impossible to conduct a full education program since the lack of space forces children to spend many school days in their cells. One facility I sued, for example, had young people assigned to a classroom every third day. Teachers did not know which young people would arrive at class at any time. Young people not in the classroom were kept in their rooms. This practice is unconscionable but not unusual.

Training Schools

Juvenile training schools are long-term treatment centers where juveniles are sent after the court finds they have committed a delinquent act. These places are usually located away from urban areas and are characterized by large land areas and clusters of cottages or residential units. A young person's length of stay averages 18 months.

The mandate of these facilities is to implement treatment that addresses the problems that contribute to young people's decisions to violate the law. Training schools provide the most opportunity for young people to receive long-term education, but there are often problems transitioning young people back into their local schools. All too often a training school's district will not transfer credits to a young person's home district, and the academic achievements and progress made during confinement will not be rewarded.

Boot Camps and Outdoor Experiential Facilities

"Boot camp" is a catch-all phrase that can apply to several different types of outdoor experiential programs. A common characteristic of these programs is that there is usually some type of intense physical requirement or guided activity that requires teamwork. Some programs impose a military atmosphere with strict discipline and constant interaction between the staff and detainees. Others place young people in situations that require trust and teamwork in order to accomplish goals or gain program rewards. The important issue with boot camps is to determine who provides education for the program. Often, boot camps will not contract with licensed providers of educational services, and they invent curricula that are not sufficient to meet the needs of youth.

Conclusion

We must muster all of our energy to assure that young people are not irretrievably lost in a system that sees them as throwaway people. Too many juvenile justice professionals cite the usual suspects: too little money, too many forms, too little leadership at the top, too many regulations at the bottom. Too few staff, too many students, files, and families to handle.

But we must be up to the task of making sure education is a right guaranteed and delivered in juvenile facilities. When children are deprived of their liberty, their best hope is education. It can be critical to a young incarcerated person that someone cares enough to assist him or her with reading or self-expression through creative writing. And there are inspiring examples: *The Beat Within* is an incredible newspaper in the California juvenile system that allows children to express themselves on many subjects while learning.

Many people have struggled mightily to bring humanity and enlightenment into young people in the darkest of circumstances. Such work has epic significance in the lives of children and their families. John Holt reminds us "that there is no difference between living and learning, that living is learning, that it is impossible, and misleading, and harmful to think of them as being separate." Let that lesson guide us toward better educational opportunities for young people in trouble with the law.

NOTES

1. *Inmates of the Boys' Training School v. Affleck*, 346 F. Supp. 1354, 1370 (D.R.I. 1972).
2. *D. B. v. Tewksbury*, 545 F. Supp. 896, 905 (D. Or. 1982); *Martarella v. Kelley*, 359 F. Supp. 478, 481 (S.D.N.Y. 1973); *Green v. Johnson*, 513 F. Supp. 965, 976 (D. Mass. 1981).
3. *Tommy P. v. Board of County Commissioners*, 645 P.2d 697, 701–704 (Wash. 1982).
4. *Martarella v. Kelley* 359 F. Supp. 478, 481.
5. 432 F. Supp. 1130 (S.D. Miss. 1977).
6. 20 U.S. Code 1401 (a) (1) (A), 1401 (a) (15), 34 Code of Federal Regulations 300.7.
7. See Loren Warboys et al. "The Prevalence of Disabilities in the Juvenile Court Population." *California Juvenile Court Special Education Manual*. San Francisco: Youth Law Center, 1994.
8. 29 U.S. Code 504 et seq.
9. *Alexander S. v. Boyd*, 876 F. Supp. 773, 801 (D.S.C. 1995).
10. 20 U.S. Code, 1401 (a) (16), 1401 (a) (17), 1401 (a) (19), 34 Code of Federal Regulations 300.16, 300.17, 300.18.

Sexual Harassment Meets Zero Tolerance: Life in K–12 Schools

NAN STEIN

Introduction: Setting the Immediate Context

On May 24, 1999, the United States Supreme Court ruled in the *Davis v. Monroe County (GA) Board of Education* case that school districts are legally and financially liable for student-to-student sexual harassment if they knew about it and did nothing to stop it. This case had begun quite a few years before, in Macon, Georgia, in the Monroe County School District. LaShonda Davis was a fifth grader who was touched, grabbed, and verbally harassed by a male classmate. The boy, who is only known by his initials, G. F., repeatedly attempted to touch LaShonda's breasts and genital area, rubbed against her in a sexual manner, constantly asked her for sex, and, in one instance, put a doorstop in his pants and acted in a sexually suggestive manner (Brake 1999). By no stretch of the imagination was this boy subtle or was his behavior ambiguous; rather, it was persistent and unrelenting.

LaShonda, on the other hand, had not remained quiet or passive. Besides telling G. F. to stop, she also told her teachers. Her parents also complained to her teachers, and asked to have LaShonda's seat moved. But her teachers and school officials did nothing, not even separate the two students, who sat next to each other. After several months of this harassment, LaShonda's grades fell and she wrote a suicide note. G. F.'s behavior was clearly having both psychological and academic consequences. LaShonda's parents filed a criminal complaint against the boy and also a federal civil rights lawsuit against the school district for permitting a sexually hostile environment to exist. In the criminal action, the boy pleaded guilty to sexual battery. And after five years of legal battles through various levels of the federal court system, the U.S. Supreme Court finally settled the case in a five-to-four decision.

The Supreme Court's ruling in the *Davis* case also ended years of disagreements among various federal courts in different parts of the country: the ninth (in a California case) and seventh (in a case in Illinois) circuits had held that schools were responsible for peer-to-peer sexual harassment, while the fifth (in a Texas case) and the eleventh (where the *Davis* case came from) circuits ruled in the opposite direction. Until the time of the Supreme Court's decision, confusion reigned nationwide, with courts making contradictory rulings, often over similar sets of facts (Stein 1999).

The *Davis* decision was lauded by many, including feminists. But, within a short period of time, it was clear that the *Davis* decision was being used by those in favor of zero tolerance as yet another excuse to suspend and expel students for conduct much less egregious than that of G. F. *Davis* landed in the midst of the national conversation about school safety, which had been overtaken and unfortunately dominated by the zero tolerance, law-and-order notion of school safety.

The Larger Context of
Sexual Harassment in Schools

First, we need to go back a bit into the last decades of the twentieth century, as the term "sexual harassment" came flying into our national discourse, no longer only residing in the realms of workplace discrimination or the vocabulary of feminists, legal scholars, law students, and some school officials. Now, the term "sexual harassment" is everywhere, even in places that we might not want it to be applied, and sometimes we may privately cringe when we hear it used. Events that may be trivial have been labeled as sexual harassment, maybe deliberately in an effort to make feminists look like we have gone too far—not only do we get labeled "antiboys," but we are described as just downright silly. But, quite frankly, that is not as disturbing as the hijacking of legal victory in the *Davis* case, which is now being used in the service of student surveillance, punishment, and control amid the law-and-order/school safety discourse that so consumes our nation.

The feminist discourse and thinking that began this work on sexual harassment years ago, and that led to the victory in the *Davis* case, has been appropriated by the zero tolerance/school safety forces, who have added sexual harassment to a long list of behaviors that school personnel may use to suspend and expel young people from schools. There are no second chances for the students, no discretion for administrators, and no teachable moments for teachers to use with their students. As a former middle-school teacher myself who had 36 students in my class (Whittier Middle School, Dayton, Ohio), I used to believe in and use the "teachable moment." But, that technique has been removed from a teacher's repertoire, an act justified under the rubric of zero tolerance.

Moreover, remembering the context in which the *Davis* case has landed helps to explain the predicament that we are in: it came one month after the April 1999 shootings at Columbine High School, in Littleton, Colorado. The *Davis* case was rapidly converted into just another justification for law and order and for zero tolerance policies—do anything to avoid a lawsuit or a school shooting. And we can't forget that this school safety mania/zero tolerance mantra is part of the larger discourse that also includes trying minors as adults (Proposition 21 in California, passed in March 2000), deterrence theories, "three strikes, you're out," mandatory sentencing, drug policy, capital punishment, and a general reduction of civil liberties. And, this feminist victory is being used by people that most feminists may not consider our allies, those who would be hard-pressed to care about feminist issues. Feminism is being used to establish new forms of control.

In September 1992, along with some colleagues from the Wellesley College Center for Research on Women, I conducted a survey on sexual harassment in schools that ran in *Seventeen* magazine (LaBlanc 1992). Among the multiple-choice questions were also two open-ended questions, one of which asked, "What do you think schools should do about sexual harassment?" One young respondent wrote, "I believe that if all girls who have ever been sexually harassed reported the guys who did it, there would no longer be any boys in school" (personal communication, 1992). At the time, I thought this was true but not likely, since when boys sexually harassed girls, if it was noticed at all by school personnel, it was treated lightly, and only rarely did the harassers get punished.

Flash forward from 1992 to the fall of 1996, when the nation focused on an incident in Lexington, N.C. Jonathan Prevette, that cute little six-year-old boy with the curly hair and the thick glasses, kissed a little six-year-old girl.

Most of the media attention that this incident generated focused on the injustice of his so-called "suspension" (I always took issue with the use of the word "suspension" in this case, as he was moved from one class to another for the day—not exactly the definition of "suspension" by any stretch of the imagination). The school officials were mocked and criticized for paying attention to the plight and distress of the little girl, yet they were made to look the fool for extending the label of sexual harassment to the behaviors of such young children. But the real culprits were made out to be the feminists who had gone too far—we were blamed for having created this world in which Jonathan was now being demonized (Stein 1999; O'Toole 1997).

During the media frenzy over this incident, ABC's *Nightline with Ted Koppel* devoted a show on October 4, 1996, to this kissing-kid episode. The guests were Verna Williams of the National Women's Law Center in Washington, D.C. (the woman who would later argue the *Davis* case in the Supreme Court); Peggy Orenstein, a San Francisco area–based journalist and author of *School Girls*; Dr. Alvin Poussaint, child psychiatrist at Harvard Medical School; and Christina Hoff Sommers, author of *Who Stole Feminism* and a former philosophy professor at Clark University, who resides currently at the American Enterprise Institute, a conservative think tank in Washington, D.C. For 30 minutes on national television, as these four people discussed the kissing-kid incident, there was no mention of the term "zero tolerance," or even the larger notion of school safety.

Yet, it was around that time that schools were required to institute zero tolerance policies to bolster school safety and ensure orderly learning environments. The Gun Free School Act, passed by Congress in 1994, required states that receive federal funds to mandate expulsion, on a case-by-case basis, for at least one year, of any student who brought a weapon to school (*Harvard Ed. Letter*, Jan./Feb. 2000). A weapon was defined as "guns, bombs, grenades, missile launchers, and poison gas; it did not include knives . . . though some states were permitted to use a broader definition of weapons" (Wasser 2001).

However, these expulsion policies have gone from a prohibition on real hardware—guns—to now including toy weapons and squirt guns, drugs, symbolic representations of drugs (like drawings of marijuana leaves, a case that the Massachusetts chapter of the American Civil Liberties Union is representing), to fighting, gang activity, threats of violence, hate offenses, and sexual harassment (*Education Week*, Jan. 26, 2000, p. 7). More and more children are being removed from school, with no place to go; only a few states have requirements to establish alternative schools for these suspended and expelled children. More and more young people are hitting the streets, becoming exiles, being criminalized, if you will. I believe this trend to expel young people is also a manifestation of the decline of our sense of collective responsibility for children and youth.

In October 1998, the Clinton White House held a conference on school safety, essentially to address the school shootings that had taken place the previous spring in Jonesboro, Arkansas, and Springfield, Oregon. Three factors were promoted at this conference as a way to create school safety: school uniforms, metal detectors, and curfews. Since then, in this post-Columbine world, some schools think that the way to ensure school safety is to remove lockers from hallways, add fencing to the school grounds, require the students to wear identification badges, and permit them to use only see-through backpacks. In addition, students have been suspended retroactively for papers they have written, thoughts they have had, and, in one case, for drawing that marijuana leaf (which could have easily been a tomato plant). This drawing was seen as a violation of the school's zero tolerance drug policy.

Moreover, zero tolerance policies have racial implications—students are being suspended disproportionately by race under these policies. According to U.S. Department of Education figures, in the 1997 school year, black children made up 17 percent of all U.S. students but 32 percent of those suspended, while white students made up 63 percent of all students and 51 percent of those suspended, and Hispanics made up 14 percent of all students and 13.5 percent of those suspended (Shepherd 2000).

Sexual Harassment and Zero Tolerance

In this era of zero tolerance, students are suspended and expelled for incidents of sexual harassment. My examples of sexual harassment come from a variety of sources: the media, parents who call me, students who e-mail me, and conversations that I have with teachers and administrators. My examples are not scientific, but, as I always say, neither are lawsuits; they are a sample size of one, but they can teach us a lot—they may be signs of where the nation might be headed. These examples may be at the margins of what is happening, but they allow us to think about whether we would want these examples to become the center, the norm, or not.

Here are a few examples of the ways in which behaviors have been framed as expellable sexual harassment or criminal sexual assault since the *Davis* case:

- An elementary school boy in Washington state sticks out his tongue at a girl and he is suspended for sexual harassment/oral sex. Remember that this was not a teenage boy making gross tongue movements toward a teenage girl, but rather, they were small children. Granted, the tongue movements still may be gross and/or inappropriate, but one must remember how often students stick out their tongues over the quality of the food that is served to them in the school cafeteria.

- Five fourth graders in Oswego, New York, are suspended for poking their straws through their milk cartons, which had photos of a female cheerleader on them. These boys poked their straws through the section of the milk carton that was her chest area (*Education Week*, Feb. 23, 2000, p. 4). What I wonder about this is what would have happened to these children if they had poked holes in the part of the milk carton that was her head: Would they have been suspended for being pre-Columbine shooters? Or, if it had been her feet, would they be considered proponents of voodoo instead of sexual harassers? Or of having a foot fetish? Indeed, if the school has rules that playing with one's food is against the school rules, then reprimands against these children certainly would have been warranted. But, to construct this incident as one of sexual harassment seems to be a stretch and an injustice.

- A mother in Colorado who has twin fifth graders (one boy and one girl) called to tell me that her son had been labeled a sexual predator for "depanting" another boy his same age on the school playground. The school principal did not think that loss of recess privileges along with an apology to the other child was sufficient. I worry about the use of an adult, criminal label for this child, and the ways in which his peers will treat him.

- In West Bath, Maine, a group of third-grade boys used force to hold down a female classmate on the playground while one of them climbed on top of her and pretended to have sexual intercourse with her. The girl, who was frightened and crying, reported the incident to the playground supervisor, who is alleged to have told her to "stay away" from the boys. Two days later, the same incident was repeated and this time the girl told her parents (MacQuarrie and Merrill 2000; Sharp 2000).

Indeed, the school district might be negligent in this incident, and the girl's parents threatened to sue the school district in federal court for sex discrimination/sexual harassment (federal law Title IX), and failure to protect their daughter on the school playground. If the girl had indeed told a school official, who failed to take any action, the school district may be found liable.

However, particularly troubling was the way this incident, as reported by the press, escalated to discussions of criminal prosecution of the boys for sexual assault. Yet, it turned out that under Maine law, nine-year-olds cannot be prosecuted for adult crimes (state juvenile facilities only take children from age eleven and up) (Merrill 2000). Indeed, school-based consequences for the boys' behavior are warranted, but to attempt to move this incident into the criminal justice system seemed to be an extreme measure, yet made fashionable by the standards imposed by zero tolerance. Moreover, when the boys, who were suspended for a few days, returned to school, the girl who had been the target was the brunt of teasing and other hostile behaviors from her peers (Merrill 2000). Once again, this school proved itself to be remiss; they seemed no better prepared to deal with the aftermath of the episode than they did to intervene or prevent the egregious behaviors in the first place. They did, however, send a letter home to all the parents, hired an extra playground supervisor, sent several teachers to a conference on bullying and harassment, and spoke to the students about "civility, bullying, and harassment" (Sharp 2000). Too bad they didn't frame the incident as one of "violence" (or even "sexual violence"), which might have conveyed to the children the seriousness of the boys' conduct toward the girl. It is ironic—in this era of zero tolerance and the mania to name so many behaviors as violent—that this one was not so named.

- An e-mail from a teenage boy appealed for help after he had been accused of sexual harassment. The point of this story is that here is a student, reaching out for understanding, for an explanation that no doubt his school has not provided to him.

Hello. My name is Stuart XXX. I am a 17-year-old, and a senior in high school. I found out today that I was being accused of sexual harassment. I was amazed and taken by surprise because I had no idea that what I had done was considered as sexual harassment. This was possibly because my school had not properly educated its student body on the facts of sexual harassment or because I am an ignorant person. About a month ago I commented on a fellow student's figure in a positive manner. That person gave little response so I continued the compliments for about three other times to still receive no response. Agitated with this reaction, I soon disliked this person. I began to annoy [her] every so often. Please keep in mind this is over a period of a month or so. Maybe twice a week. I would ask stupid questions of whether this person hated me or not. I would sometimes poke her arm with my index finger in a way that would render no danger physically. I may once in a while walk by [her] desk and graze [her] arm. Once I made a remark as to if [she] did not respond to a question, that meant [she] wanted to go on a date and become more than friends. All of this was in jest. However, due to the fact that [she] barely ever gave any response, I had no idea of the effects of my agitations. So, today I find out that it is sexual harassment. I did some research on the net and found one common recurrence. It was stated that sexual harassment had an obvious and profound effect on the work performance of the victim. So profound that tasks were beginning to become very difficult. I took this as a student's learning environment becoming drastically affected so that they were unable to learn. I feel that my remarks by no means affected this person in such a way . . . Do you have any suggestions or an answer to whether I am guilty or not? I have a conference Monday morning on the matter, so if there is any way you could reply, it would be most graciously accepted. Thank you for your time. (personal communication, January 2000)

• Likewise, teachers report to me how they are being designated, quite out of the blue, by administrators to be the "sexual harassment grievance coordinator" for the school without receiving any preparation besides reading some memos from the administrator's file. A third-grade teacher in Massachusetts told me how she was supposed to provide training for the rest of the staff and how she was clueless and worried. Administrators seem to be appointing teachers without giving them any guidance or opportunities to get training for themselves, just ordering them to do so (personal communication, January 2000).

Zero Tolerance and Feminism

Now, to return to my larger point and concern, that zero tolerance policies are antithetical to feminism. They represent an individualistic approach; there is no collective piece to them at all, and they exclude rather than try to reshape or reform the individual. And, there is no collective responsibility for the excluded person, no space for this person.

In addition, these zero tolerance policies, besides sacrificing the individual in the name of creating the supposed safe middle, also seem to be in contradiction to the whole notion of education, which is usually about trying to help children learn and improve, whether it is their reading, their grades, their curiosity, or their goals. Generally, schools don't abandon kids when they have trouble reading or writing (or at least school administrators don't publicly admit to that approach and brag about it); there are efforts to accommodate to the students' various learning styles and rates.

Strategies for Zero Indifference (Instead of Zero Tolerance) for Sexual Harassment

To achieve a gender-safe school, I think we need to employ several simultaneous strategies to ensure that sexual harassment won't have a presence there. I suggest that we call this "zero indifference," rather than "zero tolerance," which would mean that we plan to notice the behaviors, comment on them, intervene, and make corrections accordingly.

1. Institute classroom education and curriculum that is long term, engaging, fun (not lectures by the school board attorney), and age-appropriate. The more this subject of sexual harassment—and I like to also connect it to "gender or sexual violence" can be integrated into the whole curriculum and to the main texts that the students are using, the better. That way it isn't a burden to the teachers, because it is an integral part of the curriculum, and it makes more sense to the students since it is included as an integral part of the curriculum and not added on as an afterthought.
2. Train all the staff, including the administrators, custodians, school

secretaries, bus drivers, coaches, teachers, guidance counselors, play-ground and lunchroom supervisors, and psychologists. This training should last longer than a casual staff meeting or the early-release-day faculty inservice that lasts two and a half hours. How about a full day? Or repeated sessions throughout the year?

3. Designate at least one man and one woman in every building as the "ombuds" (I'm adverse to calling them the "sexual harassment griev-ance coordinators" or "complaint managers"—what students are go-ing to visit school officials with those titles?) to whom students can go with inquires or concerns and who will act on their behalf. These individuals will need extra training, and possibly release time (from their current course schedule) to serve in this capacity. The placement of their offices is also a matter for serious consideration, and their locations as well as their names should be publicized throughout the school community.

4. Develop school-based codes of discipline for sexual harassment that ensure due process rights for the accused, as well as assurances that the student who makes the complaint will be protected from the harasser and his/her friends who might consider retaliation.

5. Develop school-based restraining orders/stay-away orders that would function to protect the student(s) who have made a complaint of harassment against another student(s). Class schedules, walking routes, bus assignments, lunchtime, and other informal locations would be covered under these restraining orders.

6. Create multiple strategies for resolution, which may involve face-to-face meetings between the harasser and the target, as long as they are voluntary and adults are present in the room (it is not up to the students to solve this problem of sexual harassment). No forced me-diation should be allowed, conducted only by student mediators. These voluntary efforts, which may also include the technique "write a letter to the harasser," cannot take the place of punishment, espe-cially if the incident involved physical contact (as happened to La-Shonda Davis) and/or if it was a repeated event.

7. Offer compassionate responses to the harasser in the form of coun-seling, whether as individual counseling or in a group setting. I am working with Brookline High School in the Boston area through a National Institute of Justice/COPS grant that they received, offering

many groups, to both boys and girls—the boys are those who have harassed girls, and the girls join typically because they want to talk about the abusive relationships that they repeatedly enter into. Other schools offer such counseling groups, sometimes run by staff from the local domestic violence or sexual assault center. I have been inspired by the one in Austin, Texas—SafePlace—which has been running groups in the Austin schools for nearly 12 years, reaching hundreds of young people a year in their 24-week sessions.

8. Parents need to be involved—both through open community forums as well as in private discussions, especially if their children are involved in incidents of sexual harassment. One technique that I have seen used is providing the classroom lessons to the parents, having them do the assignments on sexual harassment and also having them view the students' work. It can be very enlightening for them.

9. Administer sexual harassment surveys that include questions that inquire about the relationship between the harasser and the target— such as, were they in a dating relationship? Did one person want to date the other, who wasn't interested? Is this harassment due to a romance (mutual or otherwise) that went sour?

10. Incorporate subjects such as dating violence and student-to-student sexual harassment into college teacher-preparation courses as well as recertification courses.

Conclusion

Above all, sexual harassment must be framed as a matter of creating a safe school environment and infusing a concern for social justice and democracy into the schools. Sexual harassment violates fundamental democratic principles, and the problem ought to be discussed in a way that highlights those principles. If schools are to be agents of democracy, helping to create citizens ready to participate in the democracy, we need to practice democracy in our schools. Which would mean at the outset that we must alter this current trend of zero tolerance, which seems antithetical to democracy. In addition, it means putting at the forefront conversations and lessons about social justice, including sexual harassment, and finding mechanisms for justice that are worthy of a democratic institution in a democratic society (Stein 1999, p. 94).

REFERENCES

Brake, D. 1999. "The Cruelest of the Gender Police: Student-to-Student Sexual Harassment and Anti-Gay Peer Harassment Under Title IX." *Georgetown Journal of Gender and the Law* 1(37): 37–108.

Davis v. Monroe County Board of Education, 526 U.S. 629 (1999).

Ferrandino, V. L., and G. N. Tirozzi. 2000. "Zero Tolerance: A Win-Lose Policy." *Education Week* 21(20) (January 26): 7.

First, J. 2000. "The Pros and Cons of Zero Tolerance: Protection for Whom? At What Price?" *Harvard Education Letter* 16(1) (January/February): 8.

Furlan, C. 2000. "Fourth Grade Harassment Alleged." *Education Week* 21(24) (February 23): 4.

LaBlanc, A. 1992. "Harassment in the Hall." *Seventeen* (September), pp. 162–65, 170.

MacQuarrie, B., and M. R. Merrill. 2000. "Maine Town Riled by School Harassment Case." *Boston Globe*, May 17 pp. 1, 19.

Merrill, M. R. 2000. "Maine Third-Graders Won't Be Prosecuted." *Boston Globe*, June 9, p. B2.

Orenstein, P. 1994. *School Girls*. New York: Doubleday.

O'Toole, L. 1997. "It Was Only an Innocent Kiss: On the Use, Misuse and Nonuse of Contexts in Public Discussion of Sexual Harassment." Paper presented at Sixth Annual Sociologists Against Sexual Harassment Conference, Toronto, Canada, August.

"School Safety and Rights: Can They Coexist?" *Bill of Rights Network* 12, pp. 1, 6. Boston: Massachusetts Civil Liberties Union Foundation.

Sharp, D. 2000. "Schoolyard Harassment Case Disturbs Maine Town." June 6. Lexis-Nexis Academic, Associated Press wire story. Http://web.lexis-nexis.com.

Shepherd, P. 2000. "Disparity by Race in School Discipline." *Boston Globe*, February 19, p. 3.

Sommers, C. H. 1994. *Who Stole Feminism: How Women Have Betrayed Women*. New York: Simon and Schuster.

Stein, N. D. 1999. *Classrooms and Courtrooms: Facing Sexual Harassment in K–12 Schools*. New York: Teachers College Press.

Wasser, J. M. 2001. "Zeroing In on Zero Tolerance." *The Journal of Law and Politics* 15(4): 747–79.

Sticks and Stones:
The Jailing of Mentally Ill Kids

CARL GINSBURG AND HELEN DEMERANVILLE

A juvenile who is suffering from mental illness should be treated in a
specialized institution under independent medical management.

—RULE 53, UNITED NATIONS RULES FOR THE PROTECTION OF
JUVENILES DEPRIVED OF THEIR LIBERTY

Nelson Smith,* a mentally ill 17-year-old, spent most of last year in
Louisiana's youth prison system. At Jetson Correctional Center for
Youth just outside Baton Rouge, a place that Nelson said "looks nice but has
bad people inside," the boy was beaten and kicked by guards. "One guard
unzipped his pants and threatened to piss on me," the boy said. "He hit me
over and over again on the head with a table until it broke. He came at me
again and hit me on the head. It was like I passed out. I can't remember. It
was like I was underwater." Nelson has a sweet, shy smile and an unfocused,
rambling way of telling his story that is consistent with his illness. He was
diagnosed at six as having Attention Deficit Hyperactivity Disorder (ADHD)
and has a long history of mental health problems, for which he has been
hospitalized several times. In recent years, he has been diagnosed with "clinical
levels of anxiety and depression."

Nelson's path to prison was a short one. It began with limits his insurance
company placed on mental healthcare. Then, his mother, desperate to provide

*A pseudonym, used at the family's request.

him with the help he needed, gave custody of the boy to the state, which promised treatment if she relinquished him. Instead, Nelson was sent to Christian Acres, a residential program four hours from home, where kids like Nelson are housed with teens just released from jail. Although the facility was supposed to provide treatment, he was taken off his medication. After fighting with another boy, he was transferred to Jetson, where the assault took place. "I felt hurt, helpless when he called me from Jetson," his mother said. "He told me, 'Mom, they tried to kill me,' and I couldn't get my hands on my child."

Nelson's mother contacted Cecile Guin, a Louisiana State University social worker who has monitored youth prisons for more than twenty years. By this time, Nelson had been moved to Tallulah Correctional Center for Youth, a prison already under federal investigation for neglect and abuse. Guin called the prison administration at Tallulah. They promised to review Nelson's case but never did.

Guin persevered and was able to confirm Nelson's story. Two Jetson guards were indicted. She learned that Nelson never underwent the required psychiatric evaluation at Jetson and received little or no medication while in jail, a serious omission for a child with Nelson's history. "This is a youth who is almost 17 years of age," Guin wrote in a confidential memo, "who never had any criminal conduct until he entered the court system for assistance. When [his mother] asked for help with her educationally deficient and emotionally disturbed son, he was set on a path to a correctional center. This case is the crux of many of the problems we are having in this state." Jetson Warden Elijah Lewis did not return phone calls. According to David Utter, director of the Juvenile Justice Project of Louisiana, "[Nelson's] case is tragically all too typical of the treatment of mentally disabled children in Louisiana's juvenile jails."

Nelson's experience reflects a larger process that many policy makers and mental health advocates are calling the criminalization of the mentally ill, which, like mental illness, often begins at an early age. Across the country each year one million kids come into contact with the juvenile justice system (and many more are sent to locked residential treatment centers). More than 90 percent are held for nonviolent offenses. The U.S. Department of Justice (DOJ) estimates that 60 percent have a recognizable mental disorder and that as many as 200,000 are seriously mentally ill. They are kids with treatable illnesses like ADHD, post-traumatic stress disorder (PTSD), anxiety disorder, bipolar disorder and early-stage schizophrenia. All these conditions are exacerbated by time spent in county jails, detention centers, boot camps and youth prisons. Sentences can be open-ended and average years, not months. Of those who are incarcerated, two-thirds are minorities. "The extent of abuse and suffering of kids with mental disorders in our juvenile correctional facilities is almost hard to comprehend," said Michael Faenza, head of the National Mental Health Association (NMHA).

A 1998 DOJ investigation found "a pattern of egregious conditions violating the federal rights of youths in Georgia juvenile facilities," including "physical abuse by staff and the abusive use of mechanical and chemical restraints on mentally ill youths." Despite an agreement to improve conditions, the state continues to operate boot camps in which kids are subjected to military-style discipline, a "bad option" for "kids with mental health problems," in the words of Georgia Judge Sammy Jones. In Connecticut, investigators at Long Lane, the state's institution for juvenile offenders, reported in late 1998 that "children [were] handcuffed to beds . . . without clinical oversight for extended periods of time." The investigation was prompted after a 15-year-old girl hanged herself in her room. At a Pennsylvania residential treatment center last December, a mentally ill boy died in restraints, the second documented death by restraint reported at that facility in the past five years. There are documented reports of abuse of mentally ill kids in juvenile facilities in Kansas, Kentucky, Maine, New York, Arkansas, South Carolina, Florida, Virginia, the District of Columbia, California, Texas, Ohio, Maryland, and Puerto Rico.

In an unprecedented action, DOJ filed suit on July 9, 1998, against all four of Louisiana's youth prisons, charging "sexual abuse and assault at each of the four facilities." Several trial dates have been scheduled and postponed as negotiations have dragged on, with attorneys for the jailed kids growing more and more frustrated by the slow pace. "Mental health conditions in the jails continue to be very poor, and kids are suffering every day because of the lack of care," said Utter. "Early this summer a boy tried to hang himself at Tallulah, and a guard just watched."

The court has received expert reports that are nothing less than astonishing. Documents reveal that at Jetson, psychiatric evaluations of children lasted between four and eight minutes. At Swanson Correctional Center for

Youth, the staff psychiatrist in charge of caring for hundreds of boys lived out of state, in Texas, and visited the prison for only twelve hours each month. According to court documents, he "failed to recognize, diagnose or treat a broad range of psychiatric conditions." Tallulah was even worse, where the DOJ reported that "juveniles with extensive psychiatric histories who self-mutilate and/or threaten suicide have never been referred to a psychiatrist."

Underlying the question of how conditions got so bad in juvenile jails is the question of how these nonviolent mentally ill kids, some never having committed a crime, were incarcerated in the first place. Among the most persuasive explanations are that the mental health field is dominated by managed-care companies with a bottom-line agenda; that child welfare authorities often recommend the transfer of custody to the state, which then opts for incarceration over treatment; and that public schools lack the resources to adequately serve children with mental disabilities. Amnesty International reported in 1998 that children in the United States were being "denied mental health care by their health maintenance organization, following which their behavior led to their involvement with the juvenile justice system."

Forty-four states pay private managed-care companies under Medicaid to care for poor or disabled mentally ill people. In a large number of those states, fees are capitated, meaning that the managed-care contractor receives a flat fee per patient, an incentive to limit or deny care. As more and more middle-class people enroll in HMOs, managed-care policies govern their access to mental healthcare, too. A 1996 federal parity law was intended to prohibit limitations on mental health coverage—some as low as $5,000 for an entire lifetime—but the law has been widely skirted by insurers, who instead now place limits on the number of treatment and hospitalization days a mentally ill person is allowed each year. The net impact is to have less mental health coverage, explained one actuary from PricewaterhouseCoopers.

According to Michael Faenza, "Managed care supports services that are short term and easy to deliver. These kids are expensive to serve. They have complex problems and need intensive services from multiple service systems. Some managed-care firms disenroll these kids, citing their behavior. Others just won't pay for the services that the kids need."

. . .

The words "behavior" and "manipulation" are often used by managed-care providers to argue that a child has a "conduct disorder" rather than a mental illness. According to Chris Siegfried, a Texas-based community health specialist, "Conduct disorder is a shorthand way of saying that a child is 'not treatable,' a way to deny traditional mental health services, and that includes medication." It is a phrase that can carry heavy consequences for kids, including discipline and punishment but not mental healthcare.

The case of Colorado teenager Randy Oaks had come to symbolize this kind of dishonest practice. On July 17, 1996, exhausted by the insomnia common to bipolar disorders, Randy lashed out at his mother, Rebecca. She took him to Dr. George Eliopulos, a psychiatrist who had been treating the boy. Dr. Eliopulos immediately recommended hospitalization, but the Jefferson Center for Mental Health, the managed-care company that by contract handles Medicaid kids for the Colorado county where Randy lived, assigned a nurse to review Randy's case, a nurse who had never seen the boy before. After half an hour with Randy she concluded that he was "manipulating," and hospitalization was denied. "The diagnosis was changed from mental illness to conduct disorder," Rebecca said. The nurse never conferred with Dr. Eliopulos or met with Randy's mother. Dr. Eliopulos, who stood by his diagnosis and treatment plan, said mental health managed-care decisions are made "around how the money flows." Dr. Eliopulos later severed his relationship with the Jefferson Center.

That day, Rebecca was summoned by Jefferson Center administrators to meet with child welfare authorities, who told her it would be necessary to surrender custody of her son to get him treatment. Having no other options, she complied.

The state then simply adopted the Jefferson Center evaluation and determined that Randy should go to a residential treatment center, not a hospital. It's almost impossible to get a kid hospitalized, according to Dr. Hildegaard Messenbaugh, a Denver-area adolescent psychiatrist. "I've had kids who were so crazy and so desperate they were cutting themselves and bleeding over the evaluator from the managed-care company. And the answer was, 'They're just manipulating.'"

Randy, who had no criminal record whatsoever, was taken away and sent to Cedar Springs, a locked facility in another city that houses many teen offenders. Cedar Springs is part of a chain that operates facilities in fifteen states and Puerto Rico.

When Rebecca went to visit, she was stunned by what she saw. "There were kids there for sexual molestation and assaults. There were kids walking around in chains." Randy complained of feces on the bathroom walls and urine everywhere. "It wasn't even fit for dogs to live in," he said. Rebecca demanded an investigation. It was a yearlong battle, but finally Colorado authorities found that "hospitalization or other alternatives should have been offered to Rebecca and Randy at the time of the evaluation."

Randy Oaks and Nelson Smith have some things in common. Neither boy had committed any crime when he was sent away from his parents. And in both cases, parents, desperate to give their children access to much-needed mental healthcare, came under pressure to give custody of their children to the state. This is not uncommon. One study, funded in part by the National Institute of Mental Health, concluded: "The practice of transfer of custody as a requirement for receiving financial aid [for children with serious emotional disorders] occurs in a majority of states, though the actual extent of this practice is not known. The major factor influencing the use of transfer of custody appears to be the absence of an appropriate and adequate system of services for children and adolescents with serious emotional disorders."

According to Chris Siegfried and other mental health advocates, in a number of states parents are encouraged to have mentally ill kids arrested because there are no mental health services available. The Department of Health and Human Services estimates that two out of every three mentally ill children under 18 never receive any mental healthcare.

Ashley Williams is a child who showed signs of mental illness before she was 9 years old. "Ashley had trouble sleeping," said Ruby Jarrett, her grandmother, who raised her in Baton Rouge. "She would cry and become hysterical." At school she was diagnosed with ADHD, placed in a class for kids with behavior disorders and disciplined harshly by teachers without special training, her grandmother said. Truancy became common for the girl, who later saw a psychiatrist and was diagnosed with manic depression. "Kids are underdiagnosed in schools because schools are not keeping up with the mentally ill," Siegfried said. "And school failure and mental illness lead to truancy."

At 13, after breaking into a neighbor's home, Ashley ended up at Jetson. She is one of the growing number of girls entering the juvenile justice system, what the DOJ calls "a significant trend." Half the girls in jail suffer from

PTSD, according to a 1998 study of the American Academy of Child and Adolescent Psychiatry.

Ashley said that while in prison she was placed in isolation on more than one occasion, was forced to sleep on the bare floor, was denied medication and counseling, and was assaulted by guards. (According to DOJ investigators, one guard at Jetson "repeatedly whipped two females with a belt.") The guards, Ashley said, were "very harsh, like someone really taking anger out on me." Jarrett tried to contact Jetson's warden for an explanation of the girl's treatment, but the warden never responded.

"Kids with emotional disturbances and mental disorders are supposed to have individualized educational plans, which include any treatment that's needed. That is almost never done," said Shannon Robshaw, NMHA's Louisiana advocate. "Basically what kids with mental illness get in the schools is expulsion. So the school system is failing them." Only 6 percent of the most severely mentally ill and emotionally disturbed kids in Louisiana receive treatment.

Federal studies have shown that more than a third of the juveniles held behind bars—at enormous cost to taxpayers—do not need locked placements and could be safely placed in community settings. In Colorado, Dr. Messenbaugh operates residential treatment programs that are distinctly unlocked. An impromptu visit to one showed kids struggling to make lives for themselves, respecting each other, sharing past disappointments and coping with mental illness. And her success rate is high, around 75 percent. In Milwaukee, the numbers are similar. Three out of four kids in home- or community-based mental health programs never break the law again. What's more, Milwaukee's program, at $9,000 per kid per year, is a significant savings over the $55,000 it costs to keep that same teenager in jail for a year. Shannon Robshaw knows this argument well. "[For] kids with real mental health problems, locking them up, incarcerating them in these juvenile prisons—not only is it bad for the kids and permanently damaging to these youths, it doesn't even save the state money. It's much cheaper to provide the community-based services, work with the family, provide community-based mental health treatment, family support services, work with the schools—the things we know actually work," she said.

In 1999, Senator Paul Wellstone announced the Mental Health Juvenile Justice Act, to remedy abusive conditions for the mentally ill in state juvenile jails. But the political trends seem to be in the opposite direction. In the past ten years, community-based juvenile mental health services have declined by 25 percent, while law-and-order politics have fueled the construction of hundreds of juvenile prisons. Today there are approximately 250 youth prisons and boot camps in the United States.

By the time they were released, Nelson Smith, Randy Oaks and Ashley Williams had spent many months in locked facilities. They returned home sicker and, in Randy's case, scared to leave the house. "He needed months of healing to go out to do the simplest task," his mother said. According to Dr. Messenbaugh, "It makes them infinitely more difficult to treat at that point because they're suspicious. They don't believe anyone really is ever going to listen or help."

"Why would anybody do something like this to another human being," Randy asked, "trap him against his will and promise to give him help when they're not really giving help?"

PART THREE

Education and Activism

A front-page story in the *Onion*, a journal of humor that describes itself as "America's greatest news source," warns of a growing epidemic among children: "An estimated 20 million U.S. children," it asserts, are believed to suffer from a "poorly understood neurological condition called YTD, or Youthful Tendency Disorder." The article details the early warning signs of YTD, including sudden episodes of shouting and singing, conversations with imaginary friends, poor impulse control with regard to sugared snacks, preferring playtime and flights of fancy to schoolwork, and confusing oneself with animals and objects like airplanes. A parent whose child was recently diagnosed with YTD expresses relief: "At least we know we weren't bad parents," she says hopefully. "We simply had a child who was born with a medical disorder."

The satire works, of course, because it offers a cracked mirror of what is actually happening in our society. In and out of school, children are the objects of a toxic barrage of labels, stereotyped reductions of their humanity and their three-dimensionality. Being young, it seems, is a pathology in need of a cure.

Education is always an arena of hope and struggle: hope for a better future, for a widened set of possibilities, for a broader horizon; and struggle over access and equity, quality and content. Education is a space where people come together to name and enact what they want for themselves and their children and society, and what they hope to overcome in their pathways. Education is where we decide what is most worthwhile to know and experience, and how to get there. It's no wonder, then, that education is often a field of conflict.

Zero tolerance as policy and as cultural index is a knife in the heart of education. Education extends opportunities and makes connections. Education opens minds and opens doors. Education is relational—its tone, intimate; its basic gesture, an embrace; its vocabulary, dialogue. Education demands assent, participation, and reexamination.

Zero tolerance is exclusionary and intolerant, and it signifies the end of dialogue, reflection, intimacy, relationship. Zero tolerance is characterized by a casting out, and it represents, therefore, the end of education as a relentlessly humanizing enterprise, and the triumph of a narrow, authoritarian view of children and youth. We can do better. We can resist.

Zero Tolerance:
A Basic Racial Report Card

REBECCA GORDON, LIBERO DELLA
PIANA, AND TERRY KELEHER

When Martin, a young African-American student at Providence's Mt. Pleasant High School, offered to help his teacher dislodge a stuck diskette from his classroom's computer, it never occurred to him that his ingenuity would wind up getting him suspended. But that is exactly what happened when he whipped out his keychain knife and bent down to eyeball the recalcitrant disk. He fell afoul of Providence's "zero tolerance" rules, which mandate automatic suspension for any student who brings a "weapon" to school.

Would Martin have been suspended if he were white? Quite possibly. On the other hand, a white student in Danville, Vermont, was neither suspended nor expelled when he explained that he'd brought a loaded shotgun to school—because it was hunting season.

These two stories demonstrate what has become all too commonplace: disparities between the experience white students and students of color have with discipline in their public school.

In 1999, the Applied Research Center, using a computer program, conducted research called *Making the Grade: A Racial Justice Report Card*. This tool looked at indicators from graduation rates to access to bilingual education. One of the most striking trends was the overrepresentation of students of color among suspended students.

In general, the Report Card data show that African-American and Latino students are more likely to be suspended or expelled from school than their

TABLE 1: SUSPENSION AND EXPULSION DATA BY RACE

	AFRICAN AMERICAN	LATINO	ASIAN/PI	NATIVE AMERICAN	OTHER	WHITE	
Austin, TX	18%	43%	2%	0%	0%	37%	All Students
	36%	45%	0%	0%	0%	18%	Susp./Exp.
Boston, MA	55%	23%	8%	0%	0%	13%	
	70%	19%	2%	1%	0%	9%	
Chicago, IL	53%	33%	3%	0%	0%	10%	
	63%	27%	1%	0%	0%	8%	
Columbia, SC	78%	0%	0%	0%	2%	20%	
	90%	0%	0%	0%	1%	9%	
Denver, CO	21%	50%	3%	1%	0%	24%	
	36%	45%	2%	1%	0%	16%	
Durham, NC	58%	4%	2%	0%	0%	36%	
	79%	2%	0%	0%	0%	18%	
Los Angeles, CA	14%	69%	7%	0%	0%	11%	
	30%	58%	3%	0%	0%	8%	
Miami-Dade County, FL	33%	53%	1%	0%	0%	12%	
	48%	43%	0%	0%	0%	8%	
Missoula, MT	0%	1%	2%	3%	0%	94%	
	NA	NA	NA	NA	NA	NA	
Providence, RI	23%	46%	11%	1%	0%	21%	
	39%	45%	3%	0%	0%	13%	
Salem, OR	1%	10%	3%	1%	0%	84%	
	4%	22%	3%	2%	0%	69%	
San Francisco, CA	18%	24%	43%	1%	0%	14%	
	56%	19%	13%	1%	0%	11%	

Courtesy Applied Research Center

white counterparts. Table 1 summarizes suspension and expulsion data for the 12 cities.

The data show that African-American students are suspended or expelled from school in numbers proportionately much greater than those of any other group. In San Francisco, for example, African-American students are suspended or expelled at more than three times their proportion in the general school population (56 percent compared to 18 percent). In no city studied were the sanction rates for African Americans equal to or less than their proportion of all students.

The experiences of Latino students were less uniform. In some cities, Latinos experienced expulsion or suspension in proportionate numbers. But in some cities, such as Salem, Oregon, Latinos were expelled or suspended in numbers two times as high as their proportion in the school population. Further study might reveal what other factors contribute to the varied experience of Latino students, examining, for example, a community's proportion of recent immigrants.

The Report Card data show that racial disparities in school suspensions are widespread. The implications of these disparities on academic achievement, outside criminal records, and career achievement for students of color are immense, particularly considering the power of new zero tolerance policies.

Zero-Tolerance Policies— Mandatory Minimums Go to School

Just as many federal and state criminal offenses now carry mandatory minimum sentences, the law now requires public schools receiving any federal funds to institute "zero tolerance" policies for certain weapons offenses. Many states and school districts have gone beyond the federal requirements to create policies that mandate serious sanctions such as out-of-school suspension or expulsion for a wide range of student behaviors. Mandatory minimum sentencing can tie the hands of the judges who in the past had certain discretion in deciding sentences. In the same way, zero tolerance school discipline policies can land a school principal in the absurd position of having to suspend a third grader for bringing a paring knife to school in her lunch box.

Most state and local zero tolerance policies have their genesis in the federal Gun-Free School Act (GFSA) of 1994. The GFSA requires each state receiving federal funds for education (i.e., every state) to have on its books a state law requiring a one-year mandatory expulsion for any public school student bringing a "weapon" to school. The act defines "weapon" explicitly as a "firearm" as described in 18 U.S.C. Section 921—in other words, a gun, bomb, grenade, rocket, missile, or mine. This definition explicitly excludes "any device which is neither designed nor redesigned for use as a weapon." The GFSA goes on to require schools to refer to the criminal justice system any student who brings a weapon to school.

The GFSA itself is not a zero tolerance law in regard to expulsion. In fact, it requires state laws to permit local school officials to modify any expulsion order for a student on a case-by-case basis. However, many states and school districts have gone far beyond the provisions of federal law by enacting policies that countermand the federal case-by-case provision or that expand the scope of covered offenses beyond those covered by federal law.

One of this study's participant organizations, Direct Action for Rights and Equality, prepared Table 2, which provides a good example of how far local zero tolerance policies may veer from the intent of the federal law. Clearly, different schools and school districts implement zero tolerance differently; one school may automatically suspend students involved in a fist-fight, while another sanctions students who bring to school any object that could conceivably be used as a weapon. Evidence suggests that schools are more willing to recognize mitigating circumstances when they perceive the student involved in an incident as having "a real future" that would be destroyed by expulsion. In disproportionate numbers, it is African-American and Latino students whose futures are wrecked by zero tolerance policies.

A recent study of Michigan's zero tolerance policies illustrates this point (Polakow-Suransky 1999). While expulsion rates are rising in many largely black Michigan school districts, this is not the case in the 94-percent-white town of Olivet. When two white Olivet students were caught with a gun in their car trunk at the start of hunting season, they got off with a 10-day suspension and 40 hours of community service. The police were not called, and the students ended up with no criminal record. School board minutes indicate that the principal "felt the most pertinent issue in this case was that he believed that there was not intent to harm by either of these students."

By comparison, in another Michigan county, a black student was expelled for cleaning his nails with a pocket knife—which he immediately handed to his teacher when asked to do so. The police were called, and the student was expelled from school.

Zero tolerance policies represent a response to the impression that our schools have become much more dangerous in the last few years. Certainly horrific events like the slaughter at Columbine High School contribute to this sense. But are the schools actually more dangerous than they were 20 years ago? Not according to the numbers. According to the National Center for Educational Statistics' 1998 Condition of Education report, the frequency of various threats reported by high school seniors changed very little between 1976 and 1996, as Table 3 illustrates.

Before schools introduced zero tolerance policies, did they allow students to bring weapons or drugs to school? Of course not. Did they suspend or

TABLE 2

FEDERAL GFSA (1994)	RHODE ISLAND STATE LAW 16-21-18 (1995)	PROVIDENCE ZERO TOLERANCE POLICY (MAY 1996)
WEAPONS INCLUDE:	WEAPONS INCLUDE:	WEAPONS INCLUDE:
▪ Guns ▪ Explosive devices that expel projectiles ▪ Silencers and mufflers ▪ Bombs, grenades, rockets, missiles, and mines	▪ Guns ▪ Explosive devices that expel projectiles ▪ Silencers and mufflers ▪ Bombs, grenades, rockets, missiles, and mines	▪ Guns ▪ Explosive devices that expel projectiles ▪ Silencers and mufflers ▪ Bombs, grenades, rockets, missiles, and mines
	AND ▪ Realistic replicas of firearms	AND ▪ Realistic replicas of firearms
		AND ▪ Knives ▪ Razors ▪ Gas repellent ▪ Mace ▪ Martial arts devices ▪ Objects which could inflict bodily harm, such as: blackjacks, chains, clubs, brass knuckles, night sticks, pipes, studded bracelets, etc. ▪ Any object which, by virtue of its shape or design, gives the appearance of any of the above.

Chart: Direct Action for Rights & Equality. Used by permission.

expel students who did these things? Of course. But rather than expanding a school's range of approaches to discipline problems, these mandatory sanction programs actually rob teachers and administrators of the flexibility they need to deal with such problems, and remove school discipline to the realm of the criminal justice system.

In the early 1990s two criminal statisticians, James Alan Fox of Northeastern University and John Dilulio of Princeton University, fueled the de-

**TABLE 3: PERCENT OF HIGH SCHOOL SENIORS
REPORTING VICTIMIZATION AT SCHOOL, 1976 AND 1996**

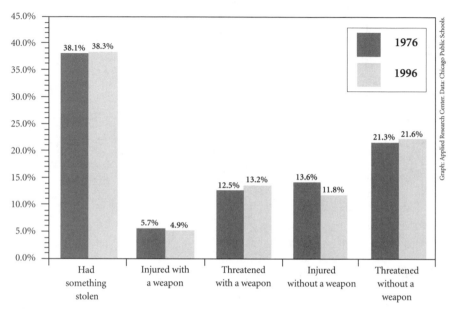

mand for zero tolerance policies. In well-publicized studies, they warned of a coming plague of juvenile crime perpetrated by a new generation of "super-predators"—"jobless, fatherless juveniles," as Dilulio put it. In fact, the plague never materialized. Public school children are no more dangerous or destructive than they were 20 years ago. But the sanctions they face are much more severe, more likely to be imposed on students of color, and more likely to severely damage their educations.

The effects of Chicago's zero tolerance policies provide a good example of the kinds of distortions these programs create. In the Chicago Public School fiscal-year 2000 final budget, in a section ironically titled "Measuring Progress Toward Goals," a chart appears of the number of student expulsions from 1993 to 2000 (Table 4). Chicago's zero tolerance policy went into effect in the middle of the 1995–96 school year. Within three years, the number of expulsions had jumped from 81 to a projected 1,000. The district's language about expulsions for the current school year is particularly revealing: rather than working to reduce the number of expulsions, the district's "proposed" figure for the 1999–2000 school year is 1,500—50 percent greater than the

**TABLE 4: STUDENT EXPULSIONS PER YEAR,
CHICAGO PUBLIC SCHOOLS, 1993–2000**

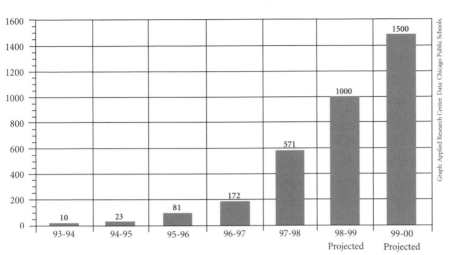

year before and 150 times as many expulsions as just six years earlier. Chicago suspends and expels African-American students at disproportionate rates, which suggests that black students will likely make up a disproportionate number of those the school district "propose[s]" to expel this year. This is a clear example of how zero tolerance policies exacerbate existing racial inequities in school discipline.

Subjective Criteria

When discipline codes define punishable behavior in subjective terms, such as "disrespect" or "defiance of authority," how the code is applied often depends on how individual teachers and administrators interpret students' behavior. Too often that interpretation is affected not only by a student's behavior but also by differences of race and ethnicity. Jeremy Lahoud works with Chicago's Generation Y, a project of the Southwest Youth Collaborative. Lahoud reports that at Hubbard High School on Chicago's southwest side, two students were suspended for six days when white school officials mistook their break-dancing poses for "gang representation."

In general, discipline codes with too much room for arbitrary interpretation may allow teachers' conscious or unconscious beliefs about their students of color to influence their decisions about how to discipline. When a school permits teachers to suspend students for ill-defined offenses, such as "defiance of authority," it can open the way for bias and cross-cultural misunderstandings to affect the discipline process.

What Can Happen When a School Takes a Race-Conscious Approach to Discipline?

That is exactly what staff at James Lick Middle School in San Francisco, California, decided to find out. Heidi Hess is Focused Effort Coordinator at James Lick. She says that teachers at her school were concerned that African-American students, who make up less than a third of the student body, receive almost half the referrals for discipline.

"The first thing we had to do," to address this disparity, says Hess, "was to really become rigorous about collecting the data. We developed forms for teachers to use which documented when a student was sent out of class (for a disciplinary referral), who sent them out, and why." Collecting this data yielded some surprising results. "We found that over 75 percent of the referrals given out last school year were for defiance of authority or disruption of class." Furthermore, most cases involved conflicts between students and teachers, rather than between students. More serious offenses, such as possession of a weapon, were rare.

Collecting the data was just the first step. "We developed a system to feed the data collected directly back to the teaching staff," Hess says, "so they can better understand what is going on" and gauge their progress. "We looked at how teachers set the rules in their classrooms, and whether and how teachers involved students in defining classroom rules." They found that when students participate in forming the rules, they are less likely to perceive them as unfairly applied.

James Lick staff began holding monthly professional development meetings to work out alternative strategies for deescalating conflict. They sought to emphasize teachers' roles in these interactions, rather than focusing solely on methods of changing students' behavior.

Although most of the power resides with the teachers, "It was a paradigm shift for the teaching staff to buy into the idea that it is their responsibility to minimize defiance situations," Hess continues. "We had to ask, 'What might be going on in the students' minds? What's going on for the teacher? And what would be alternative practices?'

"One of the best exercises we did was to role-play the beginning of a defiance scene. For example, a student walks into class and puts a soda on the table, even though no drinks are allowed in the classroom. The teacher asks the student to remove the drink. Just acting out different possible responses to this scene, with the staff taking not only the teacher's role, but also trying on the student's role—was profound."

James Lick's revamped approach to discipline is still too new to determine whether these interventions will reduce the racial disparities in suspension referrals. But already teachers are experiencing some success. Hess offers an example: "One teacher reported that she was just about to yell, from across the room, at two African-American girls who appeared to be talking and carrying on excessively. But she gave herself a few seconds to think of an alternative strategy for dealing with them. Instead, she walked over to them, and much to her surprise, found that they were talking about their work assignment. Far from yelling at them, she realized she didn't need to say anything at all."

Why Are Suspension and Expulsion Disparities Important?

Suspension and expulsion have serious effects on the life chances of students. Those who are already performing poorly in school are the most likely to be suspended, although they are the very students who can least afford to miss classes. When public schools increasingly become an entry point for young people of color to swell the ranks of the juvenile justice system, the implications are ominous. By the end of the year 2001, it is estimated that eight times as many African-American men will be in the California prison system than in the state's university system (Connolly et al. 1996).

Student leaders of Generation Y put it well when they describe the effects of suspension on their education: "You don't learn. You fall behind. You get a negative attitude about school." In fact, numerous studies back up these young people's perceptions, demonstrating that students who are suspended or expelled are more likely than their peers to drop out of school altogether (see DeRidder 1990; Hahn and Lefkowitz 1987; Wheelock 1986; Wu, Pink, and Moles 1982).

Recommendations

The bottom line is that schools must provide a challenging, respectful, and culturally appropriate learning environment, and provide training for teachers and administrators to enable them to work effectively with a multiracial, multicultural student body. Mutual respect and excitement about teaching and learning are the most effective discipline measures available to any teacher or school.

Furthermore, schools should set and annually review measurable, quantitative goals to reduce the overall numbers of suspensions and expulsions, and to eliminate racial disparities in those rates. This also requires that schools see the high suspension rates as a problem and are committed to addressing them.

Schools should also construct clear, objective discipline policies that allow for flexible application of sanctions. These policies should clearly define prohibited behaviors in ways that minimize the need for subjective interpretation by individual teachers. Administrators and teachers should resist the use of suspensions and expulsions, except in the most extreme situations.

Lawmakers should eliminate zero tolerance policies in favor of a more flexible approach to serious discipline problems. Discipline policies must protect school communities from true threats, but must also allow for consideration of mitigating circumstances and for access to due process.

Finally, no discipline policies should be implemented without taking into consideration their potential for racially disparate application and impact. This is particularly crucial in the case of policies such as zero tolerance rules, which can derail a student's education and/or give him or her a criminal record.

Given the bias built in to existing disciplinary practices and the severity of zero tolerance policies, students of color are subject to double jeopardy when it comes to school discipline. An equitable and functioning school environment is better built with equitable resources, skilled staff, and good classroom practice than get-tough zero tolerance policies.

REFERENCES

Connolly, Kathleen, Lea McDermid, Vincent Schiraldi, and Dan, Macallair. 1996. *From Classrooms to Cell Blocks: How Prison Building Affects Higher Education and African American Enrollment in California*. San Francisco: The Justice Policy Institute.

DeRidder, L. 1993. "How Suspension and Expulsion Contribute to Dropping Out." *Educational Horizons* 68 (Spring): 153–57.

Hahn, A., J. Danzerberger, and B. Lefkowitz. 1987. *Dropouts in America: Enough Is Known for Action*. Washington, DC: Institute for Educational Leadership.

Polakow-Suransky, Sasha. 1999. *Access Denied*. Ann Arbor: Student Advocacy Center of Michigan.

Wheelock, Anne. 1986. *The Way Out: Student Exclusion Practices in Boston Middle Schools*. Boston: Massachusetts Advocacy Center.

Wu, S., W. Pink, and O. Moles. 1982. "Student Suspension: A Critical Reappraisal." *The Urban Review* 14(4): 245–316.

When Is Disproportionality Discrimination? The Overrepresentation of Black Students in School Suspension[1]

RUSSELL SKIBA

The two-year expulsion of seven black students in Decatur, Illinois, in the fall of 2000 for a football game brawl has brought the issue of unequal discipline to national attention. Although the suit brought by the Reverend Jesse Jackson and Operation PUSH on behalf of those students was turned back in federal court, inequities in the application of school suspension and expulsion have begun to be widely documented. A series of reports since that incident have documented the overrepresentation of African-American students in rates of office referral, school suspension, and school expulsion (Advancement Project/Civil Rights Project 2000; Gordon, Della Piana, and Keleher 2000; Sandler 2000; Skiba et al. 2000).

Yet the unequal treatment of African-American students in school discipline is by no means a new issue. Rates of school punishment for black students that exceed rates for white students have been documented for over 25 years. In 1975, the Children's Defense Fund studied national data on school discipline and found rates of school suspension for black students that were between two and three times higher than suspension rates for white students. Since that report, disproportionate suspension for African-American students has been a highly consistent finding. Black students are also more frequently exposed to corporal punishment (Shaw and Braden 1990), and receive fewer mild disciplinary alternatives (McFadden et al. 1992). Nor does the problem appear to be lessening; recent research reports continue to find disparities in discipline in office referrals, suspension, expulsion, and corporal punishment (Costenbader and Markson 1998; Gregory 1997; Skiba, Peterson, and Williams 1997). There can be little doubt then that African-American students are in general subjected to higher rates of school suspension and other school punishments than other students.

But does minority disproportionality represent racial discrimination? That is both the central question, and the most difficult to answer. There may be any number of reasons why African-American students are disciplined more frequently than other students, and it would be extremely difficult to study any of those reasons through direct survey or observation. One might expect, for instance, that few teachers or administrators would openly admit to disciplining any group of students unfairly. Nor would it be easy to design a study allowing direct observation of blatant incidents of racism. For better or worse, unequal racial treatment in our society has become more subtle and difficult to detect.

But the issue can be addressed indirectly by looking at those explanations most often offered to explain racial disparities. Since African Americans are overrepresented in lower economic backgrounds, perhaps differences in discipline are not an issue of race, but rather an issue of social or economic class. Or perhaps black students misbehave more, forcing teachers to respond with greater rates of disciplinary consequences. If these explanations hold up, then disproportionate rates of school discipline probably do not represent racial discrimination or bias. On the other hand, if these alternate hypotheses are not sufficient to explain away findings of disproportionality, then it becomes more likely that disproportionate treatment is a sign of some form of racial discrimination.

This article outlines research that explored the disproportionate discipline of African-American students. How extensive is the unequal treatment of black students in school discipline? Where does it come from? Can it be explained away by economic status or amount of misbehavior? Ultimately, answers to these questions may provide a better indication of the extent to which disproportionality indicates discrimination.

Studying Minority Overrepresentation

Description of the database. To address the issue of minority overrepresentation in school discipline, we analyzed the disciplinary records of a major urban school district in the Midwest, one of the fifteen largest in the

FIGURE 1: DISPROPORTIONALITY IN
OFFICE REFERRALS, SUSPENSION, AND EXPULSION

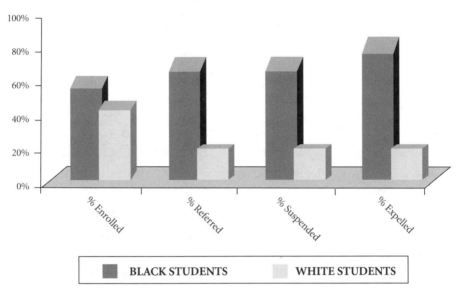

nation. We analyzed the disciplinary records for all 19 middle schools in the district over the entire 1994–95 school year. There were 11,001 middle school students in the district, of whom 56 percent were black and 42 percent white.[2]

Information on socioeconomic status was represented by qualification status for free or reduced cost lunch. Of the entire sample, 7,287 (65.3 percent) students' families met the criteria required for free lunch status. Another 2,923 (26.6 percent) students were eligible for reduced-cost lunch.

Findings

The extent of disproportionality. Across the students in the 19 middle schools, there were 16,912 referrals, 5,696 suspensions, and 47 expulsions. As in previous studies, we found large differences in rates of school discipline for black and white students. Figure 1 shows the relative proportion of office referrals, suspensions, and expulsions for black and white students. The extent of overrepresentation can be assessed by comparing the proportions of school enrollment on the left hand side, with the bars representing disciplinary actions. Thus, while African-American students constitute 52 percent of the school population, they represented 66.1 percent of the office referrals, 68.5 percent of out-of-school suspensions, and 80.9 percent of expulsions. We also found discrepancies in disciplinary treatment based on economic status. Students who were eligible for free lunch were significantly more likely to be referred to the office or suspended. It is striking that almost half (48 percent) of black students enrolled in this district were referred to the office for a disciplinary infraction at least once during the school year (compared to 21 percent of white students).

Does socioeconomic status explain racial disparities? We know from both this and previous studies that both African-American students and students in poverty are more at risk for a range of school disciplinary actions. In interviews about their high school experience, both high- and low-income students agree that low-income students tend to be punished more frequently and more severely (Brantlinger 1991). Some have suggested that the overlap of poverty and race in our society explains the apparent racial disparities in school disciplinary treatment. In its testimony before the United States Commission on Civil Rights in February 2000, the National Association of Secondary School Principals argued that "a higher incidence of ethnic and racial minority students being affected by zero tolerance policies should not be seen as disparate treatment or discrimination but in terms of an issue of socioeconomic status" (p. 3).

In order to test this theory, we retested racial differences in school disciplinary consequences while controlling for economic differences. We found that controlling for poverty status made virtually no difference in the highly significant racial differences in school suspension. These results are highly similar to those reported by Wu and colleagues (1982), who reported that racial differences in the rate of suspension remained even after controlling for socioeconomic status. Thus, although poverty status and race both place students at additional risk for being disciplined, low socioeconomic status cannot be used to explain away racial differences in referrals, suspension, or expulsion.

Where does disproportionality start? The process of suspension or expulsion is a two-step process. First, a referral to the office for a disciplinary infraction is made by a teacher or other staff member. Once a student is referred, an administrator reviews the details of that referral and determines a specific disciplinary action. Racial disparities in discipline, then, could originate at either the classroom or the office level, or both.

We found a difference in measures reflecting classroom referral versus administrative decisions. Although African-American students in this district were almost twice as likely to be referred to the office as white students, once they arrived at the office there was less evidence of racial discrepancy. This suggested to us that perhaps the black-white gap in out-of-school suspensions was due primarily to the fact that twice as many blacks as whites were referred to the office. When we retested racial differences in suspension while controlling for number of office referrals, the black-white discrepancy in school suspensions was reduced to near zero. This confirmed our hypothesis that much of the disparity in school suspension is a result of the greater rate at which African-American students are referred to the office. In our study, administrative decisions regarding school discipline were not the primary source of disparate disciplinary treatment. Rather, school suspension may function primarily to "pass along" the disproportionality that originates in referrals at the classroom level.

Some have argued that the attitudes and classroom management practices of teachers place African-American students, especially African-American male adolescents, at a disadvantage. Bullara (1993) points out that the typical classroom management style in many schools relies heavily on negative consequences, and may contribute to school rejection and dropping out of African-American youth. The problem may also be one of cultural misunderstanding. Townsend (2000) argues that many teachers, especially those of European-American background, may be unfamiliar and uncomfortable with the more active style of communication of African-American adolescents, and may interpret the impassioned and emotive manner popular among young African Americans as combative or argumentative. Fear may also play a role. Teachers who accept stereotypes of adolescent African-American males as threatening or dangerous may overreact to relatively minor threats to authority, especially if their anxiety is paired with a misunderstanding of cultural norms of social interaction. Any of these reasons might result in a higher rate of office referral for African-American students.

Do black students act out more? To this point in the analyses, it must be noted, we have no proof of bias. We know that racial disparities in suspension are real, not simply a function of the overlap of race and poverty. We have reason to believe that racial discrepancies in suspension are due not to the actions of administrators, but to the disproportionate referral of African-American students. But perhaps African-American students engage in higher rates of misbehavior. If so, higher rates of office referral and suspension would not be discriminatory, but would be an appropriate response to different levels of disruptive behavior. Are black students more likely to misbehave?

To address this question, we examined the severity of behaviors for which black and white students were referred. If African-American students are suspended more frequently because they are more unruly, we would expect them to be referred to the office for more serious infractions. Thus, we tested differences between black and white students in reasons for referral to the office, identifying which reasons for referral occurred more frequently among black students and among white students.

Prior to that analysis, however, we tested differences between boys and girls, for purposes of comparison. In this study, boys had significantly higher rates of referral, suspension, and expulsion than girls. Are boys suspended more than girls because they act out more? We indeed found that boys were referred to the office more frequently for a wide variety of offenses, ranging from minor offenses, to fighting, to indecent exposure. Girls were referred to the office more than boys for only one behavior, truancy. These findings are consistent with previous research that has consistently shown that boys have higher rates of aggression, bullying, school violence, theft, and lying, conduct disorders, and delinquency (see Skiba et al. 2000). Thus, higher rates of discipline for boys are probably not due simply to gender bias; rather, they may often be an accurate response to the tendency of boys to engage in a higher rate of misbehavior.

To test the similar hypothesis that African Americans are more unruly, we reran the same statistical analyses, this time comparing black and white office referrals. There were no differences in rate of referral between black and white students for 24 of the possible 32 reasons for disciplinary referral. Of the remaining eight reasons for referral, white students were referred significantly more often than black students for *smoking, leaving the building without permission, vandalism,* and *obscene language.* African-American students were referred more often than white students for *disrespect, excessive noise, threat,* and *loitering,* behaviors that are both more subjective and perhaps less serious. Even the most serious of the reasons for office referrals among black students, *threat*, is dependent upon perception of threat by the staff making the referral. If anything, then, African-American students appear to be referred to the office for *less* serious, more subjective reasons.

Again, these results are highly consistent with previous research. There appears to be no evidence that African-American students are punished more in school because they act out more. Although black students receive a disproportionate share of disciplinary referral, suspension, and corporal punishment, they tend to be referred to the office for less serious rule violations than white students (McFadden et al. 1992; Shaw and Braden 1990). Thus, far from supporting the hypothesis that African-American students act out more frequently, the data in general suggest that African-American students are disciplined more frequently and harshly for more subjective and less serious reasons.

Students of all races appear to be well aware of these disciplinary discrepancies. Sheets (1996) reported that both majority and ethnically diverse students in an urban high school perceived sources of racism in the application of discipline. But while white students and teachers perceived racial disparity in discipline as unintentional or unconscious, students of color saw it as conscious and deliberate, arguing that teachers often apply classroom rules and guidelines arbitrarily to exercise control or to remove students whom they do not like. In particular, African-American students felt that a lack of respect, differences in communication styles, disinterest on the part of teachers, and "being purposefully pushed to the edge" were the primary causes of many disciplinary conflicts.

Summary and Implications

In summary, our findings are highly consistent with 25 years of previous research in finding that the use of out-of-school suspension and expulsion is associated with a substantial risk of minority disproportionality, especially for African-American students. Our investigation explored two alternatives to bias as an explanation for racial disproportionality. We found that neither socioeconomic explanations nor the "increased misbehavior" hypothesis were able to account for large and consistent disparities in the discipline of black and white students. Without a plausible alternative hypothesis, it becomes more likely that disproportionality in school punishment for black students is a sign of systematic and prevalent bias in the practice of school discipline.

In particular, disproportionate rates of school suspension for African-American students seem to begin at the classroom level, with higher rates of office referrals for less objective reasons. Teacher training in appropriate and culturally competent methods of classroom management is likely then to be the most pressing need in addressing racial disparities in school discipline. Teachers consistently rate classroom management as among the most important teaching skills, yet they also report feeling most underprepared in this area (Calhoun 1987). Poorly trained to handle the challenges of disruptive classroom behavior, inexperienced teachers may engage students in power struggles that serve only to escalate disruption, especially in urban schools (Brophy and Rohrkemper 1980). Appropriate training in classroom management, appropriate rules adequately communicated to students, and the support of mental health staff and administration can all assist teachers in developing a more supportive classroom environment.

Effective teacher training must provide teachers with culturally competent practices, enabling them to meet the needs of diverse learners. Townsend (2000) lists a number of such practices, including relationship-building strategies, knowledge of linguistic patterns of African-American youth, increased opportunity for student participation in a range of school activities, and family and community partnerships. Diversity training for teachers must go beyond simplistic "we are the world" formulations to provide teachers with a complex set of skills. In the Dallas Public Schools, for example, a multicultural awareness program trained prospective teachers in a broad array of components, including community awareness, exposure to diverse communities, instructional practice, and experiences that challenge students to examine previously held assumptions (Leavell, Cowart, and Wilhelm 1999).

Racial bias in the practice of school discipline is also part of a broader debate on the issue of institutional racism in education. Although African Americans have made gains in educational opportunity since *Brown v. Board of Education*, numerous sources of racial and economic inequity in schools remain. African-American students are overrepresented in lower tracks (Oakes 1982); they are underrepresented in portrayals in school curriculum (Sleeter and Grant 1991); they have been observed to receive a lower quality of instruction in inner-city schools (Greenwood et al. 1994); they tend to attend schools with a lower quality of physical resources (Kozol 1991) and be in school districts with a lower level of school funding (Singer 1999). Thus, African-American disproportionality in school discipline is not an isolated phenomenon, but part of a larger pattern of unequal treatment.

Reducing the black-white disciplinary gap may thus require systematic reforms whose goal is to equalize educational opportunity for all students. Instead of focusing on the linguistic or cultural "deficits" of minority students, Hilliard (1999) argues that we must commit to improving the quality of educational service for all children. Brown and Peterkin (1999) propose addressing a range of factors that maintain racial and socioeconomic inequity, including districtwide standards and goals, administrative restructuring, more equitable resource distribution, and better implementation and evaluation of programs to ensure equal educational opportunity. In some cases, litigation may be required to overcome institutionalized practices that contribute to educational inequity; legal challenges to inequitable practices are beginning to be seen in the areas of tracking (Welner and Oakes 1996) and resource distribution (Dunn 1999).

Proving discrimination or bias is difficult in either research or the courtroom. But researchers can rule out alternative explanations that are often used to explain away the overdiscipline of African-American students. In this study, we ruled out two of the most common explanations for the disparity between black and white students in school suspension. African-American overrepresentation in suspension does not appear to be simply a function of an overlap with poverty status. Nor can we explain away black-white disparities in discipline through black students' misbehavior: if anything, African-American students may be referred and suspended for less objective and less serious reasons. As more of the rationalizations for a black-white discrepancy in school discipline are ruled out, we are eventually left with a simple question: What else besides discrimination can racial disproportionality be?

Findings that African Americans are overrepresented in school suspension are extremely consistent, suggesting that some form of systematic bias is inherent in the use of school suspension and expulsion. As the widespread acceptance of zero tolerance disciplinary strategies continues to expand the use of suspension (Advancement Project/Civil Rights Project 2000), we might well expect a corresponding increase in the discriminatory treatment of African-American students. Taking such data seriously does not demand that we vilify teachers as conscious racists for the overreferral of black students.

Yet whether conscious or accidental, disciplinary and educational inequities reduce the educational chances of African-American students, and demand remedies.

The debate surrounding disproportionate discipline is often framed in terms of data. Yet the most important questions that remain to be answered in this area may not be questions of knowledge but of policy. Why are data that consistently demonstrate unequal treatment of black students so often minimized? When data showing disparate treatment of African-American students are found, why is it necessary to prove that those students do not deserve unequal punishment? After 25 years of research, how much more data will it take to provide convincing proof of racial bias for those who believe that discrimination is no longer an issue in American society? Finally, what will it take to persuade the American public in general, and policy makers in particular, of the need to confront racial disparities in public education and ensure equal access to educational opportunity for all children, regardless of the color of their skin?

NOTES

1. This summarizes a more complete research study entitled "The Color of Discipline: Sources of Racial and Gender Disproportionality in School Punishment." The full report may be ordered from the Indiana Education Policy Center, 170 Smith Research Center, 2805 E. 10th Street, Bloomington, IN 47408, or accessed on the Web at www.indiana.edu/`iepc etc.
2. Since there were only relatively small proportions of students of other ethnic backgrounds (1.2% Latino, 0.7% Asian, and 0.1% Native American), we restricted our comparisons to black and white students.

REFERENCES

Advancement Project/Civil Rights Project. 2000. *Opportunities Suspended: The Devastating Consequences of Zero Tolerance and School Discipline.* Washington, D.C.: Author.

Brantlinger, E. 1991. "Social Class Distinctions in Adolescents' Reports of Problems and Punishment in School." *Behavioral Disorders* 17:36–46.

Brophy, J. E., and M. M. Rohrkemper. 1980. *Teachers' Specific Strategies for Dealing with Hostile, Aggressive Students* (Research Report No. 86). East Lansing: Michigan State University Institute for Research on Teaching.

Brown, O. S., and R. S. Peterkin. 1999. "Transforming Public Schools: An Integrated Strategy for Improving Student Academic Performance Through District Wide Resource Equity, Leadership Accountability, and Program Efficiency." *Equity and Excellence in Education* 32:37–52.

Bullara, D. T. 1993. "Classroom Management Strategies to Reduce Racially-Biased Treatment of Students." *Journal of Education and Psychological Consultation* 4:357–68.

Calhoun, S. E. 1987. "Are Our Future Teachers Prepared for the Stress that Lies Ahead?" *The Clearing House* 6:178–79.

Children's Defense Fund. 1975. *School Suspensions: Are They Helping Children?* Cambridge, MA: Washington Research Project.

Costenbader, V., and S. Markson. 1998. "School Suspension: A Study with Secondary School Students." *Journal of School Psychology* 36:59–82.

Dunn, C. 1999. "Challenging Racial Discrimination in the Public Schools of New York State." *Equity and Excellence in Education* 32:19–24.

Gordon, R., L. Della Piana, and T. Keleher. 2000. *Facing the Consequences: An Examination of Racial Discrimination in U.S. Public Schools.* Oakland, CA: Applied Research Center.

Greenwood, C. R., B. Hart, D. Walker, and T. Risley. 1994. "The Opportunity to Learn and Academic Performance Revisited: A Behavioral Theory of Developmental Retardation and Its Prevention." In R. Gardner, D. M. Sainato, J. O. Cooper, T. E. Heron, W. L. Heward, J. W. Eshleman, and T. A. Grossi (eds.), *Behavior Analysis in Education: Focus on Measurably Superior Instruction* (pp. 213–24). Pacific Grove, CA: Brooks/Cole.

Gregory, J. F. 1997. "Three Strikes and They're Out: African American Boys and American Schools' Responses to Misbehavior." *International Journal of Adolescence and Youth* 7(1):25–34.

Hilliard, A. 1999. Keynote address by Dr. Asa Hilliard III, October 19, 1998: Colloquium on Student Achievement in Multicultural School Districts. Published in *Equity and Excellence in Education* 32:70–86.

Kozol, J. 1991. *Savage Inequalities.* New York: Crown.

Leavell, A. G., M. Cowart, and R. W. Wilhelm. 1999. "Strategies for Preparing Culturally Responsive Teachers." *Equity and Excellence in Education* 32:64–71.

McFadden, A. C., G. E. Marsh, B. J. Price, and Y. Hwang. 1992. "A Study of Race and Gender Bias in the Punishment of Handicapped School Children." *Urban Review* 24:239–51.

National Association of Secondary School Principals. 2000. *Statement on Civil Rights Implications of Zero Tolerance Programs.* Testimony presented to the United States Commission on Civil Rights, Washington, D.C., February.

Oakes, J. 1982. "The Reproduction of Inequity: The Content of Secondary School Tracking." *Urban Review* 14:107–20.

Shaw, S. R., and J. P. Braden. 1990. "Race and Gender Bias in the Administration of Corporal Punishment." *School Psychology Review* 19:378–83.

Sheets, R. H. 1996. "Urban Classroom Conflict: Student-Teacher Perception: Ethnic Integrity, Solidarity, and Resistance." *The Urban Review* 28:165–83.

Skiba, R. J., R. S. Michael, A. C. Nardo, and R. Peterson. 2000. *The Color of Discipline: Sources of Racial and Gender Disproportionality in School Punishment.* Bloomington: Indiana Education Policy Center.

Skiba, R. J., R. L. Peterson, and T. Williams. 1997. "Office Referrals and Suspension: Disciplinary Intervention in Middle Schools." *Education and Treatment of Children* 20(3):295–315.

Singer, A. 1999. "American Apartheid: Race and the Politics of School Finance on Long Island, NY." *Equity and Excellence in Education* 32:25–36.

Sleeter, C. E., and C. A. Grant. 1991. "Race, Class, Gender and Disability in Current Textbooks." In M. W. Apple and L. K. Christian-Smith (eds.), *The Politics of the Textbook.* New York: Routledge and Chapman-Hall.

Townsend, B. 2000. "Disproportionate Discipline of African American Children and Youth: Culturally-Responsive Strategies for Reducing School Suspensions and Expulsions." *Exceptional Children* 66:381–91.

Welner, K. G., and J. Oakes. 1996. "(Li)Ability Grouping: The New Susceptibility of School Tracking Systems to Legal Challenges." *Harvard Educational Review* 66:451–72.

Wu, S. C., W. T. Pink, R. L. Crain, and O. Moles. 1982. "Student Suspension: A Critical Reappraisal." *The Urban Review* 14:245–303.

The ABCs of School Discipline:
Lessons from Miami-Dade County

JUDITH A. BROWNE[1]

Jonesboro, Paducah, Pearl, and Columbine. The alarm for increased safety in our public schools has been sounded and the response, zero tolerance, has been overzealous, overreaching, and detrimental to those whom we sought to protect—our children. School safety is a critical issue; guns and violence must be curbed. However, in most instances, zero tolerance exacts a price that is too high by punishing children for typical adolescent or childish, nonviolent behaviors and robbing them of opportunities to learn. It also permits schools to weed out unwanted students and label disliked students. Without a sound education, the future for these children may be bleak. For some it may lead to a life of poverty, for others a stint in prison. Zero tolerance triggers a downward spiral in the lives of children.

This essay will explore zero tolerance "in practice" and what parents, students, and communities can do to change the tide. Through case studies of four middle schools in the Miami-Dade County public school system, the first section will examine how school administrators' philosophies about discipline determine how far zero tolerance goes. The case studies illustrate that school administrators have a range of punishments available and may often reject more lenient punishments such as counseling, parental involvement, detentions, and in-school suspension for more draconian measures such as out-of-school suspension or expulsion. These harsher measures may be used to punish, deter, or get rid of students, but they are not the only answer or—in many instances—the best answer to what may be legitimate concerns about behavioral problems. The second section of this essay provides some steps communities may take to limit the reach and consequences of zero tolerance.

The Philosophy of Zero Tolerance— Evidence from Miami-Dade Public Schools

The keys to discipline lie in the hands of school officials. With the exception of offenses such as possession or use of firearms, weapons, or drugs, in most instances, student codes of conduct give school administrators broad discretionary powers to determine appropriate punishments. This latitude permits school administrators to determine how hard the "book" will be thrown at students. Thus, in schools where administrators believe in punishment for punishment's sake, students are suspended in significant numbers, but where administrators believe in compassion and rehabilitation, alternatives to suspension and expulsion are used.

A study by the Advancement Project of four middle schools in the Miami-Dade County school system illustrates how zero tolerance and other approaches to discipline are used in schools on a daily basis and how these approaches affect suspension and expulsion rates.[2] The four schools chosen for the study had comparable racial demographics and were all subject to the same student code of conduct, which is established by the school district. Although each school was subject to the same code of conduct, each principal had a different philosophy about discipline and employed different practices. As a result, the suspension rates varied widely.

The principals and other administrative staff of the four schools were interviewed and questioned about their philosophy regarding discipline. In addition, administrators were asked about the types of punishments used under various circumstances, counseling and mediation programs, and teacher/staff training. The goals of the interviews were (1) to discern whether the philosophy of principals, who are chief officers of schools, correlated to suspension rates, and (2) to better understand what other factors, in the opinion of administrators, may be responsible for wide discrepancies in discipline.

Although these case studies represent a limited sample, the patterns revealed are quite stark and suggest the need for further research. The cases indicate that philosophy determines outcomes; strict disciplinarians who believe in harsh punishments will have higher suspension and expulsion rates. However, this model of discipline does not necessarily translate into effective discipline.

The case studies also demonstrate how the varying attitudes and philosophies of principals can impact disciplinary procedures and outcomes. It is through the discretionary provisions in codes of student conduct that principals are able to act on their philosophical differences. While philosophies may not be the only factor influencing suspension rates, it is a significant one. Where the principals and administrators have adopted zero tolerance for misbehavior, suspension rates are higher. In contrast, in schools where principals do not believe that misbehavior should be punished by denying children their education, suspension rates are lower. This may indicate that, in fact, strict disciplinary models do not necessarily deter students from engaging in misconduct.

The research also revealed:

- Boredom and lack of academic challenge increase the likelihood of disruptive behavior. Administrators agreed that if students are academically challenged in class, they are less likely to misbehave. Thus, in schools that lack resources such as highly qualified teachers, textbooks, supplemental instructional materials, computers, and other resources, it is possible that students may engage in disruptive behavior more frequently and as a result, may be punished more often.

- In schools where the principal has adopted a standard that no child should be suspended, except in extreme circumstances, teachers are less likely to refer students for discipline for minor misconduct. Under these circumstances, teachers understand that their recommendations for harsh punishment are unlikely to be approved.

- Additional resources are needed in public schools to ensure meaningful educational opportunities for all students. Administrators articulated a desperate need for more counselors and behavior modification programs. These resources are essential to reducing valid disciplinary problems, providing support to teachers, and ensuring that all students may take advantage of educational opportunities.

- Teachers need to be trained in classroom management and conflict resolution. Of the four schools studied, only one provides this type of professional development training. Because teachers are the first link in the disciplinary process, they should be equipped to deal with behavioral problems using innovative strategies that emphasize defusing situations and not responding in a reactionary and arbitrary manner to trivial adolescent behavior.

- Schools should monitor disciplinary referrals by teachers to ensure fair application of disciplinary codes. Monitoring may expose problems such as poor classroom management, discriminatory treatment, or singling out of particular students. Where teachers overuse disciplinary referrals, additional training should be provided.

Miami-Dade Code of Conduct

The Miami-Dade County Public Schools Secondary Schools Code of Conduct provides guidance to parents and students about behavioral expectations, students' rights, and the range of punishments available to administrators. Relevant sections which describe the district's philosophy regarding discipline are included below.

A good school environment is best thought of as:

- positive, not negative
- helping, not punishing
- turning unacceptable conduct into acceptable conduct.

Order and discipline may be described as the absence of distractions, frictions, and disturbances which interfere with the effective functioning of the student, the class, and the school. It is also the presence of a safe, friendly, yet businesslike atmosphere in which students and school personnel work cooperatively toward mutually recognized and accepted goals.

A major consideration in the application of the code is that the most appropriate disciplinary action taken by school officials is the least extreme measure which can resolve the discipline problem. Teachers and administrators strive to use a variety of informal disciplinary or guidance strategies, prior to, during, and after formal disciplinary action.

MIAMI-DADE COUNTY CASE STUDIES

	BLACK/ LATINO STUDENTS	OUT-OF- SCHOOL SUSPENSION RATE*	IN-SCHOOL SUSPENSION RATE*	PUNISHMENT FOR A TYPICAL FIGHT
G.W. Carver	63%	2.8%	0.003%	Work assignment (cleaning, etc.) or 3 days in-school suspension
Palm Springs	94%	3.4%	19.6%	3-5 days in-school suspension
Madison	98%	16.2%	6.8%	3 days out-of-school suspension
North Dade	94%	34.1%	42.3%	10 days out-of-school suspension

*The suspension rates represent the percentage of students suspended at least once.

The Miami-Dade County Code of Student Conduct grants discretion to administrators to determine appropriate punishments. The code provides guidelines and choices. For example, a first-time fight may be punished by one or all of the following:

- Parent contact or conference.
- Administrator/teacher/student/parent conference.
- Suspension or alternative to suspension with possible recommendation to alternative school or expulsion.
- Referral of criminal acts to schools police and local police.

Repeat fighting violations require a ten-day suspension.

G. W. Carver Middle School

Philosophy: Carver's principal opposes the use of suspensions and communicates this to assistant principals and staff. The principal believes that teachers and administrators are in schools to educate—not punish. Suspensions

are used as a last resort at Carver because the principal recognizes that suspensions are a permanent mark on a student's record and thus there may be
negative long-term implications for youthful behavior. Suspensions are also
disfavored because the principal is concerned that during suspensions students are left out on the street and may get into more trouble that could
result in incarceration.

G. W. Carver has the lowest suspension rate for middle schools in the
Miami-Dade School system.[3] In 1998–99, only 2.8 percent of students were
suspended. Although G. W. Carver has fewer incidents of violence than the
other schools reviewed, there are still incidents of misconduct. The most
frequent reasons students are referred for disciplinary action are fights and
cutting class. While the Code of Student Conduct permits 10-day suspensions
for fights, the Carver administration uses its discretion to employ other punishments permitted under the Code of Conduct. For fights and cutting class,
G. W. Carver students receive one- to three-day in-school suspensions (which
are typically reduced) or are given a work assignment, such as cleaning the
cafeteria. Supervised work assignments and in-school suspension are the most
common punishments used at G. W. Carver. These punishments uphold the
ideal that disciplining children should not prevail over educating them.

Palm Springs Middle School

Philosophy: The principal's philosophy is that every student must feel like
she/he is part of the school. No child should be neglected or disregarded. The
principal will not put children on the street but insists that the school work
with them. Teachers at Palm Springs Middle School know the principal's
philosophy is to go to great lengths to meet the needs of students and that
he discourages referring students to him for disciplinary reasons.

Eleven years ago, Palm Springs Middle School had a horrible reputation; it was known for low attendance, high failure rates, low morale, and
significant gang activity. The principal instilled in staff that every child
should feel cared for and wanted. He reached out to gang members and
provided incentives to failing students. The school's attendance has improved dramatically. In 1989, it was ranked 36th in the district, and by
1998 ranked number one for attendance in the district. Student performance has improved and, as a result, more students are being promoted

to the next grade. The principal continues to care about his students; for example, he spends the two hours of lunch periods in the cafeteria, interacting with students.

Palm Springs's out-of-school suspension rate is currently 3.4 percent of students, one of the lowest rates in the district. The most frequent infraction of the Student Code of Conduct at Palm Springs is fighting. Although the district's Code of Conduct permits out-of-school suspension for fighting, students at Palm Springs are typically assigned to the School Center for Special Instruction (SCSI) in-school suspension program for three to five days. Students in this program are isolated; they spend the day in the SCSI doing their class assignments. They do not change classrooms throughout the day. There are, on average, ten students in SCSI per day. The teacher in SCSI assists students with assignments and counsels students. Other common infractions which result in assignment to SCSI include talking back to teachers, defying teachers, and not being prepared or refusing to work. Out-of-school suspensions are reserved for weapons (automatic suspension), violent fights, and severe defiance of authority.

To keep students in school and reduce student conflicts, Palm Springs has developed programs to provide resources to students, teachers, and parents. The school has an alternative education program for students with behavioral and academic problems. This program has classes for each grade level (six through eight); students stay in the same classroom for math, social studies, science, and language arts, but are permitted to take physical education and an elective with other students. There are fewer students in each class, and each class has a teacher and an aide. Students in this program are provided with nurturing, academics, and counseling. Teachers remain in regular contact with the parents of these students. The teachers in the program are more tolerant and patient. Students in the program are given the special attention they need and, as a result, are not lost.

In addition, the school has developed a successful conflict resolution and anger-management program for teachers and students. The program provides participants tools to distinguish between intelligent choices and emotional impulses. Students are also trained to serve as peer mediators, and family counseling sessions are available in the evenings.

Madison Middle School

Philosophy: The principal will not tolerate children who misbehave. She believes in strict discipline. However, before a student is referred to the principal for suspension, every possible alternative must have already been utilized. While strict discipline is employed, students are given opportunities to correct behavior before suspension is used. In fact, the disciplinary plan developed by the principal reminds teachers: "The ultimate objective is to keep students in school."

The suspension rates at Madison Middle School during the 1998–99 school year were 16.8 percent in-school and 16.2 percent out-of-school. (This is relatively low for Miami-Dade middle schools.) However, this low out-of-school suspension rate does not reflect the true number of suspensions; it represents only the percentage of children who were suspended at least once. Madison Middle School has a small group of students who are repeatedly suspended from school.

The most common violation of the Student Code of Conduct at Madison is fighting. As one assistant principal explained, sixth graders are immature; "They look at each other—they fight." Students involved in fights at Madison are suspended (out-of-school), typically for three days (ten days if the fight involves more than one person), and receive counseling upon their return. Punishments for fights are decided on a case-by-case basis. Other common Code of Conduct violations include disruptive behavior and skipping class.

To reduce disciplinary problems, the principal believes that the school needs a program that isolates disruptive students within the school. This program would provide a smaller classroom environment. In addition, the principal believes that the school needs more counselors so that they may have a meaningful opportunity to build relationships with students and their parents.

North Dade Middle School

Philosophy: The principal of North Dade Middle School believes in the zero tolerance approach to discipline. She stated clearly that she has no tolerance for nonsense or disruption in the classroom. She believes that classroom disruption is the foremost problem—if teachers can teach without constant disruptions, students would learn, test scores would rise, and students would be happy. The principal believes this justifies the high suspension rate at the school. She supports the removal of disruptive students from the classroom and believes that consistent application of zero tolerance is important.

In addition to environmental factors (drugs, poverty, and violence), the principal believes that limited parental involvement and poor preparation in elementary school contribute to the high number of disciplinary problems. In seeming contradiction, the principal asserted that disciplinary infractions arise most often because students get restless in class and as a result pass notes, talk, and engage in general disruptive conduct. She believes that good teachers do not have chronic disciplinary problems and that many teachers need more training.

Despite an acknowledgment that teachers may be to blame, at least in part, for the disciplinary problems, the suspension rates for North Dade during the 1998–99 school year were 42.3 percent in-school and 34.1 percent out-of-school. These rates are among the highest for middle schools in the Miami-Dade County school system. Madison Middle School, which has a 16.2 percent out-of-school suspension rate, has a comparable number of incidents of violence (approximately .22 incidents per student). Thus, the dramatically salient differences in suspension rates may be attributable to difference in philosophy. North Dade's principal anticipates that suspension rates at North Dade will increase for the 1999–2000 school year because of consistent application of the zero tolerance policy. Ultimately, she wants the students to be in a classroom where teachers teach, not discipline.

Discipline at North Dade Middle School was by far the harshest of the schools reviewed. Students at North Dade involved in a fight are given an automatic ten-day out-of-school suspension, one of the most drastic measures that may be taken under the district's Code of Student Conduct. (Punishments for fights may include a series of increasingly harsh steps. A ten-day suspension is required only where a student has repeatedly engaged in fighting. Other schools reported using in-school suspensions or three- to five-day out-of-school suspensions. Ten-day suspensions are reserved for brutal fights or gang-related fights.) The principal explained that she does not care what students have to say in their defense because they could have avoided a fight by seeking assistance from an administrator or security monitor. If a parent meets with a school official, the suspension may be reduced. A recent fight between rival gangs led to arrests, suspension, and a recommendation of expulsion of approximately ten students. In-school suspensions, in which children spend the entire day (including lunchtime) in a self-contained classroom, are utilized for Code of Conduct infractions such as dress code violations and talking back to a teacher.

North Dade has recently implemented a number of programs that the administration hopes will eventually reduce suspensions by addressing problems and providing alternative solutions. The school has an alternative-to-suspension program that requires counseling sessions for parents and students. In addition, the school recently purchased computer software that will permit formal monitoring of disciplinary referrals. (It is the only school of the four mentioned that has a formal monitoring system.) This program will permit the school to analyze disciplinary referral data, including the type of conduct and the referring teacher. Teachers with a high number of referrals will attend classroom management training. Title I funds have been used to hire a full-time community specialist responsible for working with parents and increasing parental involvement. The school's Peace Program provides conflict resolution and anger-management training for students.

Lessons

Each of these schools confronts different problems and challenges with regard to students, teachers, and environment, yet our visits confirmed that there is a "zero tolerance philosophy" that permeates our schools. This philosophy contributes to incredibly different suspension rates. Administrators use different approaches to discipline and have varying views about what constitutes disruptive behavior and how to handle it. Ultimately, the approach chosen depends upon whether the school leadership believes that all children should be provided meaningful educational opportunities or whether they should proceed based on the conviction that disruptive behaviors cannot be tolerated under any circumstances. Thus, these interviews confirm the need to widely promote alternative methods to suspension for dealing with disruptive behaviors and to help principals and teachers understand that children can change their behaviors without being subjected to exclusion from school. Without a change in philosophy, many schools will continue to write off and weed out children, cutting off their educational opportunities.

Putting Common Sense Back into
Discipline: Strategies for Change

Zero tolerance and school discipline measures can be changed so that children are no longer treated as predators. The following strategies for change were developed by a panel of experts (advocates, attorneys, community organizers, educators, and researchers) during the National Summit on Zero Tolerance and School Discipline convened by the Advancement Project, Rainbow/PUSH Coalition, and the Civil Rights Project at Harvard University. The following "action plan" can be accomplished by parents, students, advocates, attorneys, educators, and policy makers. (Where suggestions require the action of school boards, state education departments, educators, and policy makers, the changes may be advocated for by parents, students, community groups, and others.) To stop this trend, concerned individuals will need to organize and develop strategies appropriate to their community's circumstances; some of the following suggestions may be adapted, where appropriate.

Parents, Students, and Community Groups

- Train students and parents, and provide written materials regarding Student Code of Conduct, due process rights, and the procedures for appealing disciplinary decisions.
- Train students and parents regarding rights of children with disabilities under the Individuals with Disabilities in Education Act (IDEA).
- Collect data regarding suspensions and expulsions from local school district or State Department of Education to better understand the extent of the problem. This data should include students' race, gender, and disability, and whether they have Limited English Proficiency (LEP). Additionally, data regarding the reasons for suspensions and expulsions and the disciplinary action taken for each (in-school suspension, out-of-school suspension, or expulsion) should be collected. Data should also include the number of arrests of students for conduct in school, or the number of students referred to law enforcement agencies and the reasons, the number of students repeatedly suspended, and the number of students assigned to alternative schools. The compiled

data should be shared with concerned citizens through pamphlets, flyers, or newsletters.

- Assist in development of the codes of conduct for district, schools, and classrooms.
- Develop a network of attorneys who will represent students in disciplinary cases. Refer students and parents to these attorneys.
- Train parents and concerned community members to represent students in disciplinary hearings, where permitted.
- File complaints of discrimination on basis of race, national origin, disability, age, and gender with the U.S. Department of Education Office for Civil Rights. This may include discrimination against an individual or a group (such as African Americans, Latinos, disabled) protected by the law.

School Districts/School Administrators/Teachers

- Adopt a policy limiting the circumstances under which police may intervene in school disciplinary matters. Include in the policy that parents must be contacted immediately whenever law enforcement authorities intervene.
- Collect uniform discipline data that details race, gender, disability, LEP, the offense and the action (punishment) taken, number of students repeatedly suspended, number of arrests, number of referrals to law enforcement agencies for in-school conduct, and number of students assigned to alternative schools (by race and gender). Make this data available to the public. Also, use data to monitor teachers' disciplinary referrals, providing training for teachers with excessive referrals or discriminatory patterns.
- Incorporate classroom/behavior management and conflict resolution training during professional development days.
- Train students to serve as peer mediators.
- Involve parents and students in the development of Student Codes of Conduct for the district, school, and classrooms.
- Permit advocates (concerned community members) to act as advocates for students during disciplinary hearings. Thus, do not limit representation to parents and attorneys.

- Use suspension as a last resort. Develop programs that are alternatives to suspension. These programs should keep children on track academically and be staffed by a qualified teacher.
- Include other stakeholders (such as parents and students) on disciplinary committees.

State Departments of Education

- Require training in cultural diversity, adolescent psychology, classroom management, behavioral management, and conflict resolution for state certification.
- School accountability ratings should take into account suspension rates (for discretionary suspensions), so that high rates negatively affect ratings.
- Require that alternative schools provide academic programs that are on par with state requirements for mainstream schools.
- Require uniform data reporting from school districts to include the data mentioned above.

Conclusion

The zero tolerance phenomenon in school discipline is wreaking havoc on our children. All too often, students are caught in the web of zero tolerance as a result of nonviolent behaviors, and administrators quickly dole out punishments that do not fit students' behaviors. The consequences are dire: academic failure, loss of opportunities to learn, and, in many cases, criminal or juvenile charges. If this trend is not reversed, we will be faced with a generation of young adults who are uneducated and thus unprepared to join the workforce. To avoid losing a whole generation of Americans to hopelessness, our schools must adopt policies and programs that maintain safety and discipline while providing real educational opportunities. Schools must embrace children instead of pushing them out. Parents and communities must be involved in this process. Without concerted efforts to abandon zero tolerance for typical harmless adolescent behavior, the consequences of leaving children outside the schoolhouse doors will be far-reaching and devastating.

NOTES

1. The author is Senior Attorney with the Advancement Project, a policy and legal
   action organization advancing universal opportunity and a racially just democracy. This chapter includes excerpts from *Opportunities Suspended: The Devastating Consequences of Zero Tolerance and School Discipline*, a report coauthored
   by the Advancement Project and the Civil Rights Project at Harvard University,
   released in June 2000. A copy may be obtained by contacting the Advancement
   Project at (202) 728-9557 or visiting www.advancementproject.org or www.
   harvard.edu/groups/civilrights.
2. These case studies are discussed in more detail in *Opportunities Suspended*,
   discussed in note 1.
3. G. W. Carver, unlike the other schools in the case studies, is a magnet school
   that has an admissions process which seeks to admit high-achieving students.
   While this may differentiate Carver, this school was still important in the review
   of Miami-Dade schools because it has the lowest suspension rate of the district's
   51 middle schools.

Finding Safety Where We Least Expect It: The Role of Social Capital in Preventing School Violence

PEDRO A. NOGUERA

Americans want safe schools. In fact, unlike other public expectations related to social needs, such as health care, traffic, or the cost of living, Americans feel *entitled* to safe schools. Americans feel so strongly about the need for safe schools that the issue has in recent years become America's number one priority on the national education agenda (Pace 1996; Johnson and Immerwahr 1994–95).

The logic behind such a sense of entitlement seems fairly straightforward—since we require children to go to school, then at the very minimum shouldn't we guarantee their safety while they are there? To put it even more bluntly: even if we can't guarantee that they will learn anything when they go to school, can't we at least assure parents that no harm will come to their children while they are in a school's custody?

Such logic is appealing and compelling. In fact, it resonates so profoundly within the American population that even those without children in school agree that safety should be the highest priority (Pace 1996). Such concerns have registered with politicians. In response to incidents such as the mass shootings in Littleton, Colorado, and Jonesboro, Arkansas, policy makers have hastily crafted solutions aimed at alleviating the public's fears. Elected officials, from the president, to the Congress, to members of state legislatures and local school boards, have weighed in on the problem (Marquez 1996). Since no one is in favor of school violence, there has been relatively little debate over the kind of prevention measures that have been enacted, except among those who believe we haven't gone far enough or gotten tough enough in our efforts to make schools safe.

In the pages ahead I will analyze why it is that much of what has been done for the purpose of making schools safe, including the enactment of zero tolerance policies, has done little to allay the public's fears (Marquez 1996). I will argue that part of the discrepancy between public perception and public policy is due to the unpredictable nature of violence and the ineffectiveness of the measures most commonly adopted to curtail youth violence in particular. As an alternative to the get-tough policies commonly enacted in school districts across the country, I will argue that the most important step schools can take to promote safety is to cultivate bonds of trust and caring within the school community. Put differently, I will argue that the most effective way to create safe schools is through investments in what sociologists refer to as social capital.

Rethinking Zero Tolerance

The logic behind zero tolerance is powerful but illusory. The idea that we could make our schools safe simply by identifying and apprehending violent or potentially violent students seems to make sense. The assumption is that bad students engage in violence, and if it were possible to identify and remove all of the bad, incorrigible, deviant, and disruptive students, our schools would be safe. This is not unlike the logic behind the steady expansion of prisons and the growth in incarceration rates throughout the United States. Such thinking has also prompted several states, including most recently California, to lower the age at which children accused of committing violent crimes can be tried as adults (Nieves 2000). In a society gripped by the fear of violence and what have been termed "superpredator" juveniles, such reasoning is clearly compelling. However, what gets overlooked in the rush to increase punitive measures is the ways in which the environment of a school or community may actually promote and generate violent behavior. As a result of this oversight, the possibility that zero tolerance could promote safety is substantially reduced, if not entirely eliminated.

To illustrate this point, I will recount the experience of one school that flirted with a form of zero tolerance and then wisely backed away once the results of the policy became clear. The school in question was located in an economically depressed neighborhood in Oakland, California. For some time the school had been under pressure from district officials to raise the test scores of students. In response to repeated criticisms from the central administration, the school's faculty complained that they could not raise test scores because they simply had too many disruptive students. After much deliberation and debate, an administrator from the district office made the following proposal to the school: a special class would be created and taught by a specially trained teacher who would be assigned to work with the most disruptive students. Since all parties assumed that the most disruptive children were African-American males, the teacher—who was also an African-American male—would be provided with the latest in Afrocentric curriculum. In addition, the administrator pledged that the students would be provided with mentors, field trips, and jobs after school.

In preparation for the class, teachers at the school were asked to compile a list of the twenty most disruptive students. Once the students were identified, the students were placed in a classroom located in an isolated wing of the school. Physically separated from the rest of the school population, the students had a school day that was shortened in order to minimize their contact with other students at the school.

Within two weeks of operation, the participants manifested extreme signs of frustration and the experiment showed clear signs of failure. The district failed to live up to its promise to provide mentors, field trips, and after-school jobs, and before long, the students and the teacher realized that they had been set up: there was nothing "special" about this new class except for their strategic isolation. Resentful about being banished and feeling indignant about the apparent betrayal by the district, the students took out their anger on the teacher. Before long, the classroom was rife with conflict between the teacher and the students, with a steady escalation in name calling and personal threats. Before long, the formerly enthusiastic teacher was bitter and seriously contemplating resignation. By the end of the first month, both the teacher and the students demanded an end to the experiment.

As an observer to this experiment, I was not surprised at the response of the students and teacher. Despite the young teacher's enthusiasm, I doubted how effective he would be trapped in a classroom with twenty active students, and I never believed that the district would follow through on its pledge of support. However, what I found even more interesting is what occurred in the other classrooms at the school. When I asked teachers two weeks after the special class had been created what their classrooms were like once the most disruptive students had been removed, several teachers reported that since their departure, other children who previously had not been particularly disruptive had emerged as major behavior problems. Ironically, several suggested that if the school were provided with one more special class and specially trained teacher for disruptive students, they believed that the problem could be solved.

Fortunately, the administrators involved had the good sense to retreat from the experiment rather than expand the number of special classes for disruptive students. In its place, a discussion on the cause of disruption in classrooms ensued among the faculty. During these discussions I pointed out that I had observed all of the classrooms in the school, and not all of them were plagued by disruptive students. In fact, I noted that some of the teachers were quite skilled at maintaining an orderly classroom in which teaching and learning were the central focus. My observation prompted a much deeper and longer discussion about teacher-student relationships and the kinds of instructional strategies that seemed most effective at engaging students intellectually. After a lengthy discussion, there was general agreement among the faculty that when students were academically engaged there were few disruptions in the classroom. By the end of the meeting, the faculty began generating a list of strategies for increasing academic engagement among students, and disruptions by students were no longer seen as inevitable or unavoidable.

Increasing School Safety Through Social Capital

The experience of this Oakland middle school is instructive. One thing it shows is that when we locate the source of behavioral problems within individuals, we tend to ignore the ways in which the culture of a school and relations between teachers and students can foster and generate problematic behavior. Additionally, the case reveals that when we move beyond trying to remove and eliminate those who are seen as most likely to perpetrate violent or disruptive acts, we can actually engage in more creative discussions regarding how to promote order, safety, and learning.

Learning is, after all, what schools are supposed to be about. However, the current approaches utilized to address school violence seem to ignore this basic point. Schooling in American society is premised upon an unstated social contract: students are expected to obey authority and comply with school regulations in exchange for an opportunity to learn. However, when there is no evidence that students are learning, should they still be expected to conform to school rules? That is, if maintaining order is all that is left of the purpose of schooling, is it realistic to expect that students will obey school rules? Given that there is little evidence of learning at many schools that serve poor children (Maeroff 1988), and given that low-achieving students are typically overrepresented among disciplinary referrals, it is obvious that when the contract is broken, maintaining school order becomes much more difficult.

Let us imagine for a moment that zero tolerance policies did not exist and that instead, communities across the country were seriously grappling with ideas and proposals they hoped would make schools safe. What would happen if we started a discussion about school safety by asking ourselves the question: "What are the characteristics of a safe school, and what conditions and features seem most central to the sense of security such schools engender?" If we started there and then moved to the question "What does it take to develop a safe school?" it is doubtful that the answers generated would immediately lead to a discussion of metal detectors and surveillance cameras, or to schools governed by rigid rules and procedures more akin to military or correctional institutions. It is more likely that if we were to take the time to contemplate safety without the encumbrances created by the prevailing discourse on school violence, we might actually envision schools where safety is the natural by-product of social relationships premised on respect and responsibility. Rather than promoting a vision of schools shielded from violence by the constant presence of guards and metal detectors, the schools we might aspire to create would be pleasant, nurturing environments where children are known well by the adults who work with them, and where parents are treated with respect and actively support the goals of the school. Such schools would not only feel safe, but their design, climate, and ambiance would indicate to all who entered that this was a special place to be, a place where teachers and students focus on teaching and learning in an atmosphere free of intimidation and fear.

The amazing thing is that such schools aren't a fantasy—they actually exist. Justice Matters (June 2000) recently published a report on school violence in which several such schools located in inner-city communities throughout the country are featured and profiled. Though each school is located in a poor neighborhood, none of the schools rely upon the presence of armed guards, electronic fences, principals wielding baseball bats, or rigid zero tolerance policies. The most common characteristic of these safe schools is a strong sense of community. It is also not a coincidence that these schools are also places where students and teachers feel supported, where students are academically engaged, and where trust, respect, and norms of reciprocity are sufficient to promote behavior that is conducive to the maintenance of safe and caring environments. Such schools also exhibit high levels of involvement and support from the parents and the communities they serve. Safety at these schools is a by-product of supportive social relationships achieved through development of social capital, one of few school reforms that actually cost very little.

Social Capital and School Safety

The concept of social capital was developed by sociologists as a way to characterize and make tangible the benefits individuals derive from their membership within groups (i.e., families, churches, civic organizations) and their association within social networks. Social capital theorists argue that connections between people generate bonds of reciprocity which can result in the acquisition of tangible benefits such as jobs, social support, advice, favors, safety, and protection (Sampson 1998; Putnam 1993). Like economic capital, social capital has value because individuals who are socially well-connected have greater access to tangible resources.

The concept of social capital is actually an extension of an idea which grew out of the work of French sociologist Emile Durkheim. Through an extensive analysis of the victims of suicide in Paris in the late nineteenth century, Durkheim came to the conclusion that connections between people actually prevented suicide (Durkheim 1951). Durkheim also concluded that suicide was a phenomenon tied to individualism, social isolation, alienation, and what he called anomie—a state of normlessness. He concluded that the more isolated an individual was, the more likely it would be that he or she would commit suicide or engage in other forms of antisocial behavior.

The notion that individuals received benefits from their participation within social networks and groups was eventually extended to an analysis of schools. In a comparative study of public and parochial schools, sociologist James Coleman argued that parochial schools, especially Catholic schools, generated social capital through bonds of obligation and accountability with the parents they served. He also argued that parochial schools were more likely to produce successful student outcomes than public schools because they elicited a greater degree of social closure (Coleman 1988). Social closure refers to the sense of accountability of mutual responsibility that exists between the adults who work within a school and the parents of the children that are enrolled. The greater the sense of connection and partnership between a school and the parents it serves, the greater the degree of social closure. Coleman argued that schools with a high degree of social closure would have fewer dropouts and disciplinary problems and a higher degree of parental satisfaction. Since social closure is made possible by shared values and aspirations between parents and school personnel, Coleman argued that it would be more difficult to achieve high levels of social closure in public schools due to their commitment to secularism and because of the heterogeneity of their clientele (Coleman 1988).

While Coleman may have been correct in his observation that parochial schools are more likely to develop a high degree of social closure because they tend to attract parents that share their core values, there are exceptions among public schools. Schools that promote a particular vision or philosophy often attract parents who embrace similar perspectives. Moreover, there is evidence that high levels of parental involvement produced by shared values and a sense of community are also common features of many charter schools (UCLA Charter School Study 1998) and even some magnet schools (Fuller and Elmore 1996).

Social Capital as a Resource for School Safety: A Blueprint for Action

Beyond parental involvement and support, it is possible to imagine a variety of other ways in which social capital might serve as a resource which could aid schools in promoting security and other important goals. Four possible strategies are described in some detail here. I have attempted to make these as clear and practical as possible, because if there is any hope that alternatives to zero tolerance will be considered, then those charged with insuring safety must be convinced of their feasibility and viability.

1. **Reduce anonymity, alienation, and the impersonal character of schools.** A common feature of many large schools is that the connections between adults and students are weak, and, as a result, many students lack consistent meaningful contact with adults. This is especially likely to be the case in secondary schools where students typically change classes and interact with several different adults in relatively short classroom periods over the course of a school day (Ayers, Klonsky, and Lyons 2000).

   Anonymity increases the vulnerability of schools to outbreaks of violence because it limits the possibility that a responsible adult will know when a student is in distress and in need of help. In several of the recent mass shootings, adults were caught offguard by the violent outbursts of students. This was even the case at Columbine High School, where the students who perpetrated the violence often dressed in long black trenchcoats and had been observed extending Nazi salutes to each other. Though in retrospect a number of teachers recalled seeing signs that the two students seemed alienated and had been harassed by peers, no adult at the school felt obligated to intervene with the students in order to determine what might have been wrong (Tebo 2000).

   There are several strategies that can be pursued in order to decrease the degree of anonymity and alienation among students. One approach might be to find ways to reduce the size of a school through the creation of academies or schools within schools (Kemple and Snipes 2000). Smaller learning communities make it possible for students to interact with a smaller number of adults and increase the probability that teachers will get to know their students well. Alienated and troubled students are easier to detect and respond to when closer relationships between students and teachers exist. Additionally, outsiders who might pose a threat to a school are more noticeable within a smaller school setting.

   Reducing the number of students assigned to guidance counselors so that counselors actually have a chance to get to know and provide counseling to the students they work with is another way of reducing anonymity. Given that a growing number of students arrive at school in need of emotional and psychological support, it is also important for schools to develop partnerships with health and social service agencies that can provide direct assistance to students. Additionally, in-school and out-of-school mentors can be utilized to support students' needs and to help them to develop meaningful bonds with caring adults (National Association of Black Public Administrators 1992).

2. **Promote a climate of respect by responding quickly and consistently to minor infractions.** Advocates of community-based policing have suggested that the presence of abandoned cars, graffiti, public consumption of alcohol, and street-level drug dealing all contribute to an environment in which major crimes are more likely (Gladwell 1998). They argue that by responding aggressively to relatively minor infractions, police officers can reduce the likelihood that major crimes will be perpetrated. Similarly, the highly acclaimed Ten-Point Program that was created to reduce youth homicides in Boston is based upon a collaboration between police and probation officers, church leaders, and community residents. Together, members of this coalition have reduced incidents of violence among juveniles by proactively responding to minor offenses such as marijuana possession and curfew violations committed by juveniles on probation (Patterson 1999).

Researchers argue that these methods of policing are effective because they create a climate in which more serious crimes are less likely to occur. Robert Sampson (1998) has argued that community policing methods can also facilitate the generation of social capital which can be instrumental in deterring crime. He suggests that in communities where residents are connected to one another by overlapping social networks and local participation in formal and informal organizations, residents "are better able to realize common values and maintain effective social controls" (p. 15).

Strategies similar to those utilized for the purpose of promoting neighborhood safety can also be applied in schools to prevent disruptive or violent behavior. The schools featured in the Justice Matters report mentioned previously (June 2000) take an aggressive stance toward discipline that is similar to the approach described here. However, what distinguishes the approach of these schools from the approach typically taken in public schools is that their disciplinary policies are not merely punitive; they are also preventive. Rather than suspending students with poor attendance and poor academic performance, these schools utilize other measures to address misbehavior. Preventative approaches to punishment are further enhanced when they are combined with counseling and regular communication with parents.

When schools respond rapidly, effectively, and consistently to offenses that are often treated as minor infractions, such as cutting class, sexual harassment, vandalism, graffiti, and hateful and disrespectful language, it will be less likely that major offenses will occur. This is because responding to minor offenses sends the strong message that any attempt to undermine the values of a school community will be addressed immediately. In this way, assertive responses to minor infractions can serve as a means of reinforcing the values and mission of the school and help in creating a climate where respect for learning and the rights of others are maintained as prevailing community norms.

3. **Adopt a preventative approach to discipline utilizing strategies that encourage students to take responsibility for their behavior and learn from their mistakes.** The most common forms of punishment utilized by schools to control behavior rely upon various forms of exclusion, humiliation, and, when resources permit, individualized therapy. With the advent of zero tolerance, the overall direction of school discipline policies has been toward increasingly severe forms of punishment. A recent study issued by the Applied Research Center (1999) identified a number of school districts where suspensions of kindergarten-age children are not uncommon. In most school districts, there is also a high correlation between academic performance and the students who are most frequently targeted for discipline. Throughout the country, a distinct pattern emerges: a disproportionate number of those disciplined are black, male, from low-income families, and identified as either low achievers or developmentally disabled (ARC 1999).

Despite the fact that there is little if any evidence that the kinds of punishments most frequently utilized by schools have the effect of deterring or modifying behavior, these methods of punishment continue to be popular. In fact, with the advent of zero tolerance policies, the number of students suspended and expelled from schools has actually increased in several school districts in the last few years (ARC 1999). In the current political climate, the efficacy of suspending truant and low-achieving students is hardly ever raised or questioned, nor are there many people challenging the merits of dispatching expelled students unsupervised to the streets.

In the place of traditional disciplinary measures, a number of psychologists have called for the use of different methods to prevent classroom disruptions and to modify student behavior (Alschuler 1994). Some of the strategies that have been recommended include: various forms of community service, mandatory after-school tutoring, additional work assignments, public apologies, and retribution for victims. The basic idea underlying these methods is that discipline should not be used to exacerbate poor attendance or academic performance. Rather, whenever possible, students should be encouraged to learn from mistakes, and punishments should be designed to encourage reflection on their behavior. Finally, for those students whose personality or family circumstance requires greater intervention, counselors and case workers should be utilized to provide individual attention, and if necessary, alternative learning environments.

An example of how such an approach can be applied can be seen in the response of a principal at a West Oakland middle school to a fight between two students. The fight occurred in a neighborhood near the school as students were walking home. After breaking up the fight and mediating the conflict between the two students, the principal required the two combatants to knock on the door of each resident on the block where the fight occurred to apologize for the disturbance. Additionally, for the remainder of the week, the two students were required to clean up the playground at school during recess. Instead of automatically suspending the students, as might typically occur under most zero tolerance policies, or pretending that the fight was not the school's concern since it occurred off school grounds, the principal felt it was most important that the students learn to accept responsibility for their actions and to recognize the destructive effect the actions had upon their community.

Such approaches strengthen the social capital of a community because they reinforce its values and the sense of mutual accountability. Of course, it must be added that it is not assertive discipline alone that reduces the likelihood of violence or disruptions in the school environment. More importantly, it is an overarching climate of respect which permeates the culture of a school and guides social interactions that ultimately is the most important element of a safe and orderly environment.

4. **Provide numerous opportunities for students to become more deeply engaged in school and activities that further their development.** Several studies have shown that students who are actively involved in school activities are more likely to do well academically and less likely to get into trouble in school (Steinberg 1996). This also is more likely to be the case for students who are involved with extracurricular activities such as sports, music, theater, clubs, or student government. Similarly, researchers have found that teachers who are able to intellectually engage their students are less likely to experience disruptions or other problematic behavior (Alschuler 1994). As one veteran teacher told me when I asked her how she managed to maintain such an orderly classroom in a school that had a reputation for being "out of control":

> My students know I don't play. When they're with me its all about the work and they respond. They have to, because they know I ain't even gonna send them to the office. If they act out in my classroom they're gonna answer to me. And they don't want that. No, in my classroom, work is not optional. That's the key: keep them busy learning and you'll never have any problems with behavior (Interview, November 1993).

There are several reasons why deepening student engagement in school is an effective strategy for promoting safety. The most obvious reason is that when students are actively involved with their academic interests or extracurricular activities, they simply have less time to get into trouble. Several clubs, and especially most sports, require students to maintain minimal grades and to participate in tutorial programs (Adler 1985). Students may also be required to spend a great deal of time after school and on weekends participating in an activity or club. With less idle time, students have fewer opportunities to engage in behavior that may be harmful to themselves or others.

Developing strategies aimed at deepening student engagement in school can also have the effect of cultivating intrinsic motivations toward learning. Since engagement cannot be forced or required, in order to achieve it educators must find ways to tap in to the intellectual curiosity of students and make learning meaningful, interesting, and relevant to them. To the extent that students become willing participants in their own education, social control ceases to be the major preoccupation of education (Kohl 1998). Schools where students are actively involved in pursuing intellectual, athletic, artistic, and vocational interests are less likely to experience discipline problems or disruptions.

Most research on learning shows that schools typically rely most heavily upon extrinsic rewards (i.e., grades, awards, admission to prestigious colleges, etc.) to motivate students to become academically engaged (Kemple and Snipes 2000). Such strategies are more likely to be effective with middle-class, college-oriented students who perceive the external rewards as valuable and desirous. Lower-class students, particularly those that are born in the United States, tend to be less motivated by the external rewards offered by schools and less likely to buy into the achievement ideology (Ogbu 1990; MacLeod 1987). Research has shown that alternative schools and career academy programs are more likely to be successful in educating students from low-income families because they promote the intrinsic interests and desires of students to learn (Kemple and Snipes 2000).

Finally, strategies that promote deeper student engagement are effective at promoting safety because when school "matters," and students perceive themselves as having a reason for doing well academically, they are less likely to engage in behavior that might jeopardize future success. Students who do buy in to the achievement ideology and who believe their performance in school can positively influence their future life chances are less likely to be delinquent or disruptive in school (MacLeod 1987). A similar tendency can be seen in a study on teen pregnancy by sociologist Kristen Luker (1996). She found that a major reason why middle-class girls were less likely to have children during adolescence than lower-class girls was their recognition that such an occurrence would decrease their chances of going to college after graduation. Similarly, students who believe that a promising future lies ahead of them will be less likely to engage in behavior that will interfere with or undermine their future goals.

Greater student engagement in school can be achieved in a variety of ways. Expanding after-school activities so that more students can participate in sports, clubs, and the arts is one way. Many alternative schools have succeeded at getting students more engaged through various forms of experiential learning (Ayers, Klonsky, and Lyons 2000). Career academies and school-to-work programs also demonstrate considerable promise in eliciting greater engagement from students of varying academic abilities (Kemple and Snipes 2000). All of these strategies are also instrumental in generating social capital because they contribute to a strengthening of ties between students and the adults who work with them. Moreover, while such measures are not cost-free, they are certainly much less costly than the measures typically associated with zero tolerance policies.

Conclusion

All educators must take seriously the need to create schools that are genuinely safe. However, much more debate is needed on the strategies and policies that are being proposed and implemented to achieve this important goal. In this paper, I have tried to make the case for strategies which personalize the school environment, which encourage students to feel responsible for their behavior, and which deepen relationships between students and teachers. This is by no means an exhaustive list, nor do I claim that these are foolproof remedies. Violence is unfortunately unpredictable, and neither the strategies I have endorsed, nor those which accompany the enactment of zero tolerance policies, can completely guarantee that schools will be free from violence.

Perhaps even as we continue to search for solutions, we should also face up to the fact that absolutely safe schools are not possible in a society such as ours that is so obsessed with violence. There is a pervasive fear of violence in American society, even though crime rates are at an all-time low and violent incidents in schools are statistically less likely today than they were twenty years ago. However, there is also widespread fascination with and interest in violence. Many Americans are repulsed by violence, especially random, indiscriminate acts, which are seen as a threat to social order and as a breakdown in the cultural norms of society. However, the fact that such acts occur with frequency and regularity in the United States suggests that the occurrence of violence may not be an aberration at all.

As repulsive as it may seem, violence is a learned behavior that follows normative patterns. There are, of course, "legitimate" forms of legally sanctioned violence, such as violent acts that are carried out by the military, the police, or the courts. Violence also serves as a form of entertainment and is featured prominently in professional sports such as football, hockey, and boxing, as well as in movies and television programs. Violence also has symbolic value and serves as a unifying national theme, which is why war heroes (e.g., John McCain and Colin Powell), famous battles (e.g., Pearl Harbor, Gettysburg, Little Big Horn, the Alamo), and events (Victory Over Japan Day celebrated on August 9 in several states following the bombing of Hiroshima and Nagasaki) are widely embraced. Finally, violence can also be seen as a form of communication, which, like speech or hand gestures, can be seen as a behavior containing its own logic and meaning. For example, little boys often hit little girls because they like them, and new members of fraternities or sports teams are abused during hazing rituals which are designed to reinforce a sense of brotherhood.

For all of these reasons, responses to violence that do not take into account the ways in which it is rationalized, legitimated, and sanctioned within schools, communities, and society are unlikely to succeed in reducing or eliminating it. Until we confront the fact that as a society we both love and fear violence and recognize that this contradictory stance hinders our ability to fully come to terms with it, we will continue to be trapped in a futile state of paralysis over what should be done to reduce violence.

REFERENCES

Adler, P. 1985. "From Idealism to Pragmatic Detachment: The Academic Performance of College Athletes." *Sociology of Education* 58:241–50.

Alschuler, A. 1994. *School Discipline: A Socially Literate Solution.* New York: McGraw-Hill.

Applied Research Center (ARC). 1999. Oakland, Calif.

Ayers, W., M. Klonsky, and G. Lyons. 2000. *A Simple Justice.* New York: Teachers College Press.

Coleman, J. 1988. "Social Capital in the Creation of Human Capital." *American Journal of Sociology* 94:S95–S120.

Durkheim, E. 1951. *Suicide.* New York: The Free Press.

Fuller, B., and R. Elmore. 1996. *Who Chooses, Who Loses?* New York: Teachers College Press.

Gladwell, M. 1998. "The Tipping Point." *New Yorker,* April, pp. 29–34.

Johnson, J., and J. Immerwahr. 1994 95. "First Things First: What Americans Expect from the Public School." *American Educator,* Winter.

Justice Matters. 2000. *Turning to Each Other, Not on Each Other: How School Communities Prevent Racial Bias in School Discipline.* June.

Kemple, J., and J. Snipes. 2000. *Career Academies: Impacts on Students' Engagement and Performance in High School.* New York: Manpower Demonstration Research Corporation.

Kohl, H. 1998. *The Discipline of Hope.* New York: Simon and Schuster.

Luker, K. 1996. *Dubious Conceptions: The Politics of Teenage Pregnancy.* Cambridge, Mass.: Harvard University Press.

MacLeod, J. 1987. *Ain't No Makin' It.* Boulder, Colo.: Westview Press.

Maeroff, G. 1988. "Withered Hopes, Stillborn Dreams: The Dismal Panorama of Urban Schools." *Phi Delta Kappan* 69:632–38.

Marquez, S. A. 1996. "Fear of Crime: Some Evidence of an Inverse Relationship." Unpublished paper. Presented at the Pacific Sociological Association Annual Meeting, Seattle, March 21–24.

National Association of Black Public Administrators. 1992. *A Leadership-Oriented Mentoring Program for At-Risk African American Youth.* Washington, D.C.

Nieves, E. 2000. "California Governor Building a Tough-on-Crime Record." *New York Times,* May 23.

Ogbu, J. 1990. "Minority Education in Comparative Perspective." *Journal of Negro Education* 59(1): 45–57.

Patterson, O. 1999. "Boston's Ten-Point Program." *New York Times,* November 12.

Policy Analysis for California Education. 1996. "Californians' View on Education: Questions and Poll Results." Berkeley: University of California at Berkeley.

Putnam, R. 1993. "The Strange Disappearance of Civic America." *American Prospect* (Winter): 34–48.

Sampson, R. 1998. "What Community Supplies." *Urban Problems and Community Development.* Edited by R. Ferguson and W. Dickens. Washington, D.C.: Brookings Institution.

Steinberg, L. 1996. *Beyond the Classroom.* New York: Simon and Schuster.

Tebo, M. G. 2000. "Zero Tolerance, Zero Sense." *American Bar Association Law Journal* (April).

UCLA Charter School Study. 1998. *Beyond the Rhetoric of Charter School Reform.*

Turning *to* Each Other, Not *on* Each Other: How School Communities Prevent Racial Bias in School Discipline

SUSAN SANDLER

Jeffrey and Jerrold are cousins. They are both in sixth grade, but go to school on opposite sides of town. They are African American.

One morning, Jeffrey goes to school and the teacher introduces a new math activity. Jeffrey starts teasing the girl sitting next to him, throwing little pieces of paper at her. The teacher reprimands Jeffrey. A little while later, Jeffrey does it again and the teacher intervenes again. When the teacher is writing on the board, another student begins throwing pieces of paper. The teacher turns around and points at Jeffrey. "That's it," she says. "I've given you two warnings, and now you're going to the office." "But I didn't do it this time," Jeffrey protests. "I don't want to hear it," the teacher replies. "You've been disrupting the class all week, and I won't have it disrupted anymore."

In the office, Jeffrey waits for the crowd of students before him to have their turn talking to the counselor. When it's Jeffrey's turn, the counselor calls Jeffrey's home, but there is no answer. "Your mother isn't home again. She never seems to be home," he adds with frustration. "Don't talk about my mom like that!" shouts Jeffrey. "Don't you use that tone of voice with me!" the counselor yells. "You better take back what you said! You don't know what you're talking about!" shouts Jeffrey, standing up. "That's it," the counselor says. "You're going home."

Meanwhile, Jerrold is also starting his school day. When he enters the school building, one of the teachers, Ms. Martin, is doing "morning duty," greeting students and parents. "Good morning, Jerrold," she says. "Give me that big smile of yours." " 'Morning, Grandma," says Jerrold, calling her by the nickname that the students have for her.

Like his cousin, Jerrold is starting his morning with math and is throwing wads of paper at his neighbor. His teacher comes up to his desk and speaks quietly so that no one else can hear. "Jerrold, do you remember that meeting we had when you explained how you get frustrated in class when you don't understand? Do you remember the idea your mom had about thinking of questions you can ask to get help?" "Oh yeah," Jerrold says, "I forgot again." Jerrold thinks of some questions and asks his work partner for help. Ten minutes later, after another reminder from the teacher, Jerrold is calling out excitedly, "I understand it! I can do a problem all by myself. And I really understand it!" (This is a big breakthrough for him.) "That's great! I knew you could do it," the teacher says, walking over to him. "Do you want to tell the rest of the class at meeting time?"

The above descriptions of hypothetical schools form a sharp contrast to each other. The first school uses practices that are common in schools that disproportionately discipline students of color. The staff in this school are hard-working, dedicated individuals, yet their efforts resulted in practices that have disproportionately punitive outcomes for students from certain racial groups. This scenario reflects a situation that lacks the policies, practices, and staff development that would allow the school to be successful with Jeffrey. They have not actively taken on the task of eliminating institutional racism which, when ignored, results in all manner of disproportionately negative outcomes for students of color.

The problems in the first school become apparent when contrasted with the second school. At Jerrold's school, the policies, practices, and training are in place to prevent racial bias in school discipline. Such schools are featured in a recent study: *Turning to Each Other, Not on Each Other: How School Communities Prevent Racial Bias in School Discipline.* Based on a national search for schools using approaches to successfully prevent racial bias in discipline, eight schools were selected for this study. *Turning to Each Other* examines these schools, distilling lessons for how to put an end to this unacceptable problem.

These schools shatter commonly held conceptions about school discipline. The common wisdom is that some schools (often schools with many students of color and low-income students) should suspend a lot of students. If they don't, these schools will become violent, chaotic places where no one can learn.

Behind this thinking is the assumption that some kids are inherently bad or violent. These bad kids must be intimidated sufficiently or separated from the rest of the students so that everyone else may learn.

All of the schools in the *Turning* to *Each Other* study fit the profile of schools at which the conventional expectation is that many students will need to be suspended and expelled. The schools are composed predominantly of students of color. The majority of the students in most of these schools qualify for free or reduced-price lunch because of low income levels.

Yet, in fact, all of these schools are unusually safe. Their students frequently comment on how safe they feel at school. Many of these schools are also quite intellectually rigorous. Two of the high schools that are featured have graduation and college-going percentages in the high 80s and 90s. Many of the schools are well known for their exciting, challenging curricula and effective pedagogy.

These schools show that you do not have to suspend and expel "those kids" to create unusually safe, productive learning environments.

How do they do this? The Reverend Jesse Jackson, in other contexts, has challenged us to turn *to* each other, not *on* each other. These schools incorporate the idea of "turning to each other" into their policies and everyday practices, so that they consistently turn *to* the students, to the families, and to each other to solve problems, rather than turning *on* students and families of color. For example, in the scenario about Jerrold's school, the teacher turned to Jerrold and his mother for solutions. Jerrold described his experience of the situation, which led his mother to suggest a plan that Jerrold and the teacher implemented.

These schools reject the notion that some young people are just bad. These schools emphasize approaches which invest in students' growth and development rather than in writing off some students. They recognize each student's talents and moral core rather than treat some students as bad apples to be discarded before they spoil the rest. And they get results. They have structures, such as small school size, that support their approach. Much of their philosophy and approach amelioriates or directly eliminates the institutional racism that usually permeates schools and other mainstream institutions.

Schools That Can Show Us
How to Prevent Racism in Discipline

Through a national search, the *Turning to Each Other* study identified eight such schools: Central Park East Secondary School (CPESS; East Harlem, New York), DeWitt Clinton High School (Bronx, New York), El Puente Academy for Peace and Justice (Brooklyn, New York), Oakhurst Elementary School (Georgia), PSJA High School (San Juan, Texas), River East Elementary School (East Harlem, New York), San Francisco Community School (California); and Sankofa Shule (Lansing, Michigan). Both the qualitative and quantitative data collected on these schools shows that they are able to maintain safe environments without resorting to harsh, punitive, or exclusionary practices. Spanning the country and all ages within the K–12 spectrum, these schools have rich information about many practices and approaches that can transform our nation's schools. They also demonstrate how aspects of the school environment, such as size, play a very important role. This discussion describes some of the key practices they used to get their results.

Actively and Consciously Caring Culture

The *Turning to Each Other* study identified schools with caring cultures based on the idea that such school environments would buffer and protect students against institutional racism. A caring culture does not necessarily eliminate institutional racism in the school. However, the close relationships engendered in a caring school make the effects of stereotypes, ethnocentrism, and other forms of institutional racism less pernicious—students know that adults sincerely care about them and have their interests at heart. Furthermore, such schools tend to provide opportunities for school adults to learn about their students and over time reduce racism in the school.

As Table 1 illustrates, there were several practices that the schools in the study used to bring about an actively caring culture.

Of the practices listed in the table, the most significant are the explicit emphasis on a caring ethic and the school's foundation based on a mission. For most of the schools, a great deal of effort went into making a caring ethic explicitly a central part of the school. DeWitt Clinton High School is a good example of this. There is something in the air, a feeling of respect and caring,

TABLE 1

	CPESS	DEWITT CLINTON	EL PUENTE	OAKHURST	PSJA	RIVER EAST	SF COMM.	SANKOFA SHULE
Caring ethic is explicitly a central part of school	Yes*	Yes	Yes	Yes		Yes	Yes	
Started school based on a mission	Yes	No	Yes	No	No	Yes	Yes	Yes
Resources (time, staff) devoted to building strong relationships	Yes	Yes	Yes	Yes	Yes	Yes	Yes	
Parents play important role in school					Yes		Yes	
Invests in bringing students into school culture			Yes					Yes
Curriculum and pedagogy oriented to child/youth interests, modalities			Yes	Yes		Yes		Yes
Emphasizes celebrations, clubs, and trips		Yes	Yes	Yes			Yes	Yes
Schoolwide problem-solving or conflict resolution approaches					Yes		Yes	

*Note: A cell that says "Yes" means that this area came up as a major area of emphasis in the school. A blank cell means that the research did not identify this area for the school. Given the limits of the investigation, it is possible that schools that are blank in a certain category may upon further investigation turn out to be a "Yes."

that staff and students encounter when they first come to the school, and that draws them into its culture.

This climate, "the Clinton way," is supported by a caring staff at all levels. "All levels" includes the custodians and cafeteria workers, who are considered important parts of the Clinton family. In fact, the custodial team is considered to play a very important role in maintaining the special climate at the school as they collaborate with other staff to make sure that all graffiti is painted over immediately and that the school is kept spotless.

The caring atmosphere is also supported by a "house" structure that brings a sense of personal caring to each student. The school is broken down into twelve houses. Each house has a supervisor, guidance counselor, coordinator, and family outreach assistant. Students can take courses throughout the school's curriculum, but the house staffs follow them throughout their four years. The result is that each student has specific people he or she can go to with a question or problem. If a student misses a few days at school, one of the house staff will call him or her or go to his or her house—not to intrude, but to show they care.

All of these efforts successfully communicate the caring culture to students who are known to say things about the school such as, "This is like my second home . . . no . . . this is like my *first* home."

Most of the schools draw heavily on a mission that supports them in creating a caring culture. Five of the schools were actually founded with a specific mission or vision, which they have maintained. This mission in turn unifies the school, shapes the school's practices and policies, and serves as criteria for hiring new staff. The mission of these schools seems to play an important role in the development of innovative practices that embody caring and respect for all members of the school community.

For example, El Puente (which means "the Bridge" in Spanish) has the mission to inspire and nurture indigenous leadership for peace and justice. This mission shapes the myriad practices that differentiate El Puente from other schools. El Puente's focus on "indigenous" leadership—that is, leadership from the surrounding Brooklyn neighborhood—means that many of the staff grew up and live in the neighborhood. It also means that students are seen as indigenous leaders, and school staff are there to facilitate their emerging leadership rather than to do all the leading themselves. Accordingly, staff are referred to as facilitators, not teachers, and are called by their first names. Classes are often arranged so that everyone sits in a circle, underlining the point that everyone is learning from each other.

A peaceful community does not have to lock its members out for protection. Just as families do not have lockers in their homes to guard their possessions from each other, El Puente does not have lockers for students' possessions. And indeed, theft has been an extremely rare occurrence.

School Culture Grounded in the Cultures and Realities of the Students

In some cases, schools engage in practices that directly eliminate institutional racism. Through being grounded in the students' cultures and social realities, the staffs at these schools are less likely to project negative stereotypes onto students of color and are more likely to be knowledgeable about who their students are and what they bring to school. Rather than ignoring or devaluing their students' cultures, these schools built their programs on the cultures of the students.

Sankofa Shule is an African-centered school. *Sankofa* is an Akan word that means "go back and fetch it," and Shule "school." *Sankofa* speaks to the school's philosophy that African-American children need to know where they come from to know who they are and where they are going.

What is an African-centered school? In part, it is the curriculum, which is grounded in the history and culture of African people. African-centered schools tend to use pedagogical approaches that go beyond traditional strategies to include experiential lessons, oral performance, and creative use of rhythm, gestures, and so on. At Sankofa Shule the day starts with classes in martial arts, dance, drumming, and foreign language (French, Japanese, Kiswahili, and Spanish). Subjects that are not usually thought of as active or experiential are made so. A math class might involve activities such as shooting baskets as a way to learn about fractions and percentages. Students also participate in numerous field trips, some to nearby places and others to out-of-state or even international locations.

Sankofa Shule is founded on a set of African-based cultural principles. These principles shape all aspects of school life. For example, one important principle is "Heshima," a basic concept of African philosophy, which means respect for life. Every day, in the morning and afternoon, the school comes together for "affirmations." These affirmations include chanting the ethical principles in call and response, reviewing the purpose of the day in light of one of the principles, and singing and other activities. In other settings throughout the school, the ethical principles are much discussed.

In addition to gathering information on ways in which schools might be grounded in students' cultures, the study also looked at school practices that explicitly address racism, cultural differences, and other social realities students face. Some schools speak deeply to the struggles, outrage, hopes, and dreams of students and their families.

El Puente is an example of a school that throws its lot in with that of its students and their community. The school studies the conditions that students, their families, and neighborhood face, and then takes action to improve these conditions. One year the school studied asthma, an illness that affects many of the students' families. They used epidemiological approaches to conduct a survey, through which they discovered that the neighborhood asthma rate was almost three times higher than the national average. They also discovered that women of a certain age were most likely to suffer from asthma—and since these women often work in sweatshops, this discovery related to other research projects the school conducted on the garment industry. El Puente students went on to conduct a public education program about the issue, creating community murals and taking other action to address this major neighborhood problem. Practices such as these create a school environment which overcomes common barriers between students and schools. Rather than feeling school to be a hostile environment in which their social realities and the injustices they face are invisible, students feel seen and supported as people with cultures, histories, and strengths who are contending with social injustices.

Meaningful Approach to Discipline

The schools in the study also used practices that directly addressed the discipline approach itself. Whereas previously discussed practices addressed the overall school environment, which can produce racial bias in school discipline, these practices made sure not to exclude, reject, or demean students of color within the discipline process itself.

It turns out that the school's mission plays a fundamental role in its approach to discipline. Most of the discipline practices that the schools used were based on applying their missions in the discipline context. For example, at Central Park East Secondary School (CPESS), critical thinking as described in the school's five "habits of mind" is a major part of the school's mission. At most schools, when an incident occurs (for example, something is stolen), many students accused of wrongdoing feel that no one ever really cares about or wants to hear their side of the story. At CPESS, however, the accused person is actively encouraged to argue his or her case and also to present evidence. It seems that the habits of mind such as examination of evidence and considering multiple viewpoints apply to all aspects of school life.

This practice is a hallmark of how CPESS consistently emphasizes critical thinking through nurturing young people to think for themselves in all settings rather than telling them what to do. This general approach is referred to as "coaching." Through coaching, school adults, rather than taking center-stage through lecturing, are on the sidelines providing support and guidance to students, who are the main actors.

When it comes to discipline, coaching means not having a "compliance" mentality that focuses on adults making students follow rules. Rather, the idea is that everyone in the school belongs to a community with common values, and adults support students in figuring out how to apply these values and involve them as participants in a collaborative process when the values are not upheld. Accordingly, the school emphasizes values and has few rules. When there is a discipline issue, much of the intervention involves helping the student reflect and learn, which makes talking (with the student, family, etc.) one of the major interventions.

What It Takes for Schools to Achieve These Qualities — Process and Resources

What enabled the schools in the study to achieve what they did? Their practices and policies were made possible by many things—a process of school transformation that took place over time and included resources, structures, staffing, and so forth. Table 2 summarizes these various supports.

The three factors that seemed to play a role in the greatest number of

TABLE 2

	CPESS	DEWITT CLINTON	EL PUENTE	OAKHURST	PSJA	RIVER EAST	SF COMM.	SANKOFA SHULE
Small size	Yes*	No	Yes	Yes	No	Yes	Yes	Yes
Additional funding	Yes	Yes	Yes	Yes	Yes		Yes	Yes
Highly selective hiring				Yes		Yes		
Willingness to remove staff from school		Yes				Yes		
Multiyear process		Yes	Yes	Yes				
Substantial planning/ meeting time	Yes					Yes	Yes	Yes
Emphasizes professional development				Yes			Yes	
Deploys staff so as to build relationships	Yes	Yes	Yes		Yes	Yes		
Principal leadership plays major role		Yes		Yes	Yes			Yes

*Note: The same methodology was used here as for Table 1.

schools are small size, additional funding, and the deployment of staff so as to build relationships.

Small size seems to play a vital role in the success of many of the schools. Six of the schools are small. Almost everyone at these schools commented on how vital the small size is to their ability to create a caring community. Smallness makes it possible for students and staff to know each other well and creates a sense of intimacy. However, the study found that carefully structured large schools were able to replicate many of the qualities of a small school. DeWitt Clinton High School has 4,300 students and creates a caring community through a strong schoolwide culture, through breaking the student body into twelve houses, and through community-building events, clubs, and activities.

All of the schools except one mentioned that additional funding supports their ability to implement an outstanding school climate and meaningful approach to discipline. This funding mainly goes to support institutional structures and staffing through the creation of planning time, provision of professional development, and addition of staff. It also supports programmatic activities such as trips and events.

Five of the schools shape staff members' duties so as to build strong relationships with students and families. DeWitt Clinton created a series of positions associated with each house that focused on paying careful attention to all of the students in the house. At CPESS and El Puente, certain people play a coordinating role that supports the rest of the staff in meeting with students and parents. At PSJA and CPESS, every teacher is an advisor to a group of students. At River East, support staff work directly with students.

Conclusion

The schools in the *Turning* to *Each Other* study are inspiring, and they challenge us. They explode the myth that it is not necessary to choose between high discipline rates for students of color and safe, academically productive schools. They show that schools can be humane, caring places where discipline issues are minimal and, when they do occur, they contribute to everyone's growth and development.

We must act on the lessons from these schools. We must not allow our children to continue to be thrown away when alternatives are available. We must find a way for people in all schools to turn *to* each other, not *on* each other.

The Role of Law in Policing Abusive Disciplinary Practices: Why School Discipline Is a Civil Rights Issue

DANIEL J. LOSEN
AND CHRISTOPHER EDLEY, JR.

Introduction

All citizens should be concerned about the rising tide of harsh discipline flooding our public schools. Our democratic values are at stake.[1] The wave of school exclusionary policies, in effect and process, is undermining one of the main purposes of public education recognized in law: to prepare children to be effective, responsible members of society and participants in democratic self-governance. For most children, school attendance is their first formal relationship with government. For minorities, the unyielding form of government intervention represented by zero tolerance teaches impressionable youth that the government can take away their right to an education without giving them or their parents a meaningful opportunity to be heard.

The message of zero tolerance is clearly one of obedience, not participation. It reinforces in all children, and especially minority children, that they are excluded by, and powerless against, the government.

The use of suspension and expulsion for school-aged children, except as a measure of last resort, also contradicts our fundamental understanding of child development. As two leading child psychiatrists, James P. Comer and Alvin F. Poussaint, have written, "When punishment is necessary, it should not be harsh and traumatic for minor incidents. . . . When parents, teachers, principals, and others convey to the child that we want you, like you, and would like to have you in this school and this classroom, but there are certain things we expect of you, the response is often miraculous."[2] Overly harsh punishment, on the other hand, "either destroys a child's spirit, has no effect at all, worsens the problem, or makes it more difficult . . . to work with the child in school."[3]

The statistics on school discipline are deeply disturbing. According to the United States Department of Education's Office for Civil Rights (OCR), our annual suspension rate has nearly doubled since the mid-1970s, from 1.7 million students in 1974 to 3.2 million in 1998.[4] While fights or aggression are among the most common offenses, "[suspension] is also commonly used for a number of relatively minor offenses. . . . In fact, students are suspended for the most serious offenses (drugs, weapons, vandalism, assaults on teachers) relatively infrequently . . . and with greater frequency in urban areas than in suburban or rural schools."[5] This frequent use of suspension for minor infractions occurs despite the fact that removal from school can have a profound impact on minority students, may do irreversible damage to self-esteem, and cause negative attitudes about school.[6]

Moreover, in 1998–99, African-American students accounted for 33 percent of all those suspended and 31 percent of all those expelled, yet made up only 17 percent of all students.[7] Furthermore, earlier data show that on a national scale, boys of most racial and ethnic subgroups, including white boys, are overrepresented and are always disciplined more harshly than girls from the same subgroup.[8]

When race and gender are combined, statistics show that African-American males are disciplined more often and more severely than any other group.[9] According to the U.S. Department of Education's publication, *The Condition of Education 1997*, almost 25 percent of all African-American males were suspended at least once over a four-year period.[10] African-American males from the wealthiest families are almost as likely to be expelled or suspended as white males from the poorest families.[11] The overrepresentation of African Americans among suspended students is consistent with similar data showing criminal punishments meted out disproportionately to minority juvenile offenders.[12]

Special education students are also significantly overrepresented among the ranks of the suspended, in many districts representing one third or more of all suspensions.[13] Improper special education labeling and placement of minority children, and especially the mislabeling of African-American children as having "mental retardation," is a national concern formally recognized by Congress.[14] Therefore, the overrepresentation of children with disabilities in school discipline has particularly strong implications for minority children. Ultimately, many minority children are in double jeopardy of discrimination in discipline, first by race/ethnicity and again by disability.

Ostensibly neutral policies that effectively deny minorities access to equal educational opportunity may be rooted in a social context of intentional discrimination. Historically, minorities, and most notably African-American males, have been branded as dangerous undesirables and targeted for exclusion from school on one pretext or another. African-American students have been suspended and expelled at nearly twice the rate of white students for quite some time, but since zero tolerance has spread across the nation, the suspension and expulsion rate in some minority communities (Durham, North Carolina, for example) has soared to encompass as many as two thirds of the African Americans enrolled.[15] In Chicago, a tremendous increase in suspensions and expulsions has been noted after new discipline codes went into effect, yet the school district set a goal of doubling student expulsions for the 1999–2000 school year.[16]

Draconian discipline codes, presented as race-neutral safety precautions, perpetuate the marginalization and disenfranchisement of minorities and people with disabilities. Proponents often respond that if minority students are breaking school rules more often, then there is no unfair discrimination in excluding them more often. Children's safety must come first. But as these statistics and at least one recent study suggest, minorities and students with disabilities are receiving more frequent, severe, and longer-lasting punishments for both violent and nonviolent misbehavior compared with similarly behaving majority students.[17]

The point of civil rights law is to protect the powerless and disenfranchised from the tyranny of the majority. Since the 1994 passage of the Gun-Free Schools Act, requiring automatic discipline for gun and drug possession, expansive "zero tolerance" policies, which go far beyond guns and drugs to encompass everything from bad language to absenteeism, were implemented by state and local officials, who were typically neither minorities nor persons with disabilities.

Some argue that the "tyranny of the majority" concern is diminished by the fact that minority as well as white school authorities have backed zero tolerance policies. But the advent of zero tolerance needs to be considered in a larger national context. Swept up in a political maelstrom, government officials at all levels have been responding to the "get tough" demands of their constituents. Equally concerned with school safety as their white counterparts, and with few questioning the efficacy or fairness of zero tolerance, minority politicians and school authorities have been under great pressure to embrace stricter discipline measures. Abuses in meting out discipline existed long before zero tolerance became a buzzword, but news of the gross disparate impact of school disciplinary policy on minority youth and students with disabilities nationwide has only recently been brought to light by civil rights activists.

When school policy is at issue, courts often defer to the authority of educators. The rationale invariably refers to the courts' lack of expertise and the sanctity of local control over public schools. As a result, many practices such as tracking and high-stakes testing, which harm minority and poor children disproportionately, have been allowed to stand. But where policies have caused complete exclusion from school, as zero tolerance does, the Supreme Court has sometimes expressed greater willingness to scrutinize the educational justification.[18] Nonetheless, to stop this tsunami of intolerance, advocates must develop more effective media, policy, and legal arguments.

This essay examines the legal framework for challenging discriminatory educational practice based on race or ethnicity. The next section describes avenues through which to challenge zero tolerance under civil rights statutes. Part three provides guidance to lawyers, community activists, and parents. However, this general writing should not be considered "legal advice." Because each case is unique, it is always advisable to speak with an experienced attorney before acting.

The legal framework for challenging zero tolerance can serve a dual function: to inform legal strategy and to serve as a touchstone for policy debates and political action. Because court challenges are expensive and time consuming, we recommend extra-legal community responses that keep one foot in the courthouse door. This essay concludes by suggesting a parallelism between racial profiling on the highways and the disparate identification of minority students as rule violators in our schools.

I. The Equal Protection and Title VI Framework

The Equal Protection Clause of the Fourteenth Amendment to the U.S. Constitution and Title VI of the Civil Rights Act of 1964 each prohibit discrimination on the basis of race, color, and national origin. The Constitution applies to all schools, and Title VI applies to all schools that receive federal funding (virtually all do). There are other constitutional rights implicated, but not addressed here, such as First Amendment rights and "due process" rights. In the latter, parents can challenge a decision to suspend or expel for lack of notice or if a hearing was not properly held. Challenges on the basis of inadequate process are important, but are only relevant to a discrimination case if a minority child was denied the same process as a white child. However, as Nadine Strossen has pointed out, "It is no coincidence" that the leading case on school discipline and due process, *Goss v. Lopes*, "involved the sweeping, indiscriminate suspension of black students from Columbus, Ohio, public schools for allegedly taking part in demonstrations following Black History Month."[19]

Students and their advocates should also be aware of state constitutions and state statutes that offer similar or even more extensive protections against zero tolerance policies. Some states, for instance, guarantee the fundamental right to education, a right that is not guaranteed under the federal Constitution. Many states also have administrative agencies that focus on educational rights or on the enforcement of state antidiscrimination laws. Students and their advocates should consult with attorneys and education specialists for more information on state laws.

The two basic legal frameworks for challenging racial discrimination in school discipline are called *different treatment* and *disparate impact*. These two challenges also apply where the alleged discrimination is on the basis of gender or disability. Although beyond the scope of this essay, readers should know that there are critical additional legal safeguards against discrimination in discipline on the basis of disability.[20]

Readers should also note three important caveats about these challenges. The first is that the Title VI "disparate impact" cause of action is only available under the regulations. Second, the Supreme Court recently ruled in *Alexander v. Sandoval* that there is no "implied right of action" to enforce the Title VI disparate impact regulations in court.[21] However, Justice Stevens, dissenting, stated that it was "*likely*" that plaintiffs could still enforce the disparate impact regulations in court under a civil rights statute called "Section 1983" (42 U.S.C. § 1983, a provision of the Civil Rights Act of 1871, which was enacted after the Civil War to secure the rights of African Americans). This important legal distinction means that court actions against public schools might still be viable, despite the *Sandoval* ruling. Further, the ruling in *Sandoval* does not change the fact that a public school district can be challenged on disparate impact grounds in a complaint made to the Office for Civil Rights. Third, the "different treatment" legal framework, although available under both Title VI and the Constitution, requires proof of intent as illustrated in the examples below.

a. Different Treatment

While investigating a 1995 complaint against the Benedictine Military School in Georgia, the United States Department of Education Office for Civil Rights found that white students who had committed similar offenses as African-American students received substantially lighter sanctions. The school's discipline system was based on a point system for infractions, a disciplinary committee that met when a student reached 20 points, and a headmaster's discretion to accept or reject the committee's recommendations. OCR revealed that African-American students were routinely expelled under the point system but white students were neither expelled nor suspended for similar and even graver offenses.[22]

Most allegations of different treatment in discipline are not systemic challenges like the one above, but are brought by parents when they believe their own child has been disciplined unfairly. Despite some blatant examples, it is often difficult for parents to find enough proof of different treatment to be successful in court. Advocates and investigators have expressed a need for careful preparation in bringing a different treatment claim and suggest that all the counterarguments should be considered first. For example, if the minority student had a longer history of infractions, that difference may justify a harsher punishment for a subsequent offense.

Parents should enlist help to review disciplinary statistics and interview students in order to establish forceful claims under different treatment. In some cases, it may be wise to enlist the support of a community group to help gather a series of examples from the same district that depict a pattern of different treatment over time. Moreover, for an administrative complaint, community groups should also gather witnesses who can testify to federal investigators about their perception of the discipline code. However, parents must consider the time limits for filing complaints before they delay their claim. Once filed, claims can sometimes be joined by others. In the end, the collected evidence may prove extremely valuable to media and policy debates. Schools may be more willing to reach a negotiated settlement and change their policy if the facts of a specific case generate public outcry. But anecdotal evidence is even more effective when multiple claims are made and the statistics shout, "This is not an isolated injustice!"

b. The Intent Standard

The most difficult obstacle to proving discrimination is the fact that under the Constitution, and Title VI, the courts require plaintiffs to show proof of intentional discrimination. Parents and advocates, however, should not be too discouraged by this legal hurdle. Under the regulations to Title VI, a claim of "disparate impact" (see next section) can be brought and proof of intent is not required to make the case. A "different treatment" claim, on the other hand, does not escape the intent requirement, even under the regulations.

Intent can be established from statements or writings of policy makers, disciplinarians, and witnesses. In one successful case handed down in 1985, the court cited evidence that faculty members had referred to African-American students as "niggers," "blue gums," and "coon."[23] The court also highlighted the testimony from one teacher who had witnessed another administer corporal punishment to an African-American student until the child's skin was ruptured and bleeding, but who had never seen a white child subjected to such harsh punishment in her nine years at the school.[24]

In some cases where direct evidence is sparse, there is a way around the "intent" requirement that does not rely on the "disparate impact" regulations. In some states, if the school district is under a court order to desegregate, and the current effect of a zero tolerance policy can be tied to prior unlawful school segregation, the court may allow a plaintiff to prevail, without requiring new proof of intent.[25] The reasoning behind this desegregation exception is that if a school policy that has a racially adverse impact is connected to the old segregated system, the past intentional discrimination is still at work and the unlawful intent may be presumed.[26] Parents and advocates wishing to challenge a district's zero tolerance policy should request records directly from a court *and from the school district* to discover whether the district in question is under court order, and if so, whether discriminatory discipline had been raised as a concern in the past.[27]

c. No Intent Required—Disparate Impact Under the Regulations

Parents suspecting unlawful discrimination can sue in court or file a federal complaint with the Office for Civil Rights. To date, "disparate impact" issues have been raised infrequently compared to allegations of "different treatment."[28]

Although disparate impact claims have been underutilized, a number of class-action lawsuits that relied heavily on statistical disparities have resulted in productive settlements. In *Ross v. Saltmarsh*, for example, the court required the school district to set a goal to reduce the overall number of suspensions in order to reduce the racial disparity in suspensions.[29]

It is important to note that the Title VI regulations, setting forth the disparate impact grounds, were developed so that subtle forms of intentional discrimination could be scrutinized. The doctrine also represents Congress's intent to protect historically oppressed groups from facially neutral actions that pile on additional disadvantages.

Specifically, the Title VI regulations make it unlawful for a school to use "criteria or methods of administration which have the effect of subjecting individuals to discrimination because of their race, color or national origin, or have the effect of defeating or substantially impairing the accomplishment of the objectives of the program as respect individuals of a particular race, color or national origin."[30] In other words, an "effects test" can be applied to the discipline policies of a school or district even when all agree that the policies were not intended to discriminate and that there is no direct evidence of bias or "different treatment."

II. What Can a Concerned Citizen Do?

Parents and advocates should always consider filing both a "different treatment" and a "disparate impact" complaint. Furthermore, nonlegal challenges should be pursued simultaneously with legal ones. For both disparate impact and different treatment claims, true stories of different treatment for nonviolent behavior are especially compelling.[31]

Schools often successfully counter claims of different treatment by referring to each student's history of misconduct, or by highlighting the very specific nature of each infraction. The core argument is that because every incident and every offender is different, different treatment may be warranted. In some cases where schools have adopted strict zero tolerance policy for *categories* of misconduct, these justifications for different treatment may be difficult to maintain.

Most important, a school may have a harder time, technically, defending against a "disparate impact" claim than a "different treatment" claim. Parents and advocates should point out to school boards and the media that *any* school policy can constitute unlawful discrimination if it fails the "effects" test described in the regulations. There are limitations on who can file a lawsuit in court, but advocates should keep in mind that any concerned citizen can bring a discrimination complaint on behalf of another individual or group in an administrative action.

a. Making a Disparate Impact Argument

Legally, a disparate impact claim should be treated in the following manner:[32] (1) First, it must be established that the students who were disciplined are members of a protected racial or ethnic group;[33] (2) the complaining party must establish that a district or school policy has a negative effect on the identifiable ethnic or racial group, and that the disproportionality is great enough that it is unlikely to have occurred by chance;[34] (3) once the complaining party satisfies these two elements, the burden shifts to the school district to show that the policy is an educational necessity; and (4) if the school provides a justification, parents and advocates may challenge the justification and/or show that a less discriminatory alternative could achieve the same purpose.

b. Educational Necessity?

In a disparate impact case, once the challenger establishes a significant statistical disparity, the school district *must* justify the policy. However, a school would likely defend such a policy by saying it serves the necessary educational purpose of maintaining a calm and safe learning environment. It may bring in state educational officials or other school personnel to attest to the importance of zero tolerance. Because judges generally defer to the judgment of school officials, courts have rarely required school systems to provide extensive proof that the policy is necessary or effective in meeting its purpose.

c. Overcoming the Educational Necessity Defense

Formulating an effective response to a school's justification is critical to legal arguments, public policy debate, and media discourse. In attempting to discredit a school's justification, advocates should always differentiate "zero tolerance" from firm and consistent school discipline to avoid being painted as opponents of discipline *per se*. Parents and advocates should prepare to: (1) undermine the school's justification directly, and/or (2) describe less discriminatory alternatives that would not be unreasonably expensive to implement. If the complaint is filed with the United States Department of Education's Office for Civil Rights (an administrative agency, not a court), a strong argument can be made that the federal government has the duty, as an enforcement agency, to scrutinize the justification. If the justification is sound, OCR should search for reasonable alternatives with less discriminatory impact and only side with the school if none can be found. But the depth of OCR investigations may vary and complainants should keep close track of how OCR is proceeding.

1. Undermining Educational Justifications

One of the most important aspects of a legal challenge is the highlighting of the negative disparate outcomes. Whenever possible, parents and advocates should use distinct examples to counter claims that harsh discipline is necessary to maintain a safe, calm, and productive learning environment. There is rarely an educational justification for automatic zero tolerance for non-dangerous behavior. The underlying principle of our federal education laws (and many state constitutional provisions) is that providing education for *all* children, including those who present challenges, is a public good. Unlike private schools, public schools don't get to pick and choose who benefits.

In some cases, where there are no improvements in a school's test scores *after dropouts are accounted for*, a parent or advocate can point out the lack of evidence supporting the claim that a zero tolerance is necessary for learning to take place. Where a challenged policy is fairly new, a school will likely point to other communities where a similar policy has "worked." Opponents should be prepared to question the credibility of the district's testimony on this subject by bringing in expert witnesses and by demonstrating that there are communities where similar policies have failed to make an improvement. In some cases, the policy may have been borrowed and then distorted. If a school claims to be adhering to a certain recommended approach, challengers should contact the designers to find out whether the school district has implemented the original design appropriately.

A. Countering the Fair Process Defense

Challengers may encounter the argument that zero tolerance should not be rebuttable so long as the process is fair. In response, parents should stress that the disparate impact argument is well established in the employment context. The Supreme Court held that neutral employment tests and other hiring criteria were considered discriminatory if they were unnecessary for the job at hand or if the same information about the prospective employee could be obtained in a way that did not diminish the chances of minority applicants.[35] The fact that an *unnecessarily* harsh discipline policy may be carried out with neutrally administered due process for all does not protect it from legal challenges arising from its disparate impact.

B. Questioning Claims of Deterrence

Once the fair process argument is addressed, the deterrence-as-educational-necessity argument must still be grappled with. Claims of successful deterrence must be viewed critically. Some schools point to reduced suspensions in concurrent years to claim erroneously that zero tolerance is helping students learn to improve their behavior. Statistics that may support such claims often fail to account for the fact that many disciplined students never return to school. They may attend alternative schools, drop out, or become incarcerated, but they do not necessarily return as better citizens for their experience.[36] Along these same lines, suspension rates can be reduced by making suspensions last longer, particularly because many disciplined students are repeat offenders. Whenever schools insist their discipline policy has been effective, plaintiffs should challenge the defending districts and the media to find and publicize statistics on discipline, attendance, and graduation rates that actually follow cohorts of students from grade to grade.

National claims of successful deterrence should also be viewed critically. For example, the *Report on State Implementation of the Gun-Free School Act: School Year 1997–1998* (U.S. Department of Education 1999), depicts a decrease in the number of students expelled for carrying a firearm, from 6,093 to 3,930 in 1996–97. However, the drop may be due to the fact that in the 1996–97 report, many schools did not distinguish between weapons and firearms.[37] The drop may also be due to better and more accurate reporting.[38] Dr. Paul Kingery, who has worked on the report, stated that if only the statistics on firearms were used, there may have in fact been an increase.[39]

Furthermore, if zero tolerance is truly "teaching children a lesson," then the success must be judged by looking at the victimization rate of children both in and out of school.[40] Advocates should frame the debate in terms of broad community interests. For example, a recent report in a South Bend, Indiana, newspaper highlighted a recent spate of murders in the community by 12 African-American boys.[41] The article pointed out that all were of school age, but only two had attended school that year. Where violence rates among youth continue to rise outside of schools, expulsion and suspension reductions from year to year do not evidence a lesson learned. Therefore, advocates should document crime rates among youth outside the schoolhouse, the increasing costs of incarceration, and the burden incurred by citizens in their communities. Interviews with those who work with juveniles and with others concerned with rising crime among children on the streets should be pursued for anecdotal evidence of the dangerous impact of zero tolerance.

2. Challengers Should Offer Less Discriminatory Alternatives

The other critical concept to convey is that there are school disciplinary strategies that both ensure safety and respect civil rights. By bringing to light effective violence intervention programs that do not rely on zero tolerance, advocates can provide constructive criticism that may support a negotiated settlement or political remedies such as requesting that the school board repeal or amend the policy. Educational psychologist Russ Skiba testified before the United States Commission on Civil Rights that some schools use more graduated systems of firm discipline, in which severe consequences are reserved for the most serious offenses, with more moderate responses used for less serious behavior.[42] Whenever possible, challengers should provide examples of viable alternatives that have excluded fewer children and lowered the racial disparity in discipline. In any event, if parents and advocates can gather statistical evidence of a significant disparity, the parties may reach a settlement and avoid a protracted give and take on these questions.

d. Be Wary of Alternative Schools

Anecdotal evidence indicates that alternative schools can be harmful places for children, and that minority children are more likely to be transferred to them for discipline reasons. For example, in 1999, the superintendent for Palm Beach County, Florida, entered into a resolution agreement with OCR to address a race- and disability-based complaint regarding the district's use of alternative education programs.[43] Upon further investigation,[44] OCR found "significant disproportion" by race in the number of African-American students involved in incidents where law enforcement became involved, and significant disparities in the rate of referrals and the meting out of discipline to African-American students for a wide range of offenses.[45]

Further, the idea of isolating "at risk" children is generally regarded as a recipe for failure and distinctly frowned upon in the area of special education research and law.[46] Systemic challenges sounding in both Title VI and disability law may be effective in curtailing the inappropriate use of these programs.[47] Unfortunately, some politicians appear willing to commit large numbers of poor and minority children to experimental institutions. For example, the State of Illinois passed a law on May 21, 2001, that allows schools to transfer to alternative school programs those children it labels "at risk."[48] This broad category includes any student who is either "at risk of not meeting the Illinois Learning Standards or not graduating from elementary or high school and who demonstrates a need for educational or social services beyond that provided by the regular school program.[49] This new law explicitly enables districts to provide alternative programs by contracting with juvenile justice agencies and programs operated by the department of corrections.[50]

Parents should be concerned that zero tolerance policies, when coupled with a proliferation of "alternative" schools, could fuel an abusive reliance on alternative programs. As a result, one could expect an increase in the likelihood that "at risk" minority children are isolated in separate schools, where they will receive watered-down curricula, have few positive peer models, and be held to low expectations by unqualified instructors. Although some good alternative schools may exist, parents should be wary that an alternative school might be another conduit for the school-to-jail pipeline.

e. Filing Administrative Complaints

The Office for Civil Rights has 12 regional offices. However, parents and advocates should carefully consider the reputation of the OCR office for their region, because the agency can label the complaint as meritless or negotiate an agreement that does not require the district to make significant changes. OCR prefers negotiated settlements, and if a case has merit, it will usually pressure both parties to reach a settlement short of a hearing. The following summary of a recent challenge may provide a useful window into OCR's practice when the agency has conducted a thorough review:[51]

> In June of 1996, a complaint was filed against the Alameda High School in Alameda, California, stating: (1) a racially hostile environment existed with respect to Latino students; and (2) Latino students were treated differently compared to white students in the number of referrals and suspensions and in the severity of discipline received for the same or similar offenses.[52] OCR requested and received relevant data from the school over a three-year period of investigation and negotiation. During that time, OCR interviewed parents, students, and administrative staff, and inspected student files and discipline records.

Although OCR found the evidence of "different treatment" to be inadequate, OCR's investigation revealed that the rates of discipline of Latino and African-American students were disproportionately high. The disparity was most notable in a number of discipline categories including "defiance of authority." OCR worked with the school to reduce the discipline rate in all its high schools. Particular attention was spent on how defiance of authority incidents had been distributed across racial and ethnic lines. Between 1996 and 1999, the District reported to OCR its progress in addressing the disparity and over this period, according to OCR, successfully reduced the discipline rates for all students within an acceptable range.[53]

This example involved a disparate impact analysis, but a survey of reported cases suggests that OCR more often processes discipline complaints under the intentional discrimination standard, or limits its investigation to the specific issues raised in the complaint.[54]

In addition to overcoming the potential legal obstacle presented by the *Sandoval* decision, the most significant advantages to filing with OCR are: (1) it costs very little and parents can file claims on their own; (2) OCR has broad investigation powers and can access information from schools and school districts more rapidly than plaintiffs, which may save time for advocates given the time allowances for full discovery; (3) OCR will engage the school district in negotiations early on when evidence suggests a violation; and (4) OCR can require a school to collect certain kinds of statistical data that might be unavailable to an attorney suing in court. A school's data on discipline is often inadequate. For example, a school may record disciplinary action but not the details of the offense or length of suspensions, and not all schools collect data on discipline disaggregated by race or ethnicity. If it believes the information is needed, OCR can have a school reconfigure data that it has collected or begin collecting the information OCR requests. Furthermore, OCR data, reports, and other information will be provided if requested through a Freedom of Information Act request. Advocates suing in court face more obstacles in gaining the data needed to prove the case.

There are, however, pitfalls in pursuing an administrative remedy. Although OCR may not refuse to investigate cases that have merit, they may view the facts in a very conservative light if they are under political pressure to close a case. With so many politicians at the federal level spouting zero tolerance rhetoric, these pressures may come to bear on OCR's willingness to dig for information in the course of an investigation.

The depth and quality of OCR's investigation and negotiation also can vary significantly. Parents and advocates should take advantage of the fact that OCR attorneys will "provide technical assistance" by telephone or in person without requiring a complaint to be filed. This free advice, which should be requested as "technical assistance," can give potential complainants a sense of how the specific office of OCR would deal with their case if it were to be filed. It may also be useful to ask OCR to send a representative to attend a meeting of organized parents to discuss their concerns even before a complaint is filed.

f. Legislative and Extra-Legal Regulatory Actions That Can Be Taken

While advocates should seriously consider lawsuits, even if legal technicalities pose difficult obstacles, amending a law or policy is likely easier than getting it repealed by a judge. Most school districts have adopted a zero tolerance policy in one form or another. Where policies remove discretion or require harsh penalties for minor offenses, political action on the federal, state, and local level may be the most effective response. Because state constitutions may afford more education rights, state or local policy forums may be better venues for initiatives seeking to limit the scope of zero tolerance policies. In some districts, as a first step, parents and advocates may have to prevent an already harsh discipline policy from being expanded. Preventing a new policy from being created is usually easier than overturning a policy.

Parents and advocates can also help organize local and state support for a national movement that is zeroing in on intolerant and abusive discipline practices. Parents and students can get involved in groups like the NAACP, Southern Echo, Rainbow/PUSH Coalition, and the National Coalition of Advocates for Students who are moving forward on this and related issues. Putting pressure on OCR to take more effective action against schools with abusive discipline policies is part of a national strategy. As part of this effort, some of these groups may be organizing OCR campaigns by systematically filing strong complaints of disparate impact and different treatment with the agency.[55]

g. Broad-Based Community Action Strategies

Parents and advocates should not get discouraged too easily by the conservative rulings of courts. Court fights provide an opportunity to get the media to pay attention to the gross injustice minority children must cope with in school. Court battles that have lost but received media attention have also served as conduits for newfound political energy. Administrative complaints filed with OCR can also attract media attention if the press is made aware of them. In the end, to stem the tide of harsh discipline drowning minority youth, it is the general public that must be first engaged and then enlightened.

1. PARTICIPATION AT BOARD OF EDUCATION MEETINGS

For obvious reasons, parent involvement is critical to political solutions. Parent involvement can also lay the groundwork for legal action. That is because it takes parents to produce child plaintiffs and child witnesses, and involved parents will likely be the first to notice discriminatory patterns of discipline. Parents are especially influential when they bring their children with them and testify at school committee meetings, although the legal and privacy interests of the children should always be carefully protected. Organized presentations can have an immediate impact and can have great influence if covered by the local media; pressure can be enhanced if it is applied in tandem with legal or administrative action.[56] When addressing school boards, community groups should include the following points:[57]

- Fair discipline is where the disciplinary consequences match the misbehavior. All children benefit from discipline that teaches appropriate social conduct effectively.
- Fair and effective discipline improves the safety of the entire community, inside and outside of the school.
- Overly punitive discipline is neither fair nor effective.

- A fair and effective policy should not result in children of some racial or ethnic groups being suspended and expelled significantly more often than others for minor offenses.

Advocates should also press school boards to consider at least the following actions:

- Implement a proven effective discipline policy where punishments are fair and crafted as opportunities to teach children appropriate behavior.
- Decrease size of "regular" classrooms, so teachers can better address the problems of all students.
- Increase teacher training in conflict resolution, provide teachers more support in the classrooms, provide better supports for children who appear difficult to manage, and implement programs that will increase effective early intervention.
- Train teachers so that they are multiculturally aware and able to implement positive classroom-management policies for students from diverse backgrounds.
- Involve members of the community in developing student codes of conduct for the school district, and hold parent and student training on the codes of conduct to ensure that everyone understands their rights and responsibilities.
- Limit circumstances under which police may be called to school to deal with disciplinary issues. Include that a school must call a parent immediately if a child is arrested.
- Establish a disciplinary committee at each school that includes parents and students and people of color. The committee should be given the authority to review serious disciplinary decisions, hold hearings, and overrule a decision.
- Compile data on discipline that breaks out recorded violations by type of misconduct and punishment and disaggregates the data by race, gender, age, and disability status.

2. GATHER INFORMATION

Gathering information sends a message that legal action is just around the corner. In the short term, the anticipation of a well-supported lawsuit may make districts more willing to rethink their discipline code. Even if legal action is not part of the plan, gathering the kind of information necessary for a lawsuit—the data, the identification of education experts, and the names of parents and children with compelling stories to tell—will enhance and inform a media campaign, legislative effort, or attempts to influence a school board. Spreading information about the alarming patterns and disturbing injustices will paint a stark picture for public viewing and can change the debate paradigm from an exchange of rhetoric to speaking truth to power.

3. APPLY PRESSURE TO GAIN "TELLING" DATA

As community members attempt to collect data, they will also pressure schools to collect more and better data. Activists working politically and those pursuing legal action should keep in mind the intermediate goals of requiring more accurate information about children who are disciplined. On the state and federal level, pressure is already mounting for more uniformed reporting on school suspension and expulsion. Legal action and intensified political pressure can help speed up the process. A school board that has adopted zero tolerance will be more likely to compromise and agree to improved record-keeping requirements, including recording and reporting disciplinary actions by race and ethnicity, than to rescinding the discipline policy. The same will likely apply to settlements stemming from lawsuits and OCR complaints. Many civil rights advocates believe that more accurate information will be critical to both legal and nonlegal zero tolerance challenges in the long term.

III. Conclusion

The information battle has strong parallels to the fight against racial profiling practiced by highway police. If detailed data on police stops were collected routinely and made public, advocates believe they could better demonstrate the degree of discrimination, the ineffectiveness of racial profiling for drug interdiction, and the relative benefits of less discriminatory enforcement policies.

The infliction of broad-based zero tolerance on school children in many ways resembles the racial profiling of African-American drivers. The staggering statistics suggest that teachers monitor the behavior of minority students more closely and are more likely to refer them for disciplinary action. Racial profiling on our highways is justified on the basis of drug interdiction: zero tolerance equals violence prevention.

Given the policy's origins as a narcotics enforcement scheme, it is not surprising that zero tolerance has come hand in hand with the erosion of privacy and free-speech rights for children. Schools are increasingly filing criminal charges against students, using metal detectors, locking down classrooms, placing surveillance cameras in hallways, requiring drug tests for participation in sports, making random locker searches, interpreting drawings as criminal threats, and even equipping school police with shotguns.[58] *Time* magazine recently ran a major story about profiling computer programs designed to spot unknown dangerous students lurking in the midst of normal children by electronically scanning their school records and a variety of other factors.[59] The FBI reportedly has "school shooter" profiling software that highlights as indicators: having parental troubles, experiencing a failed romance, and listening to songs with violent lyrics.[60] The police in New Jersey and California, including the under-siege Rampart neighborhood officers of Los Angeles, now admit that they practiced racial profiling because they believe it works.

"Children are not only being treated like criminals in school, but many are being shunted into the criminal justice system as schools have begun to rely heavily upon law enforcement officials to punish students."[61] And in Texas, juvenile justice officials handle the alternative education for every excluded student. Schools must be denied the use of criminal justice approaches as a tool to reform school behavior. The tide of fear that is eroding liberty and educational opportunities, especially for minority students, will unlikely peak on its own. Communities throughout the nation must wage a serious challenge to the proffered educational justification of zero tolerance. This essay has outlined a range of steps to take that we believe will be effective if put into action.

NOTES

1. See Betsy Levin, "Educating Youth for Citizenship: The Conflict Between Authority and Individual Rights in the Public School." 95 *Yale Law Journal* 1647 (1986).

2. See James P. Comer, M.D. and Alvin F. Poussaint, M.D., *Raising African-American Children*, at 197–198 (1992); see also Barbara Townsend, "The Disproportionate Discipline of African American Learners: Reducing School Suspensions and Exclusions," *Exceptional Children* 66, 3, pp. 381–391, at 388 (2000); Kevin P. Dwyer, David Osher, and Catherine C. Hoffman, "Creating Responsive Schools: Contextualizing Early Warning, Timely Response," *Exceptional Children* 66, 3, pp. 347–365, at 349 (2000).

3. Comer and Poussaint, *supra* note 2

4. That represents an overall increase from 3.7 percent to 6.9 percent. See Robert C. Johnston, "Federal Data Highlight Disparities in Discipline," June 21, 2000, *Education Week* on the Web, http://www.edweek.org/ew/ewstory.cfm?slug=41zero.h19.

5. See Russell J. Skiba, Professor of Counseling and Educational Psychology at Indiana University, Research Review Submitted to the U.S. Commission on Civil Rights, February 9, 2000, at 21 (Washington, D.C., Feb. 18, 2000).

6. As Barbara Townsend states, "When the vast majority of school exclusions are meted out to African American students who comprise a minority of the school population, it is easy for those students to interpret this disparity as rejection and to suffer from lower self-esteem as a result. A negative collective, self-fulfilling prophecy may develop as a result of the messages that African American youth receive that they are incapable of abiding by schools' social and behavioral codes. . . . Phenomena such as overrepresentation in special and remedial classes, suspensions, expulsion and other indicators of school failure can have cumulative and disastrous effects on African American males." See Townsend, *supra* note 2, at 383 (citations omitted).

7. See Robert C. Johnston, "Federal Data Highlight Disparities in Discipline," June 21, 2000, *Education Week* on the Web, http://www.edweek.org/ew/ewstory.cfm?slug=41zero.h19.

8. See Patrick Pauken and Philip T. K. Daniel, "Race Discrimination and Disability Discrimination in School Discipline: A Legal Statistical Analysis," 139 *Education Law Report* 759 (2000).

9. See, e.g. Applied Research Center, *Facing Consequences: An Examination of*

Racial Discrimination in U.S. Public Schools (Mar. 1, 2000) [hereinafter ARC Report].

10. *Id.*

11. See National Center for Education Statistics, U.S. Department of Education, *The Condition of Education, 1997* (noting Indicator 48, "Students Who Have Been Suspended From School").

12. See Building Blocks for Youth, *And Justice For Some* (May 2000) (Research funded by the U.S. Department of Justice).

13. See Kim Brooks et al., *School House Hype: Two Years Later* 19 (Justice Policy Institute/Children's Law Center, Apr. 2000) [hereinafter *School House Hype*].

14. See Public Law 105–17, June 4, 1997, section 601[c](7)(f), (8)(A)-(F). Section 601(c)(8)(C) specifically states, "Poor African-American children are 2.3 times more likely to be identified by their teacher as having mental retardation than their white counterpart." *Id.*

15. See ARC Report, *supra* note 9, at 26.

16. See *Suspended Education: A Preliminary Report on the Impact of Zero Tolerance on Chicago Public Schools.* Generation Y, a project of the Southwest Youth Collaborative, citing Chicago Public Schools End of the Year Reports to Illinois State Board of Education, 1992–93 through 1998–99.

17. See Russell J. Skiba, Robert S. Michael, Abra Carroll Nardo, and Reece Peterson, "The Color of Discipline: Sources of Racial and Gender Disproportionality in School Punishment" (Paper disseminated at the Summit on Zero Tolerance, Washington, D.C., June 15–16, 2000) [hereinafter *The Color of Discipline*].

18. See *Goss v. Lopez*, 419 U.S. 565 (1975); *Plyler v. Doe*, 457 U.S. 202 (1982); *Honig v. Doe*, 484 U.S. 305 (1988).

19. Nadine Strossen, "Protecting Student Rights Promotes Educational Opportunity: A Response to Judge Wilkinson," 1 *Michigan Law and Policy Review*, 315, 316 (1996).

20. See Eileen Ordover, "Disciplinary Exclusion of Students with Disabilities," *Clearinghouse Review,* May–June 2000; see also "Opportunities Suspended: The Devastating Consequences of Zero Tolerance and School Discipline."

21. *Alexander v. Sandoval*, 121 S. Ct 1511 (2001).

22. See *In re* Benedictine Military Sch., 22 IDELR 643 (1995). In another case described by Norma Cantú, the department's assistant secretary for civil rights, a school had implemented a very strict discipline policy in a discriminatory fashion. OCR's investigation revealed that for substantially similar misconduct, African-American students were picked up by the police and given one week

of in-school suspension consistent with the policy, while white students received counseling and no suspension or police intervention. See Norma Cantú, assistant secretary for civil rights, U.S. Department of Education, Testimony Before the United States Commission on Civil Rights, Washington D.C., Feb. 18 (2000).

23. *Sherpell v. Humnoke Sch. Dist.*, 619 F.Supp. 670 (E.D. Ark. 1985).

24. *Id.*

25. One important caveat: the Fourth, Fifth, and Eleventh Circuit Courts, which have jurisdiction over most of the Southern states, do not allow this presumption in discipline cases. For the remaining 38 states, if a prior desegregation order included a requirement to address a disparity in discipline, then the district's discipline policy may be especially vulnerable to a constitutional challenge. Once a court has declared a district "unitary," however, the district is absolved for having had a segregated school system and the presumption no longer holds.

26. See, e.g., *Simmons v. Hooks*, 843 F.Supp. 1296 (E.D. Ark. 1994); *United States v. Gadsden County Sch. Dist.*, 572 F. 2d 1049, 1050 (5th Cir. 1978); see also Daniel J. Losen, "Silent Segregation in Our Nation's Schools," 517 *Harvard CR-CL Law Rev.* 530–32 (1999).

27. To find out whether there is a desegregation court order for cases in which the United States is a party to the case, contact the Department of Justice, Civil Rights Division, at (202)514–4092.

28. Telephone interview with Barbra Shannon, Region IV past director, U.S. Department of Education Office for Civil Rights, Apr. 24 (2000).

29. See *Ross v. Saltmarsh*, 500 F. Supp. 935 (S.D.N.Y. 1980). Although school officials denied any wrongdoing, the district also agreed to convene a committee to address the disparity in discipline and to hire a consultant recommended by the plaintiff to "advise the defendants and work with the school district to develop plans to eliminate racial disparities in suspension rates." Additionally, the district agreed to provide statistical information and create a suspension log for the consultant to review—a semester report showing for each principal or superintendent: name of the student, race, grade, referring teacher, offense, date of suspension, suspending official, date of return and length of suspension. *Id.* at 940–41.

30. 34 CFR 1003 (b)(2)(1998).

31. Telephone interview with Barbra Shannon, *supra* note 28.

32. See, e.g., "The Use of Tests When Making High Stakes Decisions for Stu-

dents," U.S. Department of Education Office for Civil Rights (Draft, July 6, 2000), at 14–15.

33. The defendant must also be a recipient of federal funding.

34. For example, if African-American students constitute 10 percent of a student body population, one would expect black students to constitute 10 percent of those individuals who are suspended under a new zero tolerance policy. But if 20 percent of students suspended under the new policy are African American, there is a disproportionate impact on the black students. There are, however, no rigid mathematical thresholds for the degree of disparity; the greater the disparity, the more likely that the challenged practice caused the disparate impact. More extensive and elaborate statistical analyses can be performed but discussion of those techniques is beyond the scope of this essay.

35. See *Griggs v. Duke Power Co.*, 401 U.S. 421 (1971).

36. See Sasha Polakow-Suransky, *Access Denied: Mandatory Expulsion Requirements and the Erosion of Educational Opportunity in Michigan.* A Report by the Student Advocacy Center of Michigan (Feb. 1999).

37. See Suspension draft report, Kingery et al., *supra* note 23, at 4.

38. *Ibid.*

39. See interview with Dr. Paul Kingery, director of the Hamilton Fish Institute (HFI), (Apr. 3, 2000).

40. See HFI, *supra* note 39, at 6.

41. May Lee Johnson, "Black Males' Drop-out Rate Reaches Crisis," *South Bend Tribune* Online Edition (Apr. 9, 2000), www.southbendtribune.com.

42. See Russell J. Skiba, testimony, *supra* note 5.

43. The complainant had previously won a Commissioner's Order (Agency Case Number DOE-98-344-FOF), which included a corrective action plan developed jointly among the complaint, district administrators, and bureau staff issued on December 2, 1998.

44. See Cover Letter to Resolution Agreement from Gary Walker, Director, Atlanta Office of OCR to Superintendent Dr. Joan Kowal (Aug. 13, 1999). Despite this agreement another complaint was filed against the district that school year, alleging similar violations. This complaint resulted in a new resolution agreement signed by a new interim superintendent for the district. See Resolution Agreement, Palm Beach County School District, #04-99-1285 (Sept. 7, 2000).

45. See Letter from Gary S. Walker, Director, Atlanta Office OCR (Sept. 7, 2000). OCR's investigation also revealed that the district had disciplined one student with disabilities despite finding that the IEP and current placement was in-

appropriate, and the district neglected to conduct a manifestation hearing for another student with disabilities suspended for thirteen cumulative days.

46. See 20 U.S.C. Section 1400 et seq. (Individuals with Disabilities Education Act Amendments of 1997). The Act's Congressional findings acknowledge substantial concerns about restrictive and segregated classrooms and conclude that isolated students are usually worse off compared to similarly situated mainstreamed students. 20 U.S.C. Section 1401 (c)(4)(5).

47. See generally, Daniel J. Losen and Kevin Welner, *Disabling Discrimination in Our Public Schools: Comprehensive Legal Challenges to Inappropriate and Inadequate Special Education Services* (scheduled for publication in *The Harvard Civil Rights–Civil Liberties Law Review*, Summer 2001).

48. See H. B. 1096, "An Act concerning alternative learning opportunities." State of Illinois 92nd General Assembly Legislation. http://www.legis.state.il.us.

49. Section 13B-15.10 of Public Act 92-0042. See http://www.legis.state.il.us/publicacts/pubact92/acts/92-0042.html.

50. Section 13-B-20.15 of the same law.

51. See Paul Grossman, Chief Regional Attorney (Region IX), Letter to Dennis Chaconas, superintendent, Alameda City Unified Sch. Dist, re: Docket No. 09-06-1291, Oct. 8, 1999 [on file with The Civil Rights Project at Harvard University].

52. The discipline concerns were exacerbated when a white student, who admitted "tagging" a bathroom wall, received no punishment while a Latino youth was suspended for five days for a similar graffiti act. *Id.*

53. A letter from OCR's chief regional attorney reviewing the school's progress informed the superintendent that the case was closed. *Id.* The district had initially reduced its rate of disciplinary incidents from 2,527 during 1995–96 to 858 incidents in 1996–97. The district employed a range of strategies, including (1) analyzing its discipline data, disaggregated by race and ethnicity for disparities and reviewing it with staff; (2) developing conflict resolution teams made up of students; (3) creating peer counseling groups; (4) establishing a Latino Boys Club; and (5) holding workshops that directly addressed issues of race. Nonetheless, even though the rates of suspension continued to decrease in 1997–98 year, OCR pressed the school to reduce the disparity in discipline for African-American and Latino students. OCR did not find statistically significant disparate rates for other ethnic groups. The district responded by employing additional strategies, including holding a retreat for administrative staff on diversity awareness and issues regarding racial stereo-

typing, profiling, and communication styles. OCR reviewed data from the 1998–99 school year and found that in all categories of student discipline, including defiance of authority, Latino and African-American students were within 1.02 points of the target goals. After completing the investigation and negotiations, the agency concluded that the school district did not discriminate against Latino students in the dispensation of discipline or allow a racially hostile environment to exist. OCR closed the case based on a finding of no violation on the original claims and assurances that the district would continue to work toward reducing the discipline rates for African-American and Latino students. *Id.*

54. See The Civil Rights Project at Harvard University and the Advancement Project, *Opportunities Suspended: The Devastating Consequences of Zero Tolerance and School Discipline* 35–36, (June 2000).

55. Guidance on how to file a complaint with OCR will soon be available on the Web site of the Civil Rights Project at www.law.harvard.edu/civilrights.

56. See Interview with Abigail Trillen, Children's Legal Services, San Francisco, California (Apr. 26, 2000).

57. See Advancement Project and the Civil Rights Project, "Zero Tolerance Policies and School Discipline: What Are They, Do They Work, What Are Your Child's Rights, and What Can Your Community Do? An Action Kit for Parents and Community Groups" (2000) (on file with The Civil Rights Project at Harvard University). This action kit will soon be available on the Web site of the Civil Rights Project at www.law.harvard.edu/civilrights.

58. Jessica Porter, *L.A.* "To Equip Campus Police Force with Shotguns," Mar. 4, 1998, *Education Week* on the Web, www.edweek.org/ew/vol-17/25guns.h17.

59. See Jodie Morse, "Looking for Trouble," *Time*, Apr. 24, 2000.

60. See Linda Jacobson, "FBI 'Profiling' Help Worries Educators," *Education Week*, Oct. 6, 1999.

61. See *Opportunities Suspended*, The Advancement Project and The Civil Rights Project, Harvard University, June 2000. See also education proposal of President George W. Bush, "No Child Left Behind," seeking to circumvent existing due process by giving teachers the authority to remove persistently disruptive students and to amend the Federal Education Rights and Privacy Act to dilute further the privacy rights of children by granting greater access of heretofore private student records to law enforcement authorities. January 2001.

Zero Tolerance: Reflections on a Failed Policy That Won't Die

MICHELLE FINE AND KERSHA SMITH

Two scholarly documents on American youth arrived simultaneously in the mail. "And Justice for Some," by Eileen Poe-Yamagata and Michael Jones (report for Building Block for Youth, Youth Law Center, 2000), documents the dramatic and profound racial disparities in arrest, detention, and incarceration rates for African-American, Latino, and white youth. The authors write: "Unfortunately the cumulative disadvantage of minority youth will continue to spiral as states continue to pass more punitive laws allowing youth to be charged as adults and therefore subject to adult sanctions such as prison and the death penalty. Thus, as legislative trends push beyond the boundary of juvenile justice, [we will witness] the continued amplification of minority youth in the system" (p. 29). African-American youth constitute 15 percent of the general population, 26 percent of those arrested, and, ultimately, 58 percent of the youth admitted to state prisons. For many African-American youth, because of the historic structure and enforcement of national, state, and local policy, life choices are cut severely short in their teens and early twenties.

Arriving on our desks at the same moment was the May 2000 issue of *American Psychologist*, in which psychologist Jeffrey Jensen Arnett introduces a reconceptualization of early adulthood, which he calls "emerging adulthood"—a time of relative freedom from social expectations, a maximizing of choices, and a period of open possibilities. Arnett writes:

> [C]hanges over the past half century have altered the nature of develop-
> ment in the late teens and early twenties for young people in industri-

alized societies. Because marriage and parenthood are delayed until the mid-twenties or late twenties, for most people, it is no longer normative for the late teens and early twenties to be a time of entering and settling into long-term adult roles. On the contrary, these years are more typically a period of frequent change and exploration. . . . Emerging adulthood is distinguished by relative independence from social roles and from normative expectations. . . . Emerging adults often explore a variety of possible life directions in love, work and world views . . . [emerging adulthood is a] time of life when many different directions remain possible, when little about the future has been decided for certain . . . the most volitional years of life. (p. 469)

Indeed, both sets of writers are correct. We witness, in America, a national bifurcation, a two-class system, divided by race, ethnicity, and social class. Accordingly, we witness two versions of adolescence and young adulthood. For the wealthy—and, disproportionately, white—adolescence can indeed be filled with opportunities, challenges, dreams, and even mistakes that may be considered a "phase" and remediable. For the poor—and, disproportionately, African-American and Latino—opportunities and dreams are viciously constrained. Mistakes become life-course tattoos. The story of who is permitted the luxury of the mistakes of youth is a quintessentially American story: a story scarred by race, ethnicity, and social class inequalities.

Zero tolerance is, intuitively, a reasonable policy—until you look under the veil. Ideologically it is part of a larger political project of "accountability," in which youth of color, typically, but not only, the poor and working class, are held "accountable" for a nation that has placed them "at risk." Systematically denied equal developmental opportunities, they are pathologized, placed under surveillance, and increasingly criminalized. As in high-stakes testing, poor youth and youth of color, rather than inequitable education systems, pay an extraordinary price for inadequate funding and education. Zero tolerance focuses narrowly in on youth. Erased are the adults, educational institutions, the social history and continuity of raced and classed oppression in America. Zero tolerance disproportionately targets, criminalizes, and effectively ends the educational careers of many poor and working-class youth of color. By so doing, zero tolerance poses a frightening threat to democracy.

To assess the impact of any social policy on youth, parents, educators, activists, and students, we might ask four simple questions:

1. Is the policy effective? Does it achieve its intended purpose?

That is, under zero tolerance policies, are students being discharged primarily for possession or use of guns, and does this policy make schools safer?

The evidence in this book would suggest No. Rick Ayers, William Ayers, and Bernardine Dohrn write, "Recent research indicates that as schools become more militarized they become less safe" (p. xii). The case in Decatur, Illinois, reveals that the implementation of zero tolerance may have exacerbated school-based tensions and incited violence rather than minimized either. In Chicago, students are overwhelmingly dismissed not for guns but for nonviolent nondrug offenses (33 percent); class cutting and tardiness (33 percent); and fighting (31 percent). Indeed, youth with no records are often suspended or expelled under zero tolerance policies through misunderstandings or instances of poor judgment with lifelong consequences.

2. Are there "unintended" consequences of the policies for youth and schools?

The material, educational, and psychological consequences of zero tolerance are huge.

- Zero tolerance policies may, indeed, turn schools into places where students and teachers feel inhibited rather than creative. If schools are supposed to be sites for the development of mind and soul, academics and citizenship, creativity and engagement—places where students and teachers feel safe and free to make mistakes, indeed learn from mistakes—zero tolerance sends a contradictory chill. This is particularly troubling for youth whose lives are surrounded by violence and who need help figuring out how to respond, negotiate, or exit. Zero tolerance creates communities in which youth and adults who most need help cannot safely come forward. Problems remain underground, further threatening self, family, school, and community.
- Zero tolerance widens the divide between school and community.

Under zero tolerance policies, students and families may feel alienated from their school community after committing (or being accused of committing) an offense. Instead of educating students
toward becoming accountable for their actions, zero tolerance policies banish youth from some of the most fundamental connections
they have. These policies reinforce the message of forced exile as a
way to deal with community problems. By so doing, poor and
working-class youth grow even more alienated from, mistrustful
of, and cynical about public institutions and democratic social relations. (See Fine et al., forthcoming).

- Zero tolerance policies may turn students into citizens who ignore,
  or refuse to see, complexities, looking for easy fixes to multilayered
  problems. Zero tolerance may in fact be an easy fix—as we rid
  schools of some "difficult" youth, we also fill the prisons we are
  constructing nationally.

3. Is the policy equitable, or does it have disproportionate negative impact on some groups?

That is, does zero tolerance render African-American, Latino,
Native-American, and immigrant youth more vulnerable to suspension and expulsion?

The evidence demonstrates an emphatic Yes. Students who have
already paid the dearest price for global capitalism, persistent poverty,
and racism, from families which have suffered historically under the
brutality of class and race stratification, are indeed the prime victims
of zero tolerance. African-Americans are approximately twice as likely
to experience expulsion and suspension as whites. Since the implementation of zero tolerance, up to two-thirds of the "minority" students in some communities have been swept into the zero tolerance
frenzy. The always horrifying intersections of race and class collide in
zero tolerance: "African-American males from the wealthiest families
are almost as likely to be expelled or suspended as white males from
the poorest families" (Losen and Edley, this volume p. 231).

4. Is the policy educational? Does this social policy create opportunities for education and development?

That is, does the zero tolerance policy create spaces in schools, families, and communities to educate youth critically about conflict resolution, gun control, and alternatives to violence?

To the contrary, educators working under the regimes of zero tolerance typically lose pedagogical opportunities to teach creatively about violence, and lose opportunities to work with families and communities as partners on the toughest questions youth face. For instance, if students writing about violence cannot wander in their texts into a wide range of responses to a violent world without risking a label, then teachers may be hesitant to teach such topics openly or at all. Conversely, students who already know far too much about violence may be reluctant to write boldly, authentically, and creatively. If parents come to school primarily to respond to a call for suspension or expulsion, the likelihood of schools creating alliances with families and communities is diminished. Teachable moments may be lost in the swamp of banishment; teacher discretion and relational knowledge of youth are undermined.

Zero tolerance policies fail on all four criteria. They do not make schools safer; they produce perverse consequences for academics, school/community relations, and the development of citizens; they dramatically and disproportionately target youth of color; and they inhibit educational opportunities.

What Works to Reduce School Violence?

It seems all too clear that zero tolerance policies exacerbate the very conditions that nurture the wretched statistics of "And Justice for Some." These same policies make "emerging adulthood" virtually inaccessible to poor and working-class youth of color. And yet the question of how to create safe, intellectually vibrant schools is, indeed, no mystery. Throughout this book we read not just a critique but a set of recommendations for schools that would make them safer, equitable, and educational.

- Safe schools are small. The evidence is overwhelming that in terms of educational excellence and equity, violence, teacher satisfaction and commitment, community engagement and public accountability, small schools far surpass large schools. Indeed, Linda Powell has described small schools as an antiracist educational intervention (Powell 2000).

- Safe schools are places in which trust and respect between youth and adults, as well as among youth, is paramount. Pedro Noguera writes on trust as a form of social capital that schools can offer to and engender in youth.

- Safe schools are sites in which learning is organized as an opportunity to explore, challenge, revise, and critique the world *as it is*, and to create a world *not yet*. We must explore the pedagogical possibilities of creating spaces for and with youth in which writing on and speaking about violence becomes a way to manage a world of terror, rather than creating a place which censors youth imagination.

- Safe schools work with communities so that social and ethical transgressions by youth become moral lessons for community-building and individual development; they become opportunities to support rather than purge, to build social capital, trust, and community sustenance. Youth, scholars, practitioners, activists, and everyday people agree that the best insurance for public safety is a community and schools bonded by respect, trust, security, early intervention, appreciation for mistakes, community organizing, and rich civic engagement. Strong and safe schools work with communities, and police, to craft policies that have powerful educational and safety consequences.

How Do We Organize Communities for Safer Schools and Against Zero Tolerance Policies?

Drawing from the rich collection of essays in this book, we imagine projects that parents and community activists can undertake with educators and students interested in creating and sustaining schools that are safe and nurturing, rigorous and caring, excellent and equitable.

1. Collect data. Gather the stated and written zero tolerance policies; find out if and how students are informed about the policies and about their rights; demand data—desegregated by race, ethnicity, gender, and special education status—on who is suspended, expelled, or otherwise punished because of zero tolerance.

2. Create speak-outs for youth. Orchestrate public opportunities for youth to speak out about local policies and how they are differentially affected—and with what consequences economically, academically, socially, and psychologically.

3. Invite educators to join the conversation. Many of the essays in this book reveal how deeply offended some educators are by zero tolerance policies. Powerful coalitions can emerge between educators, parents, and students. Find those educators and figure out ways to join forces.

4. Launch lawsuits. Brought on the basis of differential impact, class-action lawsuits are being tried in a number of communities on the basis of race, ethnicity, language, and special education bias.

5. Develop statewide "ZT-Squared Coalitions"—that is, zero tolerance for zero tolerance. Collect statewide data correlating school-specific racial and socioeconomic status distributions of students and staff, percent of certified/credentialed teachers, school size, and per capita financing of the school with rates of suspensions and expulsions. The racialized trends can be staggering and important to uncover and publicize for statewide and local organizing.

6. Reverse the rhetoric. Focus parent and community organizing onto zero tolerance for state-initiated violence—that is, we need to ask how much more "state-initiated violence" can/should poor communities endure, such as financial inequities, lack of certified or credentialed teachers, crumbling facilities, old books, the closing of branch libraries, and huge high schools with watered-down curricula and astronomical drop-out rates. Indeed, the "real" violence—of class and race-based inequities in and around schools—can be tolerated no longer.

7. Undertake youth-based activist research projects. Youth-based activist research projects can be undertaken easily and dramatically in local communities and then strung together across states and the country to demonstrate the high costs, lack of accountability, and differential race/class-based consequences of zero tolerance, e.g.:

   ▪ Document increased school, court, and criminal justice expenses, as well as the transportation and incarceration expenses of this new "accountability" system. That is, reveal the school-prison-industrial complex, which is lavishly funded, without any public monitoring, in the name of "accountability." If public education is expensive, what about mass incarceration?

- Correlate local school financing statistics, drop-out rates, and incarceration rates by neighborhood.
- Survey youth about their experiences with school- and community-based surveillance—how does the experience of being viewed as "suspicious" bear consequences for democracy and participatory citizenship?
- Design a participatory action research project in which educators, administrators, parents, and youth are questioned about why persons in these different statuses may endorse different views of zero tolerance. Then try to design a policy that speaks from several perspectives at once.

Perhaps America has always blamed youth, and youth of color in particular, for our national troubles. But today the stakes seem precariously high. Zero tolerance, combined with the proliferation of high-stakes testing, the refusal to assure high-quality educators in the poorest neighborhoods, the national unwillingness to legislate gun controls, the massive criminalization and incarceration of youth of color, and the second-chance mentality for more privileged youth, creates a system of few options for the many and many options for the few. This is an abdication of educational duty. In contrast, and in response, this book is a call to responsibility for all adults—parents, educators, activists, and community members. Our youth are under attack. What will we do?

REFERENCES

Fine, M., N. Freudenberg, Y. Payne, T. Perkins, L. Smith, and K. Walzer. "Anything Can Happen When the Police are Around! Youth Perspectives on Public Surveillance." *Journal of Social Issues* (forthcoming).

Permissions

"Ground Zero" by Gregory Michie. Reprinted with permission of the author. This article previously appeared, in somewhat different form, in the *Chicago Reader*, September 8, 2000.

"Two Punches, Expelled for Life" by Rick Ayers. Originally printed as "La Silent: What Is to Be Done?" This article is reprinted with permission of the author and the Institute for Democracy in Education. It first appeared in *Democracy and Education*, volume 12, issue 3, 1998. For additional information, contact IDE at democracy@ohiou.edu.

"From the Jail Yard to the School Yard" by Tony DeMarco. Originally published as "Suspension/Expulsion—Punitive Sanctions from the Jail Yard to the School Yard," 34 New Eng. L. Rev. 565 (2000). Reprinted with permission of the *New England Law Review*.

" 'Look Out Kid, / It's Something You Did' " by Bernardine Dohrn. Reprinted, in revised form, by permission of the publisher from Polakow, V., *The Public Assault on America's Children* (New York: Teachers College Press, © 2000 by Teachers College, Columbia University. All rights reserved), chapter 7 by Dohrn, B.

"Sticks and Stones: The Jailing of Mentally Ill Kids" by Carl Ginsburg and Helen Demeranville. Reprinted with permission from the December 20, 1999, issue of *The Nation*.

"When Is Disproportionality Discrimination?" by Russell Skiba. Reprinted with permission of the author and the Indiana Education Policy Center.

"The ABCs of School Discipline: Lessons from Miami-Date County" by Judith A. Browne. Originally published as "Caught in the Web: The Case of Miami-Dade County." Revised and reprinted by permission of the author.